Like the encyclical itself, these essays aim through and beyond the Roman Catholic public to all of us eartl carry forward *Laudato si's* mission—which species matters, is of paramount importanc

Drew Univ

In the light of the crisis we face in the planetary community of life, *Laudato si'* may well be the most important Catholic teaching document of the twenty-first century. It brings commitment to Earth, to its lands, seas, and rivers, to all of its creatures, to the center of Christian faith and practice, and teaches us to hold this together with a commitment to social justice in "integral ecology." The authors of the twelve chapters of *All Creation Is Connected* engage in important conversations with *Laudato si'* from a wide range of contexts and disciplines. They bring fresh insights into a reading of the text by means of the kind of dialogue about our common home to which Pope Francis calls us all. This is an important book that not only provides important insights, but like *Laudato si'* itself, can inspire the reader to a deeper ecological conversion.

—Denis Edwards
Australian Catholic University

The authors of the dozen essays in this excellent book make up a "dream team" of engaged scholars and activists dedicated to honing an unflinching religious response to the environmental crisis. Each deserves a membership card in that rare club of energetic teachers possessing a true knack for offering highly accessible messages on important topics. Every chapter of this book sheds abundant light on the crucial appeal of Pope Francis in *Laudato si'* for deeper environmental concern and care for our common home. Providing an eloquent witness to the power of ecological conversion, this volume will enhance your knowledge and spark your energy to make ecology the priority it must be today.

—Thomas Massaro, SJ
Jesuit School of Theology of Santa Clara University

All Creation Is Connected contains many finely crafted and engaging articles reflecting on the environmental crisis in light of *Laudato si'*. Drawing upon an impressive community of American-based scholars, *All Creation Is Connected* treats the roots of the crisis and the response required clearly and with a keen sense of urgency and passion. [A]n invaluable resource for anyone interested in the future of our 'common home,' and especially for those inspired and shaped by the Gospel.

—Pádraig Joseph Corkery
St. Patrick's College

All Creation Is Connected opens *Laudato si'* to a wider theological, scientific, and historical context. It shows how the encyclical can be integrated within varied strains of Catholic ethics such as the virtue approach or liberationist ethics. Together with the excellent bibliography and suggested study materials it can serve as an excellent supplementary educational tool for the encyclical.

—John T. Pawlikowski, OSM
Catholic Theological Union

Few encyclicals have been awaited as eagerly as *Laudato si'*. Pope Francis's letter is long and complex, as well as fascinating and significant. For that reason, readers will benefit greatly from these essays. Thirteen recognized and respected scholars explore not only the encyclical itself, but situate the document within contexts of liturgy, Catholic social teaching, liberation theology, science, ethics, sociology, peacebuilding, and mysticism. Taken together the essays in this volume provide a wealth of data and information that help us appreciate *Laudato si'*—its wisdom, its challenge, and its importance for the life of the planet.

—Kenneth R. Himes, OFM
Boston College

This is an excellent volume of carefully selected essays that illuminates the breadth and depth of Pope Francis' encyclical, *Laudato si'*. Dan DiLeo has skillfully woven together a comprehensive portrait of the encyclical that provides substantive insight on its theological, cosmological, and ethical vision for a renewed human community and planetary ethics. The reflective questions and suggested readings at the end of each chapter make this book a very helpful tool for educational forums and discussion groups. I highly recommend it.

—Ilia Delio, OSF
Villanova University

I strongly endorse *All Creation Is Connected: Voices in Response to Pope Francis's Encyclical on Ecology*. The essays are an excellent companion to deepen understanding of the critical theological, social, and ecological insights and claims woven throughout *Laudato si'*. The early chapters show both the continuity and new ground that *Laudato si'* makes with earlier Catholic social teaching. The later essays, on Pope Francis's critical contribution of the themes "Integral Ecology" and "Ecological Conversion," are especially compelling. The connections several authors make to Leonardo Boff's liberation theology and Teilhard de Chardin's and Thomas Berry's cosmological theologies ground *Laudato si'* in important contemporary theological conversations. Especially important for theologians is Richard Miller's stellar chapter, "The Cry of the Earth: The Scientific Background" . . . a clear and thorough discussion of the implications of breaching "planetary boundaries" through escalating climate change brought about by human activities—the central problem addressed in *Laudato si'*. This book will generate and ground critical conversations and active responses to Pope Francis's call for a global ecological conversion.

—Daniel T. Spencer
University of Montana

Editor Acknowledgments

Just as "no man is an island," no publication is the work only one person—particularly an edited volume, and especially a volume that emerges from a conference. Since this book was developed out of the conference *"Laudato si'* and the American Catholic Church," cosponsored by Catholic Climate Covenant, the U.S. Conference of Catholic Bishops (USCCB), and the Institute for Policy Research & Catholic Studies at The Catholic University of America (see "Introduction"), several acknowledgements are thus in order.

I would first like to thank the leadership of those organizations that cosponsored the abovementioned conference: Daniel J. Misleh, Executive Director of Catholic Climate Covenant; USCCB Department of Justice, Peace and Human Development staff; Stephen F. Schneck, Ph.D., Director of the Institute for Policy Research & Catholic Studies at the Catholic University of America; and Maria Mazzenga, Assistant Director of the Institute for Policy Research & Catholic Studies at the Catholic University of America. I would also especially like to thank those organizations' personnel who helped arrange and administer the conference: Wesley Cocozello, former Director of Operations at Catholic Climate Covenant; Woinishet Negash, Office Manager of the Institute for Policy Research & Catholic Studies at The Catholic University of America; and Lydia Andrews, Assistant to the Director of the Institute for Policy Research & Catholic Studies at The Catholic University of America.

In addition to those who helped organize *"Laudato si'* and the American Catholic Church," I am grateful to the authors who generously contributed to this volume and the professionals who intrepidly shepherded the production process: Bradley Harmon, Maura Thompson Hagarty, and Beth Erickson of Anselm Academic.

Finally, I would like to thank my spouse, Katie Corey DiLeo, whose love and support empowers my work and made this volume possible.

Publisher Acknowledgments

Thank you to the following individuals who reviewed this work in progress:

Elizabeth Groppe, *Xavier University, Cincinnati, Ohio*
John F. Haught, *Georgetown University, Washington, DC*
Joseph Mudd, *Gonzaga University, Spokane, Washington*

All Creation Is Connected

Voices in Response to Pope Francis's Encyclical on Ecology

Daniel R. DiLeo, editor

Dedication

This volume is dedicated to Daniel J. Misleh, founding Executive Director of Catholic Climate Covenant, whose commitment and witness to Catholic teaching on climate change inspires people of faith and goodwill to better *care for our common home*.

Created by the publishing team of Anselm Academic.

Cover image: Shutterstock

Printed in the United States of America

7082

ISBN 978-1-59982-874-9

Contents

Introduction

DANIEL R. DILEO

"Why care about the environment?" A 2017 Gallup poll suggests that many Americans may be asking this question. The poll indicated that from January 2016 to April 2017, Americans consistently ranked the environment as one of the least important issues facing the United States.[1]

Animated by Pope Francis's encyclical *Laudato si'* (*LS*), the short answer to this question is the title of this book: *All Creation is Connected.*[2] The longer answer, at least in part, comes from six paragraphs of *Laudato si'*. First, all of creation—its discrete parts and its totality—has inherent goodness and value (*LS* 76). Second, God is in and throughout creation, which God makes and sustains (*LS* 80). Third, humans are called to lovingly and prudently "cultivate and care for" God's creation (*LS* 66, cf. Gen. 2:15). Fourth, humans are creatures such that environmental degradation kills and injures human persons and communities (*LS* 139). Relatedly, the poor and marginalized are often most harmed by environmental degradation even though they typically contribute least to it (*LS* 48). Finally, human-caused "climate change is a global problem with grave implications" for humans and non-human creation (*LS* 25).

Grounded in *Laudato si'*, and in continuity with traditional Roman Catholic teaching, one might thus respond to the question of "Why care about the environment?" by highlighting the innate value of creation for which humans are called to care and in which God is present; the suffering and death that environmental degradation brings to human creatures (especially the poor who often do

---

1. Gallup, "Economy Top Problem in a Crowded Field," n.d., *http://www.gallup .com/poll/200105/economy-top-problem-crowded-field.aspx?g_source=Economy&g _medium=newsfeed&g_campaign=tiles*; Gallup, "Most Important Problem," April 2017, *http://www.gallup.com/poll/1675/most-important-problem.aspx*.

2. Pope Francis, *Laudato si': On Care for Our Common Home*, June 18, 2015, *http:// w2.vatican.va/content/francesco/en/encyclicals/documents/papa-francesco_20150524 _enciclica-laudato-si.html*.

relatively little to harm creation); and the particular urgency of climate change, which may soon become runaway and irreversible.

There is more to *Laudato si* than the above insights, but these help to illustrate that *Laudato si* can offer thoughtful answers to real questions. *All Creation Is Connected* invites you to consider what leading Catholic voices in the United States have to say about this groundbreaking encyclical.

Laudato si': On Care for Our Common Home

On June 18, 2015, Pope Francis released his highly anticipated encyclical *Laudato si': On Care for Our Common Home*.[3] Six months later Cardinal Peter Turkson, President of the Pontifical Council for Justine and Peace, which helped the pope draft the encyclical, urged bishops to engage in widespread interdisciplinary dialogue to operationalize *Laudato si'* and "help bring about the huge action needed to address the world's environmental issues."[4] This volume emerges out of a gathering that embodied Cardinal Turkson's sentiments.

Genesis and Structure of This Volume

In November 2015, Catholic Climate Covenant, the U.S. Conference of Catholic Bishops, and the Institute for Policy Research & Catholic Studies at The Catholic University of America held a three-day conference titled "*Laudato si'* and the American Catholic Church" to catalyze informed, practical dialogue around the encyclical. The conference sought to inspire and equip pastoral action that thoughtfully integrates *Laudato si*, and to this end brought together prominent Catholic thinkers and social ministry leaders for a series of presentations and conversations.

Although the meeting was convened to help social ministry leaders incorporate *Laudato si* into their work, it became evident during

---

3. An encyclical is an extended letter from a pope on some topic. *Laudato si'* is the first encyclical that focuses on ecology.

4. Cardinal Peter Turkson, "Catholicism and the Environment: Reflections on *Laudato si',*" Vatican Radio, January 22, 2016, *http://en.radiovaticana.va/news/2016/01/22/cardinal_turkson_bishops_should_promote_laudato_si/1202931*.

and after the conference that the scholars' presentations could help a broader audience better understand and respond to *Laudato si*. In order to act on that recognition, this volume has brought together many of those presentations along with additional complementary essays.[5]

The twelve chapters in this work are organized into five sections. Part 1, "Background and Reception," outlines the theological and sociological contexts from which *Laudato si'* came and into which it has been received. In chapter 1, Monsignor Kevin W. Irwin reviews the conciliar and papal background of *Laudato si'* and suggests how the encyclical develops precedent Catholic teaching on ecology. In chapter 2, Walter E. Grazer provides further reflections on the ecclesial background and innovative theological dimensions of *Laudato si'*. In particular, Grazer reflects on *Laudato si* in light of previous teachings on ecology from the U.S. Catholic bishops. In chapter 3, Michael Agliardo, SJ, provides sociological analysis of how *Laudato si'* has been received in the environmental, interfaith, political, and Catholic arenas of American society.

Part 2, "The Cosmos," considers how Pope Francis understands the nature, history, and future of the universe. In chapter 4, Mary Evelyn Tucker and John Grim outline the cosmological vision of *Laudato si'* and compare Francis's perspective with those of previous popes, Pierre Teilhard de Chardin, SJ, Thomas Berry, and the *Earth Charter*. In chapter 5, Drew Christiansen, SJ, describes the role of particularity, diversity, unity, and harmony in the cosmology of *Laudato si'*. Christiansen also considers how Pope Francis sees the relationship between technology, mysticism, and aestheticism.

Part 3, "Integral Ecology," unpacks this concept, which is central to *Laudato si'*. The term itself is not a neologism; it has been used, for example, by scholars to describe an interdisciplinary (or "postdisciplinary") approach to the interconnectedness of all reality.[6] *Laudato si'*, however, is the first papal encyclical to employ the term and uses the phrase to communicate the foundational claim

---

5. The views and opinions expressed in this volume are those of the respective contributors and do not necessarily reflect the official positions of Catholic Climate Covenant, the U.S. Conference of Catholic Bishops, or the Institute for Policy Research & Catholic Studies at The Catholic University of America.

6. Sean Esbjorn-Hargens and Michael E. Zimmerman, *Integral Ecology: Uniting Multiple Perspectives on the Natural World* (Boston: Integral Books, 2011), 47.

that "everything"—God, humans, non-human creation, econom-
ics, politics, culture, spirituality, etc.—"is connected" (*LS* 91). Against
this background, Dawn M. Nothwehr, OSF, describes in chapter 6
how Leonardo Boff and his Franciscan Liberation Ecological Theology influenced the use of integral ecology in *Laudato si'*. In chapter 7,
Richard W. Miller utilizes the nine processes of the planetary boundary framework to provide scientific grounding for the core claim of
integral ecology that all of creation is "interconnected" (*LS* 240).

Part 4, "Ecological Conversion," assesses how persons and communities might respond to Pope Francis's call for what essentially
amounts to an ecologically-sensitive *metanoia*.[7] In chapter 8, Jame
Schaefer suggests how persons and communities can cultivate and
respond to an "ecological consciousness" that promotes the flourishing of all creation. In chapter 9, Nancy Rourke considers the relationship between character development and action, and outlines
the role of virtue ethics in *Laudato si'*. In chapter 10, David Cloutier underscores that ecological sustainability requires a conversion
of both individuals' hearts, which animate personal actions, and the
social structures that shape and are shaped by human choices.

Part 5, "Catholic Social Ethics," examines *Laudato si'* in light of
"the body of the Church's social teaching" of which it is part (*LS* 15).
In chapter 11, Daniel P. Scheid describes how *Laudato si'* utilizes and
expands three key concepts of Catholic social teaching: the common
good, solidarity, and the preferential option for the poor. In chapter 12, Tobias Winright suggests that the connections in *Laudato si'*
between peace and integral ecology—connections made in 1990 by
Pope John Paul II and in 2010 by Pope Benedict XVI—merit the
development of a new approach to the ethics of war and peace: "integral peacebuilding."

Conclusion

At the beginning of *Laudato si'*, Pope Francis outlines "what is happening to our common home" (*LS* 17). Before he begins this account,
however, he emphasizes, "Our goal is not to amass information or to
satisfy curiosity, but rather to become painfully aware, to dare to turn

---

7. Greek for "conversion, repentance, change of mind."

what is happening to the world into our own personal suffering and thus to discover what each of us can do about it" (*LS* 19). That is to say, inquiry and reflection for this pope must translate into concrete activities; we must be "contemplatives in action," in the words of the Society of Jesus (Jesuits) to which Pope Francis belongs.

The chapters in this volume are intended to help readers better understand and more deeply engage with *Laudato si'*. In the spirit of Pope Francis's sentiment above, however, the goal of this volume is not to provide content for speculative reflection only. Rather, the purpose of this work is to help readers appreciate *Laudato si'* in ways that might inspire ecological conversions that produce corresponding actions and advocacy. To that end, let us now, as Pope Francis says at the beginning of *Laudato si'*, "enter into dialogue . . . about our common home" (*LS* 3).

PART 1

Background and Reception

CHAPTER 1

Background to and Contributions of *Laudato si': On Care for Our Common Home*

KEVIN W. IRWIN

This chapter offers a summary of documents on ecology, published before *Laudato si': On Care for Our Common Home*, from the Catholic magisterium,[1] and indicates important contributions that Pope Francis makes to the growing body of Catholic teaching on ecology.[2] The chapter[3] is divided into four unequal sections: (1) the Second Vatican Council, (2) papal teachings from Pope Paul VI up to and including Francis, (3) teachings from conferences of

---

1. In classical Latin, the word *magister* meant "master," not only in the sense of schoolmaster or teacher, but in the many ways one can be a "master" of an art, a craft, or a trade. Hence the term carries connotations of the role or the authority of one who is a master. In modern Catholic usage, the term *magisterium* has come to be associated almost exclusively with the teaching role and authority of the hierarchy—the pope and the bishops. Today, *magisterium* more commonly refers not only to the teachings themselves but also to those who exercise authority in teaching—again, the pope and the bishops.

2. Pope Francis, *Laudato si': On Care for Our Common Home*, June 18, 2015, *http://w2.vatican.va/content/francesco/en/encyclicals/documents/papa-francesco_20150524_enciclica-laudato-si.html*.

3. The review that follows is meant to express and summarize salient themes from a number of authoritative Catholic Church sources. Given the breadth and depth of what Pope Francis offers in the encyclical (as can be seen by reviewing its table of contents), this review cannot be exhaustive in terms of laying out the magisterial background for the number of varied themes in the encyclical and the sources on which the pope relies, such as theologians, spiritual writers, and authors of works relating to faith and science.

Catholic bishops, and (4) a summary of the major theological contributions in *Laudato si'*.

Vatican II on the Environment

The Second Vatican Council, convened between 1962 and 1965,
was a meeting in Rome of the world's Catholic bishops to discuss
a range of issues regarding the Catholic Church and its relationship to the world. Among its many documents, the Council's 1965
Pastoral Constitution on the Church in the Modern World (*Gaudium et spes*) most clearly addresses the environment.[4] In this regard,
however, the text is actually more notable for what it does not say,
or for what it says cryptically, about creation and the environment
generally, or for what it says about resources specifically.[5] Wherever
the document notes ecological issues, it speaks about them from
anthropological and ethical perspectives, naming human beings as
the center of creation (*GS* 12), responsible for respecting creation's
autonomy and insuring equitable distribution of its goods (*GS* 36,
39). In spelling out principles for a just economy, the document
identifies humans as responsible for consolidating control over creation in order to insure an economic order that respects the dignity of all human persons (*GS* 9, 33), a theme that recurs when
the text discusses the relationship between nature and culture (*GS*
33). Although the document teaches that humans have a fundamental responsibility to insure the preservation of the earth and its
resources, the text does not recognize the intrinsic goodness, value,
or dignity of creation.

---

4. Second Vatican Council, *Gaudium et spes*, December 7, 1965, *http://
www.vatican.va/archive/hist_councils/ii_vatican_council/documents/vat
-ii_const_19651207_gaudium-et-spes_en.html*.

5. In much English language literature today, the term *environment* refers to the
life context in which we live, our habitat, which Christians believe was given us by
God and for which we are responsible. *Ecology* (from the Greek *oikos*, "home") refers
to our being at home on the earth, and "ecological crisis" refers to the destruction that
has been worked to make the earth, our home, less inhabitable for a variety of species.
Creation refers to the whole created world and all living beings as gifts from God the
creator. Chapter 2 will address the distinctions Pope Francis makes between "nature"
and "creation," "ecology" and "environment."

Recent Papal Teaching on the Environment[6]

Pope Paul VI

The same anthropologically-based themes in *Gaudium et spes* are found in Pope Paul VI's 1967 encyclical *Populorum progressio* (*PP* 22–28).[7] Four years later in *Octogesima adveniens* (1971), Pope Paul spoke of the "environment" and directly chastised humans who have forsaken their responsibility and, "by an ill-considered exploitation of nature," risk "destroying it and becoming in . . . turn the victim of this degradation" (*OA* 21).[8] In connection with the United Nations sponsored Conference on the Environment at Stockholm in 1972, Pope Paul VI reiterated previously-stated concerns but also made significant additions. He recognized a symbiotic relationship between humans and non-human creation.[9] He urged people to use their native capacity for good, specifically their intelligence, to renew nature that is ravaged and exploited to the detriment of all creation.[10]

---

6. The fact that Pope Francis cites Pope John XXIII in *Laudato si'* is notable, even if it is not germane to this article. At the very beginning of *On Care for Our Common Home*, Pope Francis writes about Pope John XXIII's encyclical *Pacem in terris*, in which there are two important points to note. First, both John XXIII's *Pacem in terris* and Francis's *On Care for Our Common Home* are not addressed to the usual people inside the Church, but they include the broad expanse envisioned by John XXIII, that is, people of good will. Second, Pope Francis's citing of John XXIII, who was writing at the brink of a nuclear disaster, could well indicate that for Francis the state of the (neglected) environment is cause for similar urgent worldwide concern. In addition, it is important to note Pope Francis's reliance on the "see, judge, act" method adopted by John XXIII in *Mater et magistra* (236). The then-Archbishop Bergoglio used this explicitly in his editorial work on the CELAM document from Aparecida in 2007 (more below). In point of fact, John adopted this from Pius XII, who relied on the work of (Belgian) Cardinal Joseph Cardijn (1882–1967), who worked with the poor and adopted this triad as his approach to implementing the Church's social justice teaching.

7. Pope Paul VI, *Populorum progressio*, March 26, 1967, *http://w2.vatican.va/content /popepaul-vi/en/encyclicals/documents/hf_p-vi_enc_26031967_populorum.html*.

8. Pope Paul VI, *Octogesima adveniens*, May 14, 1971, *http://w2.vatican.va/content /popepaul-vi/en/apost_letters/documents/hf_p-vi_apl_19710514_octogesima-adveniens. html*.

9. Pope Paul VI, *Message to Mr. Maurice F. Strong, Secretary-General of the Conference on the Environment*, June 1, 1972, *http://w2.vatican.va/content/popepaul-vi/en/messages /pont-messages/documents/hf_p-vi_mess_19720605_conferenza-ambiente.html*.

10. Ibid.

He articulated the theme of interdependence (of all things on the earth), noting a corresponding solidarity among them.[11]

Five years later (occasioned by the fifth World Environment Day), Paul VI returned to the theme of responsibility to hand over a healthy environment to future generations and noted that humans have the choice whether to construct and ennoble the world about them or to destroy it and squander its goods.[12] In this text for the first time, the pope referred to humans in the key, biblically-inspired phrase "custodians of creation." He concluded with a forceful appeal, based on interdependence, of a "fraternal sharing and protection of a good environment."[13]

Pope John Paul II

John Paul II's first encyclical, *Redemptor hominis* (1979), provides an ecological touchpoint to which he repeatedly returns.[14] The pope notes that the destruction of creation is one of the things of which humans today are afraid (*RH* 15) and observes that humans have to make choices about progress or threats to creation's very existence (*RH* 16).[15] The pope focuses on the dignity of human persons, the responsibility humans bear for equitable sharing of the earth's resources, the wise use of their talents to work and produce

---

11. In noting that the environment is an urgent issue, the pope called for a radical commitment toward its preservation based on the biblical injunction (from Gen. 1:31 and 1 Tim. 4:4) that all creation was "good" and offered St. Francis of Assisi as a significant Catholic exemplar of a Christian contemplative stance that would witness to the harmony of humans with and in nature (ibid.). Then, in 1979, John Paul II named St. Francis of Assisi as patron of ecology. See Pope John Paul II, *Inter Sanctos*, November 29, 1979, *http://w2.vatican.va/content/john-paul-ii/la/apost_letters/1979/documents /hf_jp-ii_apl_19791129_inter-sanctos.html*.

12. Pope Paul VI, *Message for the Fifth World-Wide Day of Environment*, June 5, 1977, *https://w2.vatican.va/content/paul-vi/en/messages/pont-messages/documents/hf_p-vi _mess_19770605_world-day-ambiente.html*.

13. Ibid.

14. Pope John Paul II, *Redemptor hominis*, March 4, 1979, *http://w2.vatican.va /content/john-paul-ii/en/encyclicals/documents/hf_jp-ii_enc_04031979_redemptor -hominis.html*.

15. Ibid. He also discusses redemption as a "new creation" (*RH* 8).

goods, and the ways that issues of the environment are linked to the world economy.[16]

In his encyclical *Laborem excercens* (1981), the pope emphasizes that by divine intention humans reflect "the very action of the Creator of the universe" when they "subdue" and "dominate the earth" (*LE* 4; reiterated and explicated more fully in *LE* 25).[17] He asserts that "the earth" is "that fragment of the universe" that humans inhabit, as well as "the whole of the visible world insofar as it comes within range of the influence of humans and of their striving to satisfy their needs" (*LE* 4). "The earth" includes "all the resources that the earth (and indirectly the visible world) contains and which, through the activity of persons, can be discovered and used for their ends."[18] It is through work that humans become more and more the masters of the earth, exercising this task in accord with and "within the Creator's original ordering" (*LE* 4).[19] Human beings thus have responsibility to preserve and share the resources of the whole earth with all that dwell on it.

---

16. To the assertions of Paul VI about the earth's goodness, John Paul II juxtaposes the sin of Adam with the redemption of Christ, the second Adam (*RH* 8). But he articulates a less than happy picture of creation today by stating that it may well be subject to futility (citing Rom. 8) and that humans' responsibility in dominion has led to the pollution of the natural environment and to armed conflicts (*RH* 8). Humans have a dignity beyond compare in creation; humanity also, therefore, has deep responsibility for it as its "intelligent and noble 'master' and 'guardian,'" and not as a heedless 'exploiter' and 'destroyer'" (*RH* 15). Many of our fears, the pope writes, come from what humans produce or how they use their creative capacities; humans have not insured that "progress" and "development" "make human life on earth 'more human' in every aspect of that life" (*RH* 15). Because of human capacity for thought and moral action, the pope insists on the priority of "ethics over technology, . . . the primacy of the person over things, and . . . the superiority of spirit over matter" (*RH* 16). It is significant that the pope speaks about support for the world economy and the principle of solidarity to lead to "a wider and more immediate redistribution of riches and of control over them" (*RH* 16). Because humans have capacities that other orders of creation do not, they bear responsibility to preserve creation.

17. Pope John Paul II, *Laborem excercens*, September 14, 1981, *http://w2.vatican.va /content/john-paul-ii/en/encyclicals/documents/hf_jp-ii_enc_14091981_laborem-exercens .html*.

18. Ibid.

19. Ibid. "Original ordering" is an interesting phrase, especially given the more recent debates about evolution and whether one holds an evolutionary understanding of creation.

In *Sollicitudo rei socialis* (1987), John Paul II reiterates the above themes but also advances and specifies his thought about development and preserving resources (*SRS* 26).[20] He urges a "rigorous respect for justice" aimed at "a fair distribution of the results of true development" that shares the good things God has given to all (*SRS* 26, 35). In exercising dominion over creation, the pope reminds humans that they "have a certain affinity with other creatures" (*SRS* 26),[21] which "imposes limits upon the use and dominion over things" (*SRS* 29).

These limits include avoiding "*indiscriminate* possession of created things and the products of human industry" (*SRS* 29).[22] The pope warns humans not to use limited natural resources "as if they were inexhaustible, with absolute dominion (*SRS* 34)." Natural resources are not only here for the use of this generation, but "above all for generations to come" (*SRS* 34).[23] He thus states that the *dominion* granted to humans by God is not an absolute power, and he insists that one cannot speak of a freedom to "use and misuse" or to dispose of things as one pleases (*SRS* 34). The limitation imposed from the beginning by the Creator himself and expressed symbolically by the prohibition not to "eat of the fruit of the tree" (cf. Gen. 2:16–17) shows clearly that, when it comes to the natural world, humans are subject not only to biological laws, but also to moral laws that cannot be violated with impunity (*SRS* 34).

The document *Peace with God the Creator, Peace with All of Creation* (*1990 World Day of Peace Message*) is John Paul II's most focused, single-topic treatment of the "new ecological awareness" as a moral concern (*1990 WDP* 1, 5, 6, 15).[24] He reiterates previous papal

---

20. Pope John Paul II, *Sollicitudo rei socialis*, December 30, 1987, *http://w2.vatican .va/content/john-paul-ii/en/encyclicals/documents/hf_jp-ii_enc_30121987_sollicitudo-rei -socialis.html*.

21. It is noteworthy that in his 1989 Easter message Pope John Paul II speaks of the reconciliation accomplished through Christ's blood, a reconciliation of humans with God, with themselves, and with nature, and of humans' responsibility for creation. See Pope John Paul II, *Urbi et orbi*, March 26, 1989, *https://w2.vatican.va/content /john-paul-ii/it/messages/urbi/documents/hf_jp-ii_mes_19890326_easter-urbi.html*.

22. Ibid.

23. Ibid.

24. Pope John Paul II, *Peace with God the Creator, Peace with All of Creation: Message of His Holiness John Paul II for the Celebration of the World Day of Peace*, January 1, 1990, *http://w2.vatican.va/content/john-paul-ii/en/messages/peace/documents/hf_jp-ii _mes_19891208_xxiii-world-day-for-peace.html*.

teachings on the goodness of creation (*1990 WDP* 3–5), on the earth's resources as for the common good and use of all (*1990 WDP* 8), and on the responsibility of humans to insure more equitable distribution of the world's goods through a "new solidarity" (*1990 WDP* 10), especially among highly industrialized nations. In view of the relationship between the environment and poverty, war, and the lifestyle of modern society, he identifies today's ecological challenge as a "moral crisis" (*1990 WDP* 11–13). In response, he calls on men and women to adopt habits of "simplicity, moderation, discipline, . . . [and] a spirit of self-sacrifice" (*1990 WDP* 3). Since "*we cannot interfere in one area of the ecosystem without paying due attention both to the consequences of such interference in other areas and to the well-being of future generations,*" the pope characteristically encourages a true international approach to creation care (*1990 WDP* 3, italics in original).

Three additional aspects of this message are particularly innovative. First, the pope speaks of the "aesthetic value of creation," calling on humans to contemplate nature and "the works of human ingenuity" (*1990 WDP* 14). Methodologically, this assertion offers one fruitful avenue for developing even more substantial Catholic approaches to the ecological crisis.[25] Second, John Paul II invites "ecumenical and interreligious cooperation" (*1990 WDP* 15).[26] Finally, John Paul II explicitly addresses human-forced climate change by noting that the "'greenhouse effect' has now reached crisis proportions as a consequence of industrial growth, massive urban concentrations, and vastly increased energy" (*1990 WDP* 6).

In the encyclical letter *Centesimus annus* (1991), John Paul II returns to the familiar anthropological foundation for his teaching on equitable distribution of the earth's resources (*CA* 37). It is an "anthropological error," he asserts, that humans forget that the earth's goods come from "God's prior and original gift of the things that are"

---

25. This assertion should be read in light of Pope Paul's citing of St. Francis of Assisi's "contemplative stance" toward creation (see footnote 9) and with what we will term the "sacramental vision" espoused in *Centesimus annus* (37) (Pope John Paul II, *Centesimus annus*, May 1, 1991, *http://w2.vatican.va/content/john-paul-ii/en/encyclicals /documents/hf_jp-ii_enc_01051991_centesimus-annus.html*).

26. This document is particularly notable because it immediately preceded the World Council of Churches (Seventh) Assembly at Canberra, Australia (Feb. 7–20, 1991), the theme of which was "Come Holy Spirit—Renew the Whole Creation." See *Signs of the Spirit*, Official Report, Seventh Assembly, ed. Michael Kinnamon (Geneva: WCC, 1991).

(*CA* 37). The pope contextualizes and asserts the importance of safe-guarding "*the moral conditions for an authentic 'human ecology,*'" (*CA* 38, italics in original), which requires respect for the earth as gift to man and for man himself as gift. The use and meaning of the phrase "human ecology" therefore marks an important terminological development in the way the magisterium speaks about ecological issues.

In his 1995 encyclical *Evangelium vitae*, John Paul II's consideration of the dignity of the human person is stated negatively: when the sense of God is lost, then humans fail to consider themselves as "mysteriously different" from other orders of creation, which is a problem since we are not "merely one more living being" (*EV* 22).[27] Without the sense of God, furthermore, "nature itself, from being '*mater*' (mother) is now reduced to being 'matter,' and is subject to every kind of manipulation" (*EV* 22). More positively, he asserts, "There is a truth of creation that must be acknowledged, or a plan of God for life which must be respected" (*EV* 22).

In identifying positive signs about life in our day, John Paul II notes "growing attention being paid to the quality of life and to ecology, especially in more developed societies, where people's expectations are no longer concentrated so much on problems of survival as on the search for an overall improvement of living conditions" (*EV* 27). Here the pope reiterates the central place of humans within creation, especially human responsibility to exercise dominion (*EV* 34). He notes that humans alone are capable of knowing their Creator. The pope applies the Genesis text about tilling and looking after the garden (Gen. 2:15) to the moral responsibility humans have for the preservation of the natural habitats of the different species of animals and other forms of life (*EV* 42).

In a *General Audience* delivered on January 17, 2001, John Paul II refers both to the responsibility of "stewardship" and the need for "an ecological conversion" (*1-17-2001 GA* 4).[28] Because of this, the pope encourages "not only a 'physical' ecology . . . but also a 'human' ecology" in order to prepare "for future generations an environment more in conformity with the Creator's plan" (*1-17-2001 GA* 4).

---

27. Pope John Paul II, *Evangelium vitae*, March 25, 1995, *http://w2.vatican.va /content/john-paul-ii/en/encyclicals/documents/hf_jp-ii_enc_25031995_evangelium -vitae.html.*

28. Pope John Paul II, *General Audience*, January 17, 2001, *http://w2.vatican.va /content/john-paul-ii/en/audiences/2001/documents/hf_jp-ii_aud_20010117.html.*

Pope Benedict XVI

Often called "the green pope," Benedict XVI is known both for what he did in the Vatican to preserve energy (e.g., installing solar panels) and for his frequent writings on the environment.

In his encyclical letter *Caritas in veritate* (2009), Benedict asserts, "*The way humanity treats the environment influences the way it treats itself, and vice versa*" (*CV* 51, italics in original).[29] Today, he argues, there is a need for "*new life-styles*" (*CV* 52). For Benedict, nature and society/culture are integrated such that the decline and desertification of one leads to the impoverishment of the other. Additionally, the Church "must above all protect mankind from self-destruction" by promoting a "human ecology" that the Church must proclaim in the public sphere (*CV* 51). Next Benedict teaches that the problematic moral tenor of society, which often lacks respect for human life, is inconsistent with creation care and contradicts the desire for future generations to respect the natural environment (*CV* 51). Finally, Benedict reemphasizes that the ultimate source of truth and love "is not, and cannot be, mankind, but only God, who is himself Truth and Love" (*CV* 52). Therefore true development toward the protection of the environment and the betterment of society "is not based simply on human choice, but is an intrinsic part of a plan that is prior to us and constitutes for all of us a duty to be freely accepted" (*CV* 52). As such, the pope calls for "*new life-styles*" animated by, quoting John Paul II, "the quest for truth, beauty, goodness and communion with others for the sake of common growth" (*CV* 51, italics in original).

One year after *Caritas in veritate*, Benedict published *If You Want to Cultivate Peace, Protect Creation* (*2010 World Day of Peace Message*).[30] In that message, the pope built on his encyclical and gave extended treatment to ecology. He recognized that "our present crises—be they economic, food-related, environmental or social—are ultimately also moral crises, and all of them are

---

29. Pope Benedict XVI, *Caritas in veritate*, June 29, 2009, *http://w2.vatican.va /content/benedict-xvi/en/encyclicals/documents/hf_ben-xvi_enc_20090629_caritas-in -veritate.html*.

30. Pope Benedict XVI, *If You Want to Cultivate Peace, Protect Creation: Message of His Holiness Pope Benedict XVI for the Celebration of the World Day of Peace,* January 1, 2010, *https://w2.vatican.va/content/benedict-xvi/en/messages/peace/documents/hf _ben-xvi_mes_20091208_xliii-world-day-peace.html*.

interrelated" (*2010 WDP* 5). Additionally, he calls humanity to both "*review . . . our model of development*" and "consider the cost entailed—environmentally and socially—as an essential part of the overall expenses incurred" in economic transactions (*2010 WDP* 5, 7, italics in original). Moreover, he pointedly asks if humanity "can . . . remain indifferent before the problems associated with such realities as climate change" and calls for changes in the types and quantities of humans' energy consumption and distribution patterns (*2010 WDP* 9).

Pope Francis

When a Catholic bishop is elected bishop of Rome—and thus pope of the Catholic Church—he chooses a papal name to honor an ancestor in faith and identify a model whom he hopes to emulate. For Cardinal Jorge Mario Bergoglio, this model was Saint Francis of Assisi, patron saint of those who promote ecology and a person who cared for both creation and the poor.

At his formal installation Mass, Pope Francis drew on the ethic of his namesake by "ask[ing] all those who have positions of responsibility in economic, political and social life, and all men and women of goodwill: let us be 'protectors' of creation, protectors of God's plan inscribed in nature, protectors of one another and of the environment."[31] This responsibility to protect creation extends from "the beauty of the created world" (citing the book of Genesis and life of Saint Francis of Assisi) to "respecting the environment in which we live . . . protecting people . . . and showing loving concern for each and every person." While admitting that this will take hard work, Pope Francis also emphasizes that tenderness is a virtue of the strong, not the weak. Additionally, he sets in motion his papal concern for the poor by challenging himself to "open his arms to protect all of God's people and embrace, with tender affection, the whole of humanity, especially the poorest, the weakest, the least important, those whom Matthew lists in the final judgment on love: the hungry,

---

31. Pope Francis, "Homily of Pope Francis: Mass, Imposition of the Pallium and Bestowal of the Fisherman's Ring for the Beginning of the Petrine Ministry of the Bishop of Rome," March 19, 2013, *https://w2.vatican.va/content/francesco/en /homilies/2013/documents/papa-francesco_20130319_omelia-inizio-pontificato.html.*

the thirsty, the stranger, the naked, the sick and those in prison (Mt 25:31–46). Only those who serve with love are able to protect!"

As he admits, Francis's first encyclical, *On the Light of Faith* (*Lumen fidei*, 29 June 2013) was largely authored by Benedict XVI. But its sections on faith and reason are extensively quoted in *Laudato si'* regarding faith and science (*LS* 141, which quotes *LF* 34).[32] Other notable sections in *Lumen fidei* that come to bear in *Laudato si'* address faith and the common good, faith and the family, a light for life in society, and consolation and strength amid suffering (*LF* 51, 52, 54–55, 56, 57).

Later that same year, Pope Francis issued his post-synodal exhortation *Evangelii gaudium* (November 24, 2013).[33] Although its primary topic is the new evangelization, that is, sharing the gospel in the twenty-first century, the document lays much of the groundwork of *Laudato si'*. This is evidenced by the fact that *Laudato si'* repeatedly cites *Evangelii gaudium* (e.g., *LS* 56, 89, 110, 141, 152, 178, 196, 199, 216, 225), especially regarding insights that underpin the notion of interconnectedness that defines the concept of integral ecology in *Laudato si'* (e.g., invitation to dialogue with all persons and concern for the vulnerability of creation to sociopolitical and economic systems that value only profit and power, cf. *LS* 56, 181, 215, 257).

Recent Teaching on the Environment by Conferences of Bishops

In the Catholic tradition, national or international groupings of bishops, called episcopal conferences, serve the needs of the Catholic Church in their particular nation or international regions. Of the many that Francis cites in *Laudato si'*, this chapter examines the work of the conference of Latin American bishops, known as CELAM (*Consejo Episcopal Latinoamericano*), because of the influence of CELAM's *Aparecida Concluding Document* on the formation and

---

32. Pope Francis, *Lumen fidei*, June 29, 2013, *http://w2.vatican.va/content/francesco /en/encyclicals/documents/papa-francesco_20130629_enciclica-lumen-fidei.html*.

33. Pope Francis, *Evangelii gaudium*, November 24, 2013, *http://w2.vatican.va /content/francesco/en/apost_exhortations/documents/papa-francesco_esortazione -ap_20131124_evangelii-gaudium.html*.

contents of *Laudato si'*. The work of the conference of U.S. bishops will also be considered but only briefly since this topic is treated at length in chapter 2 of this volume.

CELAM *Aparecida Concluding Document*—Fifth General Conference of Bishops of Latin America and the Caribbean

In 2007, CELAM met for their Fifth General Conference in Aparecida, Brazil, to reflect on a number of issues. Their inclusive *Concluding Document* addresses "the evangelizing action of the Church" (*ACD* 1), that is, the effort to share the gospel with all people.[34] Most notably, Jorge Mario Bergoglio, then-archbishop of Buenos Aires and the future Pope Francis, was its final editor. The document skillfully and thoroughly combines evangelization with a number of related issues—including catechesis, education, liturgy, and sacraments—all in the context of evidence of decreasing participation in Church life and liturgy.

What may come as a surprise is the frequency with which and the manner in which the *Aparecida Concluding Document* deals with ecology and the environment. Many of the themes seen here are fleshed out more fully in *Laudato si'*. In effect, this is the key document that leads to the pope's encyclical. The *Aparecida Concluding Document* adopts the "see, judge, act" method of social ethics[35] in treating the theological foundations and themes of ecology (cf. *LS* 24–27, 104–13, 126, 181, 250–52), specific ecological issues (cf. *LS* 66, 83–87), and the interrelationship of ecology and other issues (cf. *LS* 114–26, 397). The document also offers positive pathways forward and cautions about the crisis at hand (cf. *LS* 471–88).

In sum, the CELAM bishops, viewing reality through a wide-angle lens, see ecology and evangelization, the environment and poverty, the teachings of the Catholic Church and deforestation,

---

34. CELAM, *Aparecida Concluding Document*, May 2007, *http://www.celam.org /aparecida/Ingles.pdf.*

35. "See, judge, act" is often used in social justice methodologies, as noted when discussing Pope John XXIII's *Mater et magistra* above. Sometimes this is expanded to include "celebrate."

as all parts of a whole. This document provides background to what the pope calls "integral ecology" in *Laudato si'*.

Catholic Bishops of the United States

Three major texts from the Catholic bishops of the United States are important with respect to *Laudato si'*. First, *Renewing the Earth* (1991)[36] asserts that the environmental crisis is a moral challenge involving the intertwined issues of environment, energy, economics, equity, and ethics. It sets forth the biblical data and principles of Catholic social teaching on ecology, recognizes humans as "God's stewards and co-creators," sounds a "call to conversion," and concludes with "a word of hope" (*RE* V). Second, *Global Climate Change: A Plea for Dialogue, Prudence and the Common Good* (2001)[37] contains two insights reiterated in *Laudato si'*: first, the fact that the climate is "part of the global commons" (cf. *LS* 23) and, second, the need for prudence in response to climate science (cf. *LS* 186). Third, *Global Climate Change* (2010)[38] is a letter written to the U.S. Congress by the United States Conference of Catholic Bishops (USCCB) and leaders of the National Religious Partnership for the Environment that outlines agreed-upon principles for approaching the environmental crisis. (A thorough examination of these documents is in chapter 2 of this volume.)

Major Contributions of *Laudato si'*

Nothing can substitute for a careful (even prayerful) reading of *Laudato si'*. In order to aid this process, here is a summary of what I regard as important and lasting contributions that Francis makes in

---

36. USCC, *Renewing the Earth: An Invitation to Reflection and Action on Environment in Light of Catholic Social Teaching*, November 14, 1991, *http://www.usccb.org/issues-and-action/human-life-and-dignity/environment/renewing-the-earth.cfm*.

37. USCCB, *Global Climate Change: A Plea for Dialogue, Prudence and the Common Good*, June 15, 2001, *http://www.usccb.org/issues-and-action/human-life-and-dignity/environment/global-climate-change-a-plea-for-dialogue-prudence-and-the-common-good.cfm*.

38. USCCB, *Global Climate Change*, February 2010, *http://www.usccb.org/issues-and-action/human-life-and-dignity/environment/global-climate-change-2010.cfm*.

the encyclical to Catholic, Christian, religious, and secular ecological discourse.

First, *Laudato si'* provides a comprehensive, inclusive theology of creation and ecology that highlights Catholicism as a theological, not fundamentalist, tradition (see *LS* 17). The foundations for this rich theology include God as Creator (*LS* 73), God as Trinity calling all of creation into God's Trinitarian communion (*LS* 238–40), and the sacramental principle,[39] which recognizes that all creation serves as "a locus where God is revealed, disclosed and experienced, and which underlies Catholic understanding of liturgy and sacraments" (*LS* 235–36).

Second, *Laudato si'* incorporates concrete methods, principles, and concerns, such as the "see, judge, act" method, the precautionary principle (which asserts that it is not necessary to know everything in order to act, *LS* 186), and a view toward universal and intergenerational communion (*LS* 93, 158).

Third, the encyclical encourages a movement from "natural" or "human" ecology to an "integral ecology." In this way, the document appeals for a turning away from a "tyrannic anthropocentrism" marked by consumerism and individualism (*LS* 34, 50, 68, 119, 162, 184, 203, 208–10), and it emphasizes the interconnectedness of all of creation (*LS* 68–70, 91–92, 114–22, 137–42, 240). This means addressing all ecological degradation (not "just" climate change and global warming, *LS* 23–26), as well as combating pollution, waste, and the "throwaway culture" (*LS* 20, 206), examining the ethical implications of food distribution practices (*LS* 32, 38, 50), upholding and advocating for the absolute right to potable water, the relative right to private property, the right to life, and the right to economic justice (*LS* 27–31, 93, 120, 154). It also means promoting intellectual honesty, transparency, and academic freedom (*LS* 16, 138–40, 188).

Fourth, the encyclical calls for the conversion of individuals and communities through contemplation and dialogue (*LS* 71, 216–21, 237), and it encourages especially the dialogue between faith and science (*LS* 62, 63, 95, 102, 105, 107, 110, 114, 131). Moreover, this conversion is to result in a new way of viewing, living in, and becoming stewards and caretakers of creation.

---

39. Kevin W. Irwin, "A Sacramental World: Sacramentality as the Primary Language for Sacraments," *Worship* 76, no. 3 (May 2002): 199.

Conclusion

Pope Francis and his papacy might well be called a "living parable." He talks the talk and walks the walk. *Laudato si'* articulates the ecological vision that animates the life of Francis, who drinks from the well of his own pastoral experience and who sits at the feet of his predecessors in the papacy and his brother bishops around the world. In reading (and hopefully rereading) this document, all people are invited to personal and collective conversion. In sum, Pope Francis inspires readers who carefully and prayerfully study *Laudato si'* to better care for our common home.

Review Questions

1. How would you describe Catholic magisterial teaching on ecology in one sentence?
2. How would you define *anthropocentrism*?
3. *Human dignity* is a recurring concept in Catholic magisterial teaching on ecology. What does this term mean to you?
4. What do you think is the difference between human ecology and integral ecology?
5. Why do you suppose Pope John Paul II said that "the ecological crisis is a moral issue" (*1990 WDP* 6)?

In-Depth Questions

1. Before reading this chapter, were you aware of Catholic magisterial teachings on ecology that came before *Laudato si'*? If not, why do you think that might have been?
2. Pope John Paul II and the U.S. Catholic bishops speak of the need for "conversion" regarding ecology. What would ecological conversion look like for an individual? For society?
3. In *Renewing the Earth*, the U.S. Catholic bishops describe humans as "co-creators" with God in creation. Why do you think the bishops use this term, and what image does it conjure up for you?

4. In *Global Climate Change: A Plea for Dialogue, Prudence, and the Common Good*, the U.S. Conference of Catholic Bishops emphasizes the need for prudence in response to climate change. How might this virtue—described by Pope Francis in *Laudato si'* as the "precautionary principle"—inform modern conversations about climate change?

5. This chapter identifies several contributions that *Laudato si'* makes to ecological discourse. To which one are you most drawn? Why is that?

Suggestions for Further Study

Pope Benedict XVI. *The Environment*. Huntington, IN: Our Sunday Visitor, 2012.

———. *Ten Commandments for the Environment: Pope Benedict XVI Speaks Out for Creation and Justice*. Notre Dame, IN: Ave Maria, 2009.

Christiansen, Drew, and Walter Grazer, eds. *And God Saw That It Was Good: Catholic Theology and the Environment*. Washington, DC: United States Catholic Conference, 1996.

Irwin, Kevin. *A Commentary on Laudato Si': Examining the Background, Contributions, Implementation, and Future of Pope Francis's Encyclical*. Mahwah, NJ: Paulist Press, 2016.

Lorbiecki, Marybeth. *Following St. Francis: John Paul II's Call for Ecological Action*. New York: Rizzoli Ex Libris, 2014.

Schaefer, Jame, and Tobias Winright, eds. *Environmental Justice and Climate Change: Assessing Pope Benedict XVI's Ecological Vision for the Catholic Church in the United States*. Lanham, MD: Lexington, 2013.

CHAPTER 2

Laudato si': Continuity, Change, and Challenge[1]

WALTER E. GRAZER

> We Christians, together with the other monotheistic religions, believe that the universe is the fruit of a loving decision by the Creator, who permits man respectfully to use creation for the good of his fellow men and for the glory of the Creator; he is not authorized to abuse it, much less to destroy it. In all religions, the environment is a fundamental good.[2]

At the beginning of his ecological encyclical, *Laudato si'*, Pope Francis says, "I would like to enter into dialogue with all people around the world about our common home" (*LS* 2). Dialogue and encounter are keys to understanding the substance of his papal mission and ministry. His urgent plea for ecumenical and interfaith dialogue is of extreme importance for the protection of the planet, for the promotion of an integral development of the human family, and for safeguarding future generations.

While *Laudato si'* is the most authoritative statement on ecology ever issued by the Roman Catholic Church, the remarkable leadership of other Christian communities needs upfront acknowledgement. The World Council of Churches, Ecumenical Patriarch Bartholomew I (spiritual leader of the world's Orthodox Christians), the mainline Protestant churches, and the U.S. evangelical, Jewish, and Muslim communities all do significant work to address

---

1. This article is an adaptation of a speech given by the author at the annual conference of the National Workshop on Christian Unity in Louisville on April 19, 2016.

2. Pope Francis, "Speech to the United Nations," *Origins* 45, no. 19 (2015): 328.

environmental concerns. Examples include the National Religious Partnership for the Environment (which includes the U.S. Conference of Catholic Bishops, National Council of Churches of Christ, Jewish Council for Public Affairs, and Evangelical Environmental Network) and Green Muslims.

This chapter focuses on Catholic contributions to ecological conversations by exploring three themes: (1) the continuity between *Laudato si'* and precedent Catholic social teaching, (2) the distinctiveness of Pope Francis's contribution to the developing thought about ecology within the Catholic tradition, and (3) the potential of *Laudato si'* to influence Catholic, ecumenical, and interdisciplinary efforts to meet contemporary ecological challenges.

Context and Continuity

Popes build on the work of their papal predecessors, and Pope Francis is no exception. In his attention to ecology and concern for climate change, Pope Francis does not—as some charge—wander into areas that are radical for the Catholic Church. Nor does he address topics that are of tangential concern to the Church. Rather, he draws on prior work of popes and bishops' conferences while deepening and extending the tradition of Catholic ecological concern. Little of the Catholic Church's effort to address ecological concerns during the past forty years has attracted wide enough public attention. The fact, however, that Pope Francis's ecological work is garnering significantly more attention does not mean that his work in this area is new for the Church. It means that more people are paying attention to what the Church has long been saying.

The chapter by Kevin Irwin in this volume especially highlights Pope Francis's continuity with his immediate predecessors—Popes Paul VI, John Paul II, and Benedict XVI. As pointed out later in this article, however, and as Msgr. Irwin suggests, one of the most significant new elements of *Laudato si'* is Pope Francis's integration and use of various statements by episcopal conferences around the world. This is truly a unique contribution of Pope Francis to papal discussions about ecology.

The United States Conference of Catholic Bishops (the organization that represents the U.S. Catholic bishops in the United States and previously existed as the separate National Conference of Catholic Bishops and the United States Catholic Conference), which Pope Francis quotes in *Laudato si'*, has been active since the early 1980s in addressing environmental concerns (*LS* 52).[3] Following the issuance of the *1990 World Day of Peace Message, Peace with God the Creator, Peace with All Creation*, by Pope John Paul II, the U.S. Catholic Bishops in 1991 released their own environment statement, *Renewing the Earth: An Invitation to Reflection and Action on the Environment in Light of Catholic Social Teaching*.[4] The bishops also initiated their own environment program, *Renewing the Earth: Environmental Justice Program*, in 1993 and joined the National Religious Partnership for the Environment. As the bishops' program's name suggests, they focused immediately on the link between "care for the poor and care for the earth [as] central to the bishops' approach to environmental concerns."[5]

In *Renewing the Earth*, the U.S. Catholic bishops take up themes now reflected more fully in *Laudato si'*. In particular, they examine their concern for the environment as a response to the Second Vatican Council's call to read the "signs of the times" recognizing the importance of addressing environmental issues. They see humans as part of nature and call for an exploration of the "link between a concern for the person and the earth, between natural ecology and social ecology." Basing their commentary on Scripture, theology, and the Church's social teaching, the bishops note that "respect for nature and respect for human life are inextricably related." With their emphasis upon the common good and the notion of "authentic development" first articulated by Pope Paul VI in 1967,[6] they strongly advocate for an option for the poor, a special concern for

---

3. E.g., United States Catholic Conference, *Reflections on the Energy Crisis: A Statement by the Committee on Social Development and World Peace*, 1981, *http://www .usccb.org/issues-and-action/human-life-and-dignity/environment/upload/reflections -energy-crisis.pdf*.

4. *Renewing the Earth: An Invitation to Reflection and Action on Environment in Light of Catholic Social Teaching*, a Pastoral Statement by the United States Conference of Catholic Bishops, 1991, *http://www.usccb.org/issues-and-action/human-life-and-dignity /environment/renewing the earth.cfm*.

5. Drew Christiansen and Walter Grazer, eds., *"And God Saw That It Was Good": Catholic Theology and the Environment* (Washington, DC: United States Conference of Catholic Bishops, 1996), p. 3.

6. *Populorem Progressio*, 1967, *http://w2.vatican.va/content/paul-vi/en/encyclicals /documents/hf_p-vi_enc_26031967_populorum.html*.

workers and for "sustainable social and economic development." The U.S. bishops also call us to "treat other creatures in the natural world not just as a means to human fulfillment but also as God's creatures, possessing an independent value, worthy of our respect and care." All this they said in 1991.

While the 1991 U.S. Catholic bishops' statement was broad in its concern, their 2001 statement on climate change, *Global Climate Change: A Plea for Dialogue, Prudence and the Common Good*, was an application of Catholic social teaching principles to one of the most challenging issues to face humanity in the twenty-first century.[7] The bishops viewed climate change from the perspective of the common good, justice for those living in poverty, and a call to dialogue. They recognized the controversy surrounding the issue in the realm of public policy, naming it a "test and an opportunity for our nation and the entire Catholic community." They perceived that climate change is "not about economic theory or political platforms, nor about partisan advantage or interest group pressure. It is about the future of God's creation and the one human family." Like *Laudato si'*, this statement accepts the science of climate change, calling for prudential action that respects all of creation and for solidarity with poorer people and nations. Finally, they urge the United States to take a leading role in addressing the issue.

The ecological and environmental themes explored by the U.S. Catholic bishops and those by other bishops' conferences quoted by Pope Francis in *Laudato si'* reflect the growing concern, consensus, and conviction that humanity faces serious environmental challenges that call for all people to dialogue and unite to care for our common home.

Change and Contribution: New Frontiers

If the themes that Pope Francis addresses in *Laudato si'* resonate with and build upon the work of his predecessors and bishops' conferences from around the world, some might ask, "Is there anything new in Pope Francis's encyclical? What is the buzz about?"

---

7. *Global Climate Change: A Plea for Dialogue, Prudence and the Common Good*, United States Conference of Catholic Bishops, June 15, 2001, *http://www.usccb.org/issues -and-action/human-life-and-dignity/environment/global-climate-change-a-plea-for -dialogue-prudence-and-the-common-good.cfm.*

The short answer is, "Yes, there is much that is new in *Laudato si'*." Although the following list is not exhaustive, there seem to be at least nine innovative aspects of *Laudato si'* with respect to Catholic ecological theology.

1. **The pope is the message.** The encyclical is significant because of Pope Francis himself. In so many ways, Pope Francis *is* the message. This is a man who seeks to live the gospel in a visible and unmistakable way. He embraces the migrants who washed up on the shores of Lampedusa and Lesbos, he eschews the traditional Vatican trappings of luxury, he lives in the Vatican guest house rather than alone in the papal apartment, he traveled the United States in a small Fiat rather than a large SUV like other foreign dignitaries. In street parlance, he walks the talk.

2. **The language is simple.** The pope's witness in *Laudato si'* is conveyed through language that is direct and easy to understand, without complicated images. Examples include the following:

- "The earth, our home, is beginning to look more and more like an immense pile of filth" (21).
- "'Who turned the wonder world of the seas into underwater cemeteries bereft of color and life?'" (41, quoting the Catholic Bishops' Conference of the Philippines).
- "We are not meant to be inundated by cement, asphalt, glass and metal, and deprived of physical contact with nature" (43).
- "'Whatever is fragile, like the environment, is defenseless before the interests of a deified market, which has become the only rule'" (56).
- "'God has joined us so closely to the world around us that we can feel the desertification of the soil almost as a physical ailment and the extinction of species as a painful disfigurement' (*Evangelii gaudium* 215)" (89).

The encyclical is full of direct, pithy language that stirs our imaginations and consciences. This type of language is new in Catholic magisterial documents and teaching.

3. **The pope uses his papal authority to address ecology.** Pope Francis addresses ecology with one of the most authoritative means

of papal teaching authority—an encyclical—to date.[8] This is especially so with his treatment of climate science, wherein he recognizes that "a very solid scientific consensus indicates that we are presently witnessing a disturbing warming of the climatic system" (*LS* 23) and invokes the "precautionary principle":

> If objective information suggests that serious and irreversible damage may result, a project should be halted or modified, even in the absence of indisputable proof. Here the burden of proof is effectively reversed, since in such cases objective and conclusive demonstrations will have to be brought forward to demonstrate that the proposed activity will not cause serious harm to the environment or to those who inhabit it. (*LS* 186)

He has done this at a critical moment in history as the world faces the prospect of runaway, effectively irreversible climate change. Timing is everything, and Pope Francis's choice to address ecology in his first major encyclical signals to all people of faith and goodwill the gravity with which he views present environmental challenges.[9]

4. **The pope goes further in promoting integral ecology.** Pope Francis seeks an integral ecology capable of promoting the common good and the flourishing of all life—of humans and of other creatures. He goes further than his predecessors in promoting integral ecology, a notion that is even more inclusive than the notion of integral development first proposed by Pope Paul VI in his 1967 encyclical *Populorum progressio* (14–21). Importantly, Pope Francis says we can no longer achieve integral human development without the simultaneous inclusion of concern for the environment in which we live. "We are faced not with two separate crises, one environmental and the other social, but rather, with one complex crisis that is both social

---

8. For more on this, see Daniel R. DiLeo, "Papal Authority and Climate Change: Preparing for Pope Francis' Encyclical," *U.S. Catholic*, May 20, 2015, *http:// www.uscatholic.org/articles/201505/papal-authority-and-climate-change-preparing -pope-francis-encyclical-30117.*

9. Pope Francis published the encyclical *Lumen fidei* in 2013. That document, however, was largely authored by his predecessor, Pope Benedict XVI, and did not receive nearly as much public attention as *Laudato si'*.

and environmental. Strategies for solution demand an integrated approach to combating poverty, restoring dignity to the excluded, and at the same time protecting nature" (*LS* 139).

5. *Laudato si'* **carries an unprecedentedly clear moral message about poverty and ecology.** Its message is about global inequality and how the plight of those who live in poverty is intimately connected with the degradation of the earth. Pope Francis sees a direct link between these situations, and this is unsurprising given his own pastoral experiences with the poor. He believes we cannot divorce the human social condition from a deteriorating environment, particularly as it affects those who live in poverty. In particular, he recognizes that the poor are most affected by environmental harm despite often doing least to cause it, and thus recognizes that an "ecological debt" exists between rich and poor nations (*LS* 51). He says that a "true ecological approach . . . must integrate questions of justice in debates on the environment so as to hear *both the cry of the earth and the cry of the poor*" (*LS* 48, italics in original). Although this message is not new for the papacy, Pope Francis emphasizes it with an unparalleled level of clarity and force.

6. *Laudato si'* **is a view from the ground up and not from the top down.** Pope Francis seeks a Church more in touch with the sheep whose pastors listen to their people and, in his words, "have the odour of sheep."[10] For Pope Francis, "collegiality" (that is, the pope governing the Church in partnership with the bishops) is a key reform goal of his papacy. He wants that style of governance to begin with him, and collegiality is thus on prominent display in this encyclical. *Laudato si'* reflects the local expression of the Church through more than twenty references to the ecological work of local episcopal conferences around the world.[11] This is the first time a pope has so extensively quoted episcopal conferences in an encyclical, and Francis uses this wisdom and local experience to advance collegiality and ground *Laudato si'* in peoples' lived ecological experiences.

---

10. Pope Francis, "Homily of Pope Francis: Chrism Mass," March 28, 2013, *https://w2.vatican.va/content/francesco/en/homilies/2013/documents/papa-francesco_20130328_messa-crismale.html*.

11. For more on this, see Kevin Ahern, "Follow the Footnotes," *America Magazine*, June 18, 2015, *http://americamagazine.org/issue/follow-footnotes*.

7. **Pope Francis is deeply concerned about the modern use of technology.** In *Laudato si'* he introduces a new term—"the technocratic paradigm"—to express his disquiet (*LS* 106). Concern about technology is not new for the Church. Francis, however, is sharper and more critical in his concern that humanity, through its technological prowess, has become "confrontational" with nature (*LS* 106). This is not to say that he is anti-technology. He praises its development and its contribution to the advancement of society and human wellbeing. In a memorable line, he emphasizes, "Nobody is suggesting a return to the Stone Age" (*LS* 114). He is worried, however, that the technocratic paradigm, which is rooted in power and control, "accepts every advance in technology with a view to profit, without concern for its potential negative impact on human beings" (*LS* 109). In response, he promotes a balanced approach to technology that does not subject humans or nature to a utilitarian experiment elevating technology or the market to a singular salvific role.

8. **The encyclical contains a call for education, spirituality, and conversion.** Pope Francis calls for rich "ecological education . . . spirituality . . . [and] conversion" in response to contemporary ecological challenges (*LS* 202–221). He decries rampant consumerism that impedes and threatens "a genuine sense of the common good" that is "inseparable from" integral ecology and warns that the "obsession with a consumerist lifestyle, above all when few people are capable of maintaining it, can only lead to violence and mutual destruction" (*LS* 156, 204). This is very strong language in a Church statement, arguably the strongest thus far regarding these topics. In response, he emphatically calls for a robust program of education, spirituality, and conversion in individuals and society. In particular, he highlights the need for civic and religious institutions to raise awareness of modern environmental issues and cultivate personal virtues—good habits that can catalyze widespread, lasting care for our common home.

9. **There is a call for dialogue.** Perhaps most notably, Pope Francis makes an unprecedented call for dialogue. Dialogue with other Christians, other religions, and all people of goodwill is key to his pastoral vision. Francis thus frames *Laudato si'* in an entirely

dialogical motif. He begins the encyclical by "address[ing] every person living on this planet" and expresses his desire to enter into dialogue with all people about our common home (*LS* 3). He then celebrates not only the work of other Christians and religions but also "the reflections of numerous scientists, philosophers, theologians and civic groups, all of which have enriched the church's thinking on these questions" (*LS* 7). In particular, the pope, for the first time in a papal encyclical, uplifts the prophetic leadership and witness of an ecumenical leader, Patriarch Bartholomew I (*LS* 7–9). Moreover, Francis urges dialogue between science and religion (*LS* 62) and, especially, among and between religions and religious believers (*LS* 201).

In a groundbreaking act, Pope Francis released *Laudato si'* at a press conference led by Cardinal Peter Turkson of the Pontifical Council for Justice and Peace, Metropolitan John of Pergamon of the Greek Orthodox Church, Carolyn Woo of Catholic Relief Services, and Hans Schellnhuber of the Institute for Climate Impact in Potsdam, a leading international climate scientist and an atheist. This act illustrates the pope's hope for a broad ecological dialogue and demonstrates the viability of such dialogue across alliances of religion and secular entities. This is a new way to do Vatican business.

Impact and Future Challenges

It is too early to assess the full impact of this encyclical. The timing of its release, in the summer of 2015, was deliberate. Francis aimed to influence three international meetings expected to directly affect sustainable development and the environment: the UN Conference on Financing for Development (Addis Ababa, July 2015), the UN General Assembly meeting on Sustainable Development Goals to Replace the Millennium Development Goals (New York, September 2015), and the United Nations Framework Convention on Climate Change (Paris, November/December 2015). While we must await further research and commentary to fully assess the intended impact, anecdotal evidence suggests that ahead of these meetings, many leaders and ordinary citizens took note of the moral challenges associated with sustainable development and climate change as a result of *Laudato si'*.[12]

What about the future? Pope Francis challenges all people to care for our common home by reordering the global economy so that *it* serves *people*, rather than the other way around; addressing global poverty through sustainable development; overcoming excessive consumerism; protecting other creatures and habitats; enacting policies that promote ecological justice; harnessing technology so that it serves the common good; and addressing both the causes and consequences of human-forced climate change. These challenges are for everyone on the planet, and they call for responses from the entire religious community.

Laudato si' is wide-ranging in its biblical, spiritual, theological, and policy implications, providing ample material for reflection, dialogue, and action within the Catholic community and ecumenically. Within Catholic circles, *Laudato si'* has led to an increase in the number of conferences, studies, and commentaries on ecological concerns. Such initiatives are important and likely to continue. The Church has also responded with projects to increase the environmental sustainability of its facilities and campuses. Since these efforts take years to plan and implement, there is likely to be an increased "greening" of the Church's facilities and campuses for some time. Work will have to be done, however, to secure requisite financing and encourage leaders to take long-term financial views.

Finally, the U.S. Catholic Church, led especially by the U.S. Conference of Catholic Bishops and Catholic Climate Covenant, has advocated for public policies that reduce carbon pollution and provide funding for those most affected by climate change. Here, however, it is worth pointing out Pope Francis's insight that in current politics "there are too many special interests, and economic interests easily end up trumping the common good and manipulating information so that their own plans will not be affected" (*LS* 54).

---

12. Brian Roewe, "On Climate, Polls Begin to Show Hints of 'Francis Effect,'" *National Catholic Reporter*, November 7, 2015, *https://www.ncronline.org/blogs/eco -catholic/climate-polls-begin-show-hints-francis-effect*. Joe Ware, "COP21: Laudato Si' A Major Talking Point at Climate Change Talks in Paris," *The Tablet*, December 5, 2015, *http://www.thetablet.co.uk/news/2885/0/cop21-laudato-si-a-major-talking-point -at-climate-change-talks-in-paris*.

The Church will thus need to exercise fortitude in its advocacy on behalf of creation and the poor.

As previously noted, the breadth of ecological concerns provides fertile ground for deeper ecumenical dialogue and more robust civic collaboration to address environmental challenges. It is thus encouraging to see how many non-Catholic faith traditions and communities have embraced *Laudato si'* and celebrated Pope Francis's ecological vision. It is especially heartening that ecumenical groups like GreenFaith, Interfaith Power and Light, RENEW International, and the National Religious Partnership for the Environment (of which the U.S. Conference of Catholic Bishops is a member) have worked to integrate *Laudato si'* into concrete programs and resources.

Moving forward, there is a great need for ecumenical work to further explore the theological and moral aspects of ecological issues and cultivate shared responsibilities to promote integral ecology and address related problems of poverty. In response, existing ecumenical initiatives can be deepened by official dialogues between the leaders of Christian churches using *Laudato si'* as a basis for dialogue and other faith leaders and their ecology statements. Additionally, religious believers can work to increase these ecumenical dialogues at local judicatory levels and among local congregations in a more systematic manner. Finally, people of faith can encourage religious leaders across denominational and interfaith lines to provide more visible public leadership on issues of ecological concern. This type of witness could have a significant impact upon public discussion, public morality, and public policy regarding our ecological responsibilities, and is thus extremely important.

Just as there is a need to cultivate more widespread ecumenical work in support of *Laudato si'*, it is also important to foster ecological partnerships between faith and secular communities and institutions. Many such collaborative partnerships already exist, perhaps most notably between scientists and religious leaders who rely on them to provide information that can guide their teachings. Moving forward, religious leaders should more widely consult scientific, political, and economic experts to help shape religious programs on ecology. In particular, religious leaders should integrate the urgency of the climate crisis long identified by scientists into catechesis and legislative advocacy. Furthermore, religious and secular leaders and organizations should work to form broad-based coalitions that can elevate ecological concerns in public discourse and policy.

Conclusion

At the end of the open dialogue that defines *Laudato si'*, Pope Francis offers two prayers—one for the earth itself with all who believe in God, and another specifically for Christians to pray in unity with creation. In a spirit of collaboration and prayer, people of faith and goodwill are thus invited to take up the common work to "hear *both the cry of the earth and the cry of the poor*" (*LS* 49, italics in original), to care for our common home, and to honor the opening words of the encyclical, "*Laudato si', mi Signore*," "*Praise be to you, my Lord.*"

Review Questions

1. What themes from the U.S. Catholic bishops do you see reflected in *Laudato si'*?

2. What value do you think local bishops' conferences' statements and programs might have in building awareness and support for ecological responsibility?

3. This chapter suggests several ways that *Laudato si'* develops Catholic ecological theology. Which one do you find most interesting? Why?

4. What international meetings did Pope Francis hope to influence through the release of *Laudato si'*?

5. What Catholic and interfaith organizations are working to integrate *Laudato si'* into concrete programs and resources?

In-Depth Questions

1. Pope Francis urges dialogue as a means to promote a robust ecological ethic. Do you think concern for ecology is an area for ecumenical and interfaith dialogue, or are various religious communities too separated for active, close cooperation? Can

religion and science dialogue around this issue? If so, how? If not, why not?

2. Pope Francis proposes a notion of integral ecology, which connects human development and ecological sustainability in an inseparable way. Do you find yourself compelled by or resistant to this concept? Why?

3. Pope Francis says that an adequate approach to ecology must integrate questions of human and social justice, so as to "*hear both the cry of the earth and the cry of the poor*" (*LS* 49). Why do you think he proposes this link, and what issues might it entail?

4. What do you think about the critique in *Laudato si'* that our technological prowess has become "confrontational" with nature? If you agree with Francis, what part of his argument do you find most convincing? If you disagree with him, why?

5. *Laudato si'* calls for ecological education and conversion. What are three specific ways that each could be catalyzed at your school or in your community?

Suggestions for Further Study

Cloutier, David. *Reading, Praying, Living Pope Francis's* Laudato Si': *A Faith Formation Guide*. Collegeville, MN: Liturgical Press, 2015. See especially "Introduction," 7–14.

Irwin, Kevin W. *A Commentary on* Laudato Si': *Examining the Background, Contributions, Implementation, and Future of Pope Francis's Encyclical*. Mahwah, NJ: Paulist Press, 2016.

Kelly, Anthony J. Laudato Si': *An Integral Ecology and the Catholic Vision*. Adelaide, Australia: ATF, 2016.

Lasher, Connie, and Charles Murphy. "'With Generous Courage': Promise and Poignance in the Legacies of Pope John Paul II and Pope Benedict XVI." In *Confronting the Climate Crisis: Catholic Theological Perspectives*, edited by Jame Schaefer, 365–88. Milwaukee: Marquette University Press, 2011.

CHAPTER 3

The Reception of *Laudato si'* in the United States in Secular and Sacred Arenas

MICHAEL AGLIARDO, SJ

Vatican officials released *Laudato si'* on June 18, 2015. It is a complex and multifaceted document and its reception in different societies has varied significantly. Many people in the Philippines, which in recent years has been buffeted by unusually powerful typhoons, welcomed the document's warning cry concerning climate change. In Ecuador, its social justice imperatives resonated strongly. In India, where Catholics and other Christians are a minority, its critique of Western consumerism and its call to respect all forms of life created opportunities for dialogue with the Hindu majority. In Kenya, its notion of integral ecology points toward ways of linking religion and social justice with the country's existing commitment to wildlife preservation.[1]

This chapter sketches the reception of *Laudato si'* in the United States, taking into account the way it has intersected with a series of standing issues and local circumstances. Indeed, even within a single society, a given issue or event may resonate differently in diverse quarters. The approach here is to consider several significant "arenas" in U.S. society, how they are structured, how this structure impacts the reception of *Laudato si'*, and how *Laudato si'* may, in turn, occasion the transformation of the debates taking place in these arenas.

"Arena" here refers to a relatively coherent sphere of activity with its own ongoing activities, debates, and distinctive ways of framing

---

1. These observations derive from the author's own research in the aforementioned societies during the summer of 2016.

issues. An example would be the "environmental arena," that is, the arena where environmental issues are debated and activities associated with environmental protection and like concerns are pursued. In such an arena, people stake out positions that get defined, not just in terms of their own internal coherence, but also against one another. More broadly, the whole process of building arguments, positions, and counter-positions is a significant part of the "structuring" of an arena. Of course, the structuring of the social world involves more than rhetoric. Nonetheless, the vocabulary people employ and the arguments they build ground how individuals understand their participation in society and how their shared understandings undergird social institutions. This rhetoric constitutes the lay of the land within a given arena.[2] Accordingly, when members of society take up *Laudato si'*, they inevitably do so within a context already structured by preexisting alliances, debates, and rhetorical constructs.

To understand better the significance of *Laudato si'* in the United States, one may examine how the structuring of the following arenas has affected its reception: the social order, the environmental arena, the religious arena, the political arena, and the U.S. Catholic community. These arenas are not isolated from one another; what happens in one arena may be "entangled" with or have implications for another. In other words, how people approach environmental issues like climate change may be linked to their political or religious commitments. In the end, it appears that *Laudato si'* not only challenges how Americans think about a range of particular issues; it also challenges the way certain arenas are structured. Indeed, the capacity of Pope Francis to challenge people to rethink their standing assumptions is what makes him and *Laudato si'* so provocative.

The Arena of Society as Differentiated Social Order

In the United States, people take for granted that the spheres of law, economics, and religion operate relatively independently, each on the basis of its own principles. In this sense, when scientists go to

---

2. This approach draws on the notion of embedded logics associated with Weberian social analysis, as well as social construction theory. It is similar to approaches associated with "field analysis." However, field analysis often devotes more explicit attention to power dynamics than will be possible in the limited space afforded here.

work, they are expected to leave their religion at home. In sociological parlance, this arrangement is termed "structural differentiation." Such differentiation is not absolute, but in the modern West the trend has been to parcel human activity into increasingly distinct domains. In the United States, one landmark in this process was the adoption of the First Amendment to the Constitution, which strongly demarcated the American religious sphere from the political. Clearly, one advantage of such an arrangement has been to better preserve the integrity of each sphere.

At the same time, in societies in other parts of the world, structural differentiation, where it has been encouraged, has also led to a tendency to bracket religion. And this tendency to bracket religion does lead to a recurring dilemma: when one operates in a particular sphere such as science or economics, where do the values that guide one's activity come from?

For the sphere of religion, structural differentiation poses a somewhat different dilemma. Religious activity differs from other human activities because religion as such operates out of an ultimate frame, though admittedly that ultimate frame may recede into the background when practical issues dominate the field of view. The ultimate frame out of which religion operates can, in turn, provide social actors with guidance for thinking about values applicable in other areas of life. Thus, in our day, the Catholic Church clearly affirms that the various sciences can and should operate according to their own principles. At the same time, when it comes to grappling with the moral questions that particular spheres of activity raise, Catholic thinkers often draw on Catholic social teaching and "the natural law tradition," classically understood as a foundational moral framework rooted in the eternal law of God and accessible via reason to all persons. On the basis of Catholic social teaching, the U.S. Catholic Church has issued pastoral letters on the use of nuclear weapons,[3] the economy,[4] and the environment.[5] Thus, in the modern

---

3. National Conference of Catholic Bishops (NCCB), *The Challenge of Peace: God's Promise and Our Response* (Washington, DC: United States Catholic Conference [USCC], 1983).

4. National Conference of Catholic Bishops, *Economic Justice for All: Catholic Social Teaching and the U.S. Economy* (Washington, DC: United States Catholic Conference, 1986).

5. National Conference of Catholic Bishops, *Renewing the Earth: An Invitation to Reflection and Action on the Environment in Light of Catholic Social Teaching* (Washington, DC: United States Catholic Conference, 1991).

era, Catholic actors have developed and applied resources to both respect and negotiate this circumstance of structural differentiation.

Nonetheless, during the 1960s and 70s in the United States, when science and institutions of higher education were asserting their place in society, the prospect of religion emerging from its own activity sphere and engaging in issues primarily associated with other spheres was often treated as a "boundary violation." When the U.S. bishops wrote pastoral letters on the economy and nuclear weapons in the early 1980s, they had to make the case for speaking out about such "non-religious" matters. However, as it turns out, in the case of environmentalism, the opposite has often been the case. In fact, in 1990, a group of worldwide leading scientists issued a landmark appeal for religious leaders to lend their moral voices to the struggle to "preserve and cherish the earth."[6] They positively invited religion to cross boundaries and venture into what some had considered the exclusive territory of science. *Laudato si'* is one fruitful outcome of the Catholic religious vision brought into dialogue with the social and natural sciences.

When *Laudato si'* was published, a number of Catholic U.S. politicians tried to insulate themselves from its moral claims by arguing that the pope, as a religious figure, had no authority to comment on scientific and economic matters. Their statements reflected an unnuanced understanding of structural differentiation, one that ignored not only such precedents as the U.S. bishops' pastoral letters on nuclear weapons (1983) and the economy (1986), but also the bishops' later letters on care for the environment (1991) and climate change (2001).[7] These politicians certainly did not take into account *Laudato si's* own grasp of its participation in a larger process of dialogue.[8]

---

6. Carl Sagan et al., "Preserving and Cherishing the Earth: An Appeal for Joint Commitment in Science and Religion," *American Journal of Physics* 58, no. 7 (1990): 615–18; Peter Steinfels, "Carl Sagan Urges Clerics to Join in an Effort to Save the Globe," *The New York Times*, January 16, 1990, C4.

7. U.S. Conference of Catholic Bishops, *Global Climate Change: A Plea for Dialogue, Prudence, and the Common Good* (Washington, DC: United States Conference of Catholic Bishops, 2001).

8. *Laudato si'* itself offers reflection on the importance of the dialogue between science and religion (*LS* 62), noting that the serious ecological problems we face require input from every science and all forms of wisdom (*LS* 63). At the same time, the document warns against a "technocratic paradigm" that confuses the capacity to achieve outcomes with authentic moral wisdom (*LS* 106–7). Indeed, because science and technology tend to be analytic in approach, they often lose sight of the larger whole, a shortcoming that religion is aptly suited to remedy (*LS* 110).

By contrast, other social commentators—including spokespersons for the Union of Concerned Scientists, members of the American Sociological Association, and scientists and lawyers working at various secular environmental organizations—have engaged the substance of the document, rather than dismiss it because of its religious provenance.[9] These developments, coupled with the reception of the pope at the White House and Congress on the heels of the publication of *Laudato si'*, underscore the extent to which *Laudato si'* represents a precedent challenging static notions of structural differentiation in contemporary society.[10] It does so as it brings together considerations of social justice, respect for non-human entities, atmospheric science, economics, and more into a holistic vision that would otherwise escape each particular sphere or domain.

The Environmental Arena and Climate Change

The history of environmentalism in the United States is long and complex, and that complexity is reflected in the structuring of the environmental arena today. "Classical environmentalism" emerged in the United States in the mid-1800s with the appearance of two related but distinct frames: the "conservationist" frame, which views nature as a source of raw materials and prioritizes the collective, scientific management of resources in the interest of long-term sustainability; and the "preservationist" frame, in which nature is viewed as a source of beauty and inspiration. The preservationist impulse has led Americans to safeguard the Redwoods and places such as the Grand Canyon, not as resources to be converted into something else, but for their own sake. Both the conservationist and preservationist

9. The number of "secular" environmental organizations that devoted extensive coverage to *Laudato si'* on their websites and in newsletters was impressive, ranging from the Sierra Club and the World Wildlife Fund to Greenpeace and the National Resources Defense Council.

10. On the front of public opinion, researchers at Yale and George Mason University also documented an uptick in the percentage of Americans who believe climate change to be a moral issue (rising from 32 percent to 38 percent, and from 34 percent to 42 percent for Catholics specifically) and a religious issue (rising from 8 percent to 12 percent, and from 6 percent to 13 percent for Catholics specifically), attributing these rises to Pope Francis. See Edward Maibach et al., *The Francis Effect: How Pope Francis Changed the Conversation about Global Warming* (Fairfax, VA: George Mason University Center for Climate Change Communication, 2015).

expressions of classical environmentalism share the assumption, to a greater or lesser degree, that "nature" and "the environment" are entities "out there," beyond the confines of human society. They view nature as an "object" to be managed or as the exotic "other," a source of wonder and fascination. In that sense they tend to reflect and perpetuate a certain human alienation from nature.

When it became apparent in the 1960s that our impact on the environment "out there" could, in fact, compromise human well-being, a new frame termed *protectionism* or *reform environmentalism* emerged. In the post-sixties era, more radical frames emerged. These frames question the kind of society we maintain and whether capitalism, patriarchy, or anthropocentrism are the root cause of our environmental woes. It is also worth noting that many American environmental frames have been largely secular, drawing on scientific and technocratic bases, rather than religious ones.

Overall, up through the mid-1970s, environmental protection, in general, was a broadly supported, popular cause. Then a series of environmental counter-movements arose. One was the Wise Use movement, which claimed to oppose not environmentalism as such, but "excessive" environmentalism. Its proponents opposed environmentalism insofar as it entailed government regulation and encroached upon property rights. At a time when the United States, under the Reagan administration, was engaged in a Cold War competition with the Soviet Union, those opposing environmental regulation sometimes cast it as hampering the economy, and hence, as compromising the nation in its struggle with communism. In fact, given its generally secular cast and the emergence of certain radical strands within the environmental movement, some social commentators then cleverly constructed a rhetorical opposition between American values, the free market, and religion, on the one hand, and socialism, environmentalism, and secularism, on the other.

When U.S. religious communities increasingly took up environmental causes toward the end of the decade, many did so through the lens of their standing commitments to social justice. These commitments broadened the environmental agenda to focus consideration on how environmental issues affect the poor, vulnerable, and minority communities. Some groups, such as the Evangelical Environmental Network, also explicitly worked to dismantle the Reagan-era polarity that pitted environmentalism against religion *per se*. Yet in certain conservative religious circles, that polarity lingers to this day.

Today *Laudato si'* challenges assumptions that continue to structure the American environmental arena. Drawing on the spirituality of Saint Francis of Assisi, it calls for reverence for other creatures, promoting a view that would overcome our estrangement from nature. At the same time, it maintains the standing commitment to social justice of many American religious groups by addressing creation care as simultaneously care for "our common home." In this way, it stands to deconstruct the opposition between anthropocentrism (excessive concern for humanity vis-à-vis non-human creation) and biocentrism (lack of concern for humanity vis-à-vis non-human creation) that marks the environmental arena. Moreover, by explicitly rooting its analysis in the gospel, the document challenges any facile alignment of environmentalism with secularism.

Laudato si' has made it difficult for proponents of the environmental counter-movement to advance their standard arguments. Some bloggers have tried to paint Pope Francis as a Latin American Marxist theologian attempting to smuggle an un-American ideology into the United States. However, among the think tanks and pundits who online and elsewhere regularly criticize environmental regulation and deny climate change, most have been respectful, careful not to alienate the Catholic community.[11] Nonetheless, *Laudato si'* is still taken up in an environmental arena structured by the opposition between market advocacy and concerns that link environmentalism with excessive government regulation.

One notable source of rhetoric maintaining this opposition is the Acton Institute, a think tank dedicated to free market advocacy, which, as it turns out, is headed by a Catholic priest, Father Robert Sirico. Time and again, Sirico has challenged Pope Francis and worked to domesticate *Laudato si'*. Sirico repeatedly sets up a dichotomy between free market capitalism and some deleterious alternative, contending that the pope "just doesn't understand economics very well." He writes, "The free economy, I would suggest, is better suited to attaining the material goals outlined in *Laudato si'* than many of the means suggested by some commentators and, if I

---

11. Insofar as many count Catholics among their members and allies, this caution reflects a significant interlinking between the environmental and religious arenas.

may respectfully suggest, even a better means than some of the policy suggestions contained in the encyclical itself."[12]

Other commentators, such as Bishop Robert Barron,[13] have countered that *Laudato si'* remains consistent with traditional Catholic social teaching in that it does not argue for doing away with the market. Rather, it argues for regulating market economics with laws that more directly take into account the common good and put the powerless and the Earth before profit-seeking. Here he draws on the principle of subsidiarity, which calls for protection of the common good at the lowest possible but *highest necessary* level for society. Commentators such as Barron avoid pitting environmentalism against economic wellbeing, science against religion, or people against nature, oppositions that have been used to stall the environmental movement in the United States. In doing so, they are drawing on *Laudato si'* in an endeavor to reconstruct the rhetoric of the environmental arena.

The Religious Arena and Interfaith Relations

American Catholicism operates in a larger religious arena that includes the Jewish community, Protestant and other Christian groups, Muslims, Buddhists, and a range of other faiths. With regard to environmental issues, the U.S. bishops established the Environmental Justice Program in 1993, and it became their arm for participation in the National Religious Partnership for the Environment, which also includes the National Council of Churches, the Coalition on the Environment and Jewish Life, and the Evangelical Environmental Network.[14] This broad coordinating body allows for mutual

---

12. Amanda Erickson, "Sowing Confusion," *The Washington Post*, September 18, 2015, *http://www.washingtonpost.com/sf/local/2015/09/18/francis-is-a-global-sensation-but-to-certain-traditional-catholics-his-message-rings-hollow/?utm_term=. eb48546dbd44*; Robert Sirico, "*Laudato Si'*—Free Markets and the Environment: Allies not Enemies—Testimony to the Senate Committee on Environment and Public Works," U.S. Senate Committee on Environment and Public Works, April 13, 2016, 7, *https://www.epw.senate.gov/public/_cache/files/b6b74390-9cad-49a0-9ab7-f16efb1b0341/sirico-testimony.pdf*.

13. Robert Barron, "A Prophetic Pope and the Tradition of Catholic Social Teaching," *Word on Fire*, July 14, 2015, *http://www.wordonfire.org/resources/article/a-prophetic-pope-and-the-tradition-of-catholic-social-teaching/4825/*.

14. National Religious Partnership for the Environment, "About," *http://www.nrpe.org/*.

engagement while each member organization operates according to the insights of its own tradition. Thus, even before the publication of *Laudato si'*, there was a history of collaboration in public life between U.S. religious groups, and when it came to environmental issues, key representative organizations operated along parallel but mutually supportive tracks.

Even given this history, when *Laudato si'* was released, it garnered remarkable expressions of support. Within a month, the Presbyterian Church U.S.A. had published a seven-session *Laudato si'* study guide, while a resource team within the Evangelical Lutheran Church of America had published a four-week study course by November. The *Connecticut Jewish Ledger* opined, "*Laudato Si'*, Pope Francis' powerful new encyclical, is likely to go down in history as the most important religious text of our time," adding, "*Laudato Si'* may be Catholic teaching but it is also a very Jewish document."[15] A gathering in Istanbul, representing Muslims worldwide, published an "Islamic Declaration on Global Climate Change"[16] that they noted was issued "in harmony with the Papal Encyclical" and with "the support of the Pontifical Council on Justice and Peace of the Holy See." And within the United States, the encyclical likewise inspired Muslims to speak from their own tradition in response to climate change and environmental degradation. Of course, not all religious authorities were equally enthusiastic about *Laudato si'*. Albert Mohler, president of the Southern Baptist Theological Seminary, worried that Pope Francis had strayed into uncertain scientific terrain, a diversion that could prove regrettable,[17] adding that as a Baptist he recognized neither the authority of papal encyclicals nor of the pope. While such distancing was sometimes evident, overall in the U.S. context *Laudato si'* has been the occasion for expressions of solidarity among faiths regarding an issue of mutual concern. In addition, in the religious arena it also won unprecedented appreciation of the moral and religious

---

15. "The Pope's Encyclical," *Connecticut Jewish Ledger*, June 24, 2015, *http://www.jewishledger.com/2015/06/the-popes-encyclical/*.

16. International Islamic Climate Change Symposium, "Islamic Declaration on Global Climate Change," 2015, *http://islamicclimatedeclaration.org/islamic-declaration-on-global-climate-change/*.

17. Albert Mohler Jr., "Mohler Responds to Pope Francis' 'Laudato si'," June 18, 2015, *http://news.sbts.edu/2015/06/18/mohler-responds-to-pope-francis-laudato-si/*.

leadership of the Catholic Bishop of Rome. To be sure, as much as the content of the document itself, these developments reflect the personal style of Pope Francis, who exercises moral leadership in a fraternal way. Nonetheless, *Laudato si'* has clearly contributed to a restructuring of the religious arena in a direction that promotes ecumenical and interfaith collaboration.

The Political Arena and the U.S. Culture Wars

The U.S. political arena is dominated by two political parties, the Democratic Party and the Republican Party. The binary character of this arena is largely the result of elections taking place within districts that allow for only one winner. In a district-by-district, winner-take-all system, there does not appear to be space for a viable third party. In addition to American politics being binary, many analysts are struck by the degree to which it has become increasingly polarized and viciously combative.

The polarization of the U.S. political arena has been exacerbated by the moral disagreements associated with the U.S. "culture wars." According to James Davison Hunter, the sociologist who proposed the "culture wars" thesis,[18] culture wars are disagreements not only about core moral issues but about the process of moral reasoning itself. While some advance a more pragmatic, relativistic approach to moral issues, others assert that there are substantive values that take concrete, normative form. Thus culture wars adversaries disagree about whether to view abortion from the perspective of subjective personal choice or from the perspective of the objective destruction of human life. While most ordinary Americans deploy a more complex "both-and" logic when it comes to the moral issues facing society, political parties just as often seek to polarize the debate so as to better mobilize support, with Democrats most often siding with individual choice and Republicans advocating objective values and norms.

The Catholic Church has developed a fairly consistent body of moral reasoning from which substantive moral principles may be derived. Known as Catholic social teaching, it covers areas as

---

18. James Davison Hunter, *Culture Wars: The Struggle to Define America* (New York: BasicBooks, 1991).

diverse as sexual morality and environmental protection. In recent decades it has found increasing support for many of its positions concerning family-related matters within the Republican Party. When the Obama Administration proposed a health care law requiring employers to pay for forms of contraception that violate official Catholic moral teaching, many U.S. bishops then waged a vociferous campaign opposing the law. That campaign exacerbated tensions between the Church and the Democratic Party and fed into Democratic-Republican polarization in the political arena.

In the midst of the healthcare controversy, the Pope announced that he would issue an encyclical focusing on the environment. In the U.S., environmentalism was originally a bipartisan issue. President Richard Nixon, a Republican, signed into law more pro-environmental legislation than any president before or since. It was only in the 1980s, when Republicans began to rhetorically equate environmental legislation with economy-crippling regulation and dysfunctional government that it increasingly became a partisan issue, setting up an ideological divide that few Republicans have dared to cross. As a result, Catholic social teaching on the environment generally has come to favor positions staked out by the Democratic Party. However, while Catholic bishops did write about the environment, they never put the energy behind those pronouncements that they did behind their "culture wars" positions. Accordingly, Republican eschewal of environmentalism did not threaten their standing among politically conservative Catholics.

Enter *Laudato si'*. Here was a Catholic pronouncement that supported the Obama administration's position on climate change. If the Catholic bishops amplified the document's message, it could erode Republican support among Catholics. And every pro-environmental and pro-Democratic group in America has been aware that *Laudato si'* can be cited to that effect, as well. In reaction to a leaked draft of *Laudato si'*, Catholic Republican presidential contender Jeb Bush issued his own now-famous, "I don't get economic policy from my bishops or my cardinal or my pope" pronouncement. Two other Catholic Republican hopefuls, Marco Rubio and Rick Santorum also tried to pirouette their way around the document. To complicate matters further, the pope was already scheduled to visit the United States in September 2015 for the World Meeting of Families, and in connection with that visit, House Speaker John Boehner, a Republican and a staunch Catholic, had already arranged for the pope to address a joint session of Congress in September 2015. After the publication of *Laudato si'*, as the pope's visit approached, Democrats waxed gleeful while Republicans braced.

All told, the culture wars, the Obama healthcare initiative, standing positions on social justice and climate change, hostility to environmental regulation, advocacy of free-market economics, and a binary political culture have brought about an intense interlinking of arguments and interests, alliances and oppositions that have structured the political arena within which *Laudato si'* is taken up. That lends a significance to *Laudato si'* apart from the contents of the document itself. In the face of this convoluted set of tensions and constructs, just prior to the visit of Pope Francis to the United States, Chris Gibson, a Catholic Republican Congressman from New York, and ten colleagues introduced a resolution calling for dialogue in Congress on climate change. It was a modest attempt to depoliticize climate change, searching for, as he put it, "common ground on how to address it." Issued in the wake of *Laudato si'*, Gibson's resolution was an attempt to restructure the rhetorical divide that has held progress on climate change hostage to polarization in the political arena.

During the Clinton-Trump presidential debates, the issue of climate change was barely mentioned, and neither candidate spoke about their environmental policy. Given the gravity of contemporary environmental issues, this silence left commentators scratching their heads. And while key U.S. bishops spoke out on immigration reform and the need to admit refugees to our shores, most remained silent on climate and the environment. And while the 2015 edition of Forming Consciences for Faithful Citizenship (a document the U.S. Catholic bishops collectively issue at the time of national elections) did mention climate change and repeatedly cite *Laudato si'*, few bishops chose to speak out on environmental issues, certainly not to the degree they did on immigration reform or the imperative to admit refugees to our shores.[19] Then when Donald Trump won office—despite losing the popular vote

---

19. U.S. Conference of Catholic Bishops, *Forming Consciences for Faithful Citizenship*, 2015, *http://www.usccb.org/issues-and-action/faithful-citizenship/upload/forming-consciences-for-faithful-citizenship.pdf.*

by a significant margin—he assumed a mandate to strip down the Environmental Protection Agency, roll back President Obama's Climate Action Plan, and withdraw the United States from the COP21 Paris Accords. In response, the U.S. Conference of Catholic Bishops is further lifting up *Laudato si'* and urging the Trump Administration to care for our common home and uphold existing U.S. environmental policy commitments.[20] Given these developments, all constituencies in the U.S. Catholic Church are facing the challenge of lending greater priority to climate change, environmental protection, and the social justice questions that stem from these issues. In the past, the U.S. Church has spoken prophetically and powerfully across partisan political divides to bring the common good back into focus. Will it muster the institutional will to do so in defense of our common home moving forward?

Catholicism in the United States in the Post-*Laudato si'* Era

The Catholic community in the United States is large and complex. It includes dioceses and the parishes they contain, religious orders, schools, hospitals, media outlets, retreat centers, and myriad other ministries, each with its own dynamic culture. Here we review the typical engagement with *Laudato si'* of American religious orders, Catholic universities, the Catholic theological community, lay Catholics, the U.S. bishops, and Catholic NGOs.[21]

Communities of Catholic religious orders, such as the Franciscans and the Sisters of Saint Joseph, have their own constitutions and governing structures, as well as their own history and spiritual traditions. Given these distinctive foundations for culture and institutional life, religious orders can operate somewhat independently

20. See, for example, U.S. Conference of Catholic Bishops, "Letter to Secretary of the Treasury Regarding Our Shared Obligation to Care for the Environment," May 5, 2017, *http://www.usccb.org/issues-and-action/human-life-and-dignity/environment/usccb-crs-letter-to-treasury-secretary-mnuchin-on-environment-2017-05-05.cfm.*

21. An NGO is a non-governmental organization. NGOs are nonprofit organizations that provide services for individuals and for the community at large, and while they may cooperate with government agencies, in the United States they operate independently.

not only of the culture of society at large, but also of the culture of the larger Church. With regard to environmental issues, women religious, in particular, have long advocated for spirituality and forms of ministry informed by an ecological ethic. Women religious have thus constituted a sort of ecological vanguard of the U.S. Catholic Church. In the past decade or so, male religious have been catching up. When *Laudato si'* was published, its words resonated strongly with many communities of U.S. religious. Moreover, given that the Leadership Conference of Women Religious, the coordinating body for most groups of U.S. women religious, had been under Vatican scrutiny until late spring 2015, the publication of *Laudato si'* represented a significant vindication of their work on ecology.

In addition to religious orders, the Catholic theological community and Catholic universities often serve as sites of cultural innovation in the U.S. Catholic Church. These are sites institutionally committed to reflection on the tradition and its relevance to contemporary society. It is estimated that during the first year and a half following the publication of *Laudato si'* over sixty of the more than two hundred Catholic-affiliated institutions of higher education held public events devoted to the document, some of which extended across several days. And an increasing number of U.S. Catholic theologians have begun to consider the implications of *Laudato si'* for the life of the Church.

The reaction to *Laudato si'* of various lay constituencies within the U.S. Catholic community has varied across a spectrum. One end of the spectrum is defined by those willing to adopt a critical take on contemporary American consumerism and the value set that promotes and legitimates such patterns of consumption. Many such Catholics have formed Creation Care Teams to discuss and implement *Laudato si'* in their parishes;[22] they have brought *Laudato si'* into the public sphere in the op-eds and letters to the editors they have written; and, citing *Laudato si'*, they have added a Catholic perspective to events such as the People's Climate March.[23] The other end of the spectrum is marked by Catholics who have staked out a

---

22. Creation Care Teams have been organized throughout the country with the support of Catholic Climate Covenant, an organization that works in cooperation with the U.S. Conference of Catholic Bishops and more than a dozen other national Catholic organizations.

23. The People's Climate March took place in Washington, D.C., on April 29, 2017.

counter-cultural position of a different sort. Standing up to secular culture and the individualism that makes personal preference a universal moral yardstick, they affirm traditional faith and substantive moral commitments. This often involves pro-life positions rooted in an appreciation of the sacredness of human life. Insofar as *Laudato si'* affirms the sacredness of God's creation as well, it poses a challenge to simplistic assumptions regarding the distinctive place of human beings. Stefano Gennarini, Director of Legal Studies at the Center for Family and Human Rights, laments that the encyclical does not present a "more comprehensive discussion of the sanctity of human life, the evil of the global abortion industry and population control, as well as their eugenic origins.[24] For Gennarini and many in the pro-life movement their emphasis on the sanctity of human life is tied to a worldview in which human life is uniquely sacred, and the definitions of good and evil are tied clearly to this insight. By stressing the sacredness of creation itself, *Laudato si'* may require that they rework the logic of their "pro-life" position and its attendant worldview.

R. R. Reno, editor of the influential journal of opinion *First Things*, offers some balanced commentary on *Laudato si'*, but toward the end of his lead editorial he makes this pronouncement: "The modern encyclical tradition, however, is a teaching tradition, not a homiletic one, and *Laudato si'* provides too little teaching."[25] Here his point seems to be that the document is *homiletic*, rather than *doctrinal*. The implication is that therefore it is not binding, and so may safely be dismissed. Insofar as *First Things* is published by "an educational institute aiming to advance a religiously informed public philosophy,"[26] it is caught up in the American culture wars. While the pronouncements of Pope Benedict and Pope John Paul II tended to be more objective and doctrinal, shoring up positions favored by the readership of *First Things*, *Laudato si'* does not square so neatly. Indeed, not only does Reno's dismissal of *Laudato si'* seem to reflect the cultural logic of the American culture wars. The vicious

---

24. Pete Baklinski, "Pro-life Leaders Praise, Express Concerns about Papal Environment Encyclical," *LifeSite News*, June 18, 2015, *https://www.lifesitenews.com/news /pro-life-leaders-praise-express-concerns-about-papal-environment-encyclical*.

25. R. R. Reno, "The Weakness of *Laudato Si'*," *First Things*, July 1, 2015, *https:// www.firstthings.com/web-exclusives/2015/07/the-weakness-of-laudato-si*.

26. *First Things* Masthead, *https://www.firstthings.com/masthead*.

polarization of its rhetoric surfaces there, too. In places, Reno's tone is not just critical but snide and disrespectful. For example, he charges the document with making "heavy use of . . . familiar, technocratic conceits," then announces, "So much for the bold cultural revolution." He also takes Pope Francis to task for endorsing the *Earth Charter* "a secular initiative." The *Earth Charter* is an ethical framework for international cooperation in building a just and sustainable order.[27] While it is not a religious document itself, it explicitly affirms the role of religions in this endeavor. Nonetheless, it is viewed by conservatives in the American culture wars as promoting relativism at best. In any case, promoting secularism and relativism are hardly the agenda of *Laudato si'*, despite Reno's protestations. In substance and in style *Laudato si'* challenges not only so-called "progressive" Catholics to link their faith to what may have otherwise seemed secular causes; it also challenges the standing syntheses of faith and issues of more traditionalist Catholics in ways that make them uncomfortable.

The response of the U.S. bishops has been described as muted. At their semi-annual meeting in June 2015, just prior to the release of *Laudato si'*, Cardinal Theodore McCarrick noted that none of the bishops had advocated that the environment should be a top priority for the U.S. Conference of Catholic Bishops (USCCB) in the coming years.[28] But McCarrick was sure that once the pope's encyclical came out and the bishops had time to digest it, they would line up behind it. In fact, some 110 out of the more than 170 ordinaries (bishops in charge of a diocese have since issued) statements welcoming the encyclical, and the USCCB has incorporated the document into subsequent ecological statements.[29] Yet challenges at the diocesan level

---

27. For more on the *Earth Charter*, especially vis-à-vis Church teaching, see chapter 4 in this volume, "Cosmology and Ecology in *Laudato si'*" by Mary Evelyn Tucker and John Grim.

28. Laurie Goodstein, "Pope Francis May Find Wariness among U.S. Bishops on Climate Change," *The New York Times*, June 13, 2015, *http://www.nytimes.com/2015/06/14/us/pope-francis-may-find-wariness-among-us-bishops-on-climate-change.html?_r=0*.

29. Individual bishops' statements can be found on the website of Catholic Climate Covenant at *http://www.catholicclimatecovenant.org/us-bishops-statements-on-laudato-si*. USCCB statements on ecology can be found at *http://www.usccb.org/issues-and-action/human-life-and-dignity/environment/index.cfm*.

remain, and the circumstance of Louisville Archbishop Joseph E. Kurtz, recent president of the U.S. Conference of Catholic Bishops, is perhaps emblematic of many U.S. bishops. His diocese resides in a state whose economy depends in part on coal, and whose senator was the Republican majority leader at the time *Laudato si'* was released. Kurtz has held press appearances in Washington, D.C., and Rome underscoring the importance of *Laudato si'*, and in his diocese, Catholic organizations like the Earth and Spirit Center and Catholic Charities integrate the document into their active ministries. Yet, given all the priorities of his diocese, concerns about the immediate economic well-being of his flock, and the way *Laudato si'* is entangled in the politics of many intersecting arenas, it may take time to determine how to articulate a leading pastoral response concerning the myriad issues raised by *Laudato si'*. So, for the moment, and in addition to the bishops' work mentioned in the previous section, leading advocacy of the document within the U.S. Catholic community seems in many ways to rest with religious orders, Catholic universities, Catholic NGOs, and the theological community.

Conclusion

As people think about the kind of society they endeavor to build together, they both collaborate and take opposing positions in various arenas. In framing their positions, they draw on a range of resources. Since its publication, *Laudato si'* has been one such resource in multiple arenas. In taking up *Laudato si'*, social actors don't simply reinforce standing positions, they also reframe issues and challenge the way certain domains within society are structured. In that sense, *Laudato si'* has a dynamism of its own, one that already has contributed to notable developments in the Catholic, inter-religious, environmental, and political arenas in American society.

Review Questions

1. What were some of the precedents in Catholic social teaching that paved the way for the reception of *Laudato si'* in the United States?

2. What are some of the frames and counter-frames that influence how environmental issues are taken up in the United States and how the environmental arena has come to be structured?
3. How have different non-Catholic religious communities in the United States responded to *Laudato si'*?
4. How have assorted political contests and divisions in the United States complicated the reception of *Laudato si'*?
5. What has been the reaction to *Laudato si'* of various sectors within the U.S. Catholic community?

In–Depth Questions

1. In the United States context, some commentators cast nature as a concern distinct from human affairs, or they pitch economic well-being against environmentalism broadly conceived. What effect does that way of constructing the matter have on public debate? Are there other ways to frame these matters? How does *Laudato si'* challenge this way of framing the debate?
2. Have you ever witnessed or experienced the presence of a "culture war" in society or in the Church? If so, how did you feel and respond?
3. What does *Laudato si'* teach us about the role of religion in contemporary society?
4. Have you seen *Laudato si'* discussed and acted upon by institutions with which you are involved (e.g., school, church, diocese, local newspaper)? If so, describe these activities. If not, what do you think have been some of the barriers to such engagement?
5. Despite its enthusiastic reception in some quarters, the transformative potential of *Laudato si'* has yet to be tapped, even within the Catholic community. Is it just a matter of time? What might inspire Catholics in sectors of the Church that have not given priority to the document to take a second look?

Suggestions for Further Study

Agliardo, Michael, SJ. "Restoring Creation and Redressing the Public Square: Religious Environmentalism and the Columbia River Pastoral." In *Green Discipleship: Catholic Theological Ethics and the Environment*, edited by Tobias L. Winright, 37–59. Winona, MN: Anselm Academic, 2011.

———. "The U.S. Catholic Response to Climate Change." In *How the World's Religions Are Responding to Climate Change: Social Scientific Investigations*, edited by Robin Globus Veldman, Andrew Szasz, and Randolph Haluza-DeLay, 174–92. New York: Routledge, 2013.

Curran, Charles E. *The Social Mission of the U.S. Catholic Church*. Washington, DC: Georgetown University Press, 2010.

Haluza-DeLay, Randolph, Robin Globus Veldman, and Andrew Szasz. "Social Science, Religions, and Climate Change." In *How the World's Religions Are Responding to Climate Change: Social Scientific Investigations*, edited by Robin Globus Veldman, Andrew Szasz, and Randolph Haluza-DeLay, 3–20. New York: Routledge, 2013.

Norgaard, Kari Marie. "Climate Denial: Emotion, Psychology, Culture, and Political Economy." In *The Oxford Handbook of Climate Change and Society*, edited by John S. Dryzek, Richard B. Norgaard, and David Schlosberg, 399–413. New York: Oxford University Press, 2011.

Shwom, Rachael L., Aaron M. McCright, and Steven R. Brechin. "Public Opinion on Climate Change." In *Climate Change and Society: Sociological Perspectives*, ed. Riley E. Dunlap and Robert J. Brulle, 269–299. New York: Oxford University Press, 2015.

Steinfels, Margaret O'Brien. *American Catholics and Civic Engagement: A Distinctive Voice*. Lanham, MD: Sheed & Ward, 2003.

PART 2

The Cosmos

CHAPTER 4

Cosmology and Ecology in *Laudato si'*

MARY EVELYN TUCKER AND JOHN GRIM

The enormous problems we face as a human community with regard to environmental degradation and social inequity are highlighted throughout *Laudato si'*. The sense of our destiny as linked to that of Earth and all creation is noted in many passages as well. Our larger cosmic story is in the background of this encyclical, while our wanton destruction of nature is in the foreground. Related to this interface of cosmology and ecology are influences on the encyclical coming from such major Catholic thinkers as Teilhard de Chardin and Thomas Berry. Teilhard is directly cited in footnote 53 of the encyclical. Thomas Berry's influence comes into the encyclical through the works of Leonardo Boff and Sean McDonagh, theologians who have been inspired by Berry (as well as Teilhard) and contributed to the drafting of *Laudato si'*. In this essay we explore these influences as well as the connections with the *Earth Charter* and the *Journey of the Universe* project.

These interconnected themes of cosmology and ecology are elaborated in this essay. The encyclical confirms the understanding of Pierre Teilhard de Chardin—a Jesuit paleontologist and geologist—that our fate is bound with nature and the story of our emergence from the deep time of the universe. Both Teilhard and *Laudato si'* seek to ignite human energy toward creating a flourishing future (*LS* 83, note 53). *Laudato si'* expresses a profound wonder at creation and tremendous sorrow at what is being lost in this moment in the natural world and thus in the human psyche. The encyclical asks, how can we find our way forward?

> ## Pierre Teilhard de Chardin
>
> Pierre Teilhard de Chardin (1881–1955), a Roman Catholic priest in the Society of Jesus (Jesuits), was both a paleontologist and geologist.[1] "The sense of the earth and its evolution was a source of inspiration in both his scientific work and his theological reflections. Teilhard was continually meditating on the nature and formation of the universe [and] the book of nature is where he encountered the divine. . . . Teilhard's comprehensive vision of the earth and its interconnected life processes evolving over time is a well spring of hope for the critical work ahead to create a sustainable future."[2]

Integral Ecology: Catholic Social Teaching, Humans, and Earth

Pope Francis could not have chosen a more central or pressing topic for *Laudato si'* than the human role in ecological degradation and climate change. He critiques our "technocratic paradigm" (*LS* 101, 109, 111–12, 122) and "throwaway culture" (*LS* 16, 22, 45). He calls for a transformation of the market-based economic system that he feels is destroying the planet and creating immense social inequities. Indeed, the encyclical is highly critical of unfettered capitalism and rampant consumerism. Francis's critique draws on earlier papal and Church teachings regarding the problematic dimensions of capitalism in relation to social and ecological justice. He sees unregulated economic growth as problematic for the long-term sustainability of the community of life—both human and non-human.

This might seem like a radical message, but it is also the culmination of a century of Catholic social justice teaching. By drawing on and developing the work of earlier theologians and ethicists, this encyclical makes explicit the links between social justice and our newer

---

1. For more on Teilhard, see the American Teilhard Association, *http://teilhard dechardin.org/*.

2. Mary Evelyn Tucker, "The Ecological Spirituality of Pierre Teilhard de Chardin," *Teilhard Series* 51 (2005): 1.

understanding of eco-justice. Francis also went to great lengths to cite the words and ideas of previous popes and the insights of eighteen bishops' letters from around the world. Thus the pope is drawing on earlier Church teachings that have already highlighted issues with the environment. This reflects episcopal collegiality, that is, responsibility for the universal Church shared by the pope and other bishops, in the spirit of Vatican II. Doing so is also a strategic move, lest the encyclical be seen as radical or out-of-step with Church teachings. Pope Francis draws these teachings together with the term "integral ecology," which was used in 1995 by the cultural historian and Catholic priest Thomas Berry, as well as the Catholic liberation theologian Leonardo Boff.

Cardinal Peter Kodwo Appiah Turkson, one of the key architects of the encyclical, believes understanding the phrase "integral ecology" is central to understanding the pope's message. Turkson has identified several principles of integral ecology: (1) the moral imperative of all people to be protectors of the environment, (2) care for creation as a virtue in its own right, and (3) the need for a new global solidarity to direct our search for the common good.[3]

Integral ecology, then, means that ecological integrity and social justice are linked because humans and nature are part of nurturing, interdependent life systems. Given that the poor and vulnerable are most adversely affected by an ailing planetary system, Pope Francis calls us to "hear *both the cry of the earth and the cry of the poor*" and address ecological integrity and social justice (*LS* 49, italics in original). While this summons draws on traditional Christian teachings regarding care for the poor, it also marks an important shift in the Church's conception of the relationship of humans to nature and to work.

Related Teachings of Prior Popes

We can compare Pope Francis's thinking to the writing of Pope John Paul II, who in turn builds on Pope Leo XIII's 1891 encyclical *Rerum novarum*, which focused on workers' rights.[4] In this document

---

3. See the text of Cardinal Turkson's presentation of *Laudato si'* on June 19, 2015, at Ecojesuit, *http://www.ecojesuit.com/full-text-of-the-presentation-of-cardinal-peter-kodwo-appiah-turkson/7995/*.

4. Pope Leo XIII, *Rerum novarum*, May 15, 1891, *http://w2.vatican.va/content/leo-xiii/en/encyclicals/documents/hf_l-xiii_enc_15051891_rerum-novarum.html*.

Leo XIII highlighted "the condition of the workers"; their labor had become a mere commodity in an economic milieu that gave primacy to the free market and unregulated exploitation of workers.

In *Centessimus annus*, his 1991 encyclical to celebrate the one-hundred-year anniversary of *Rerum novarum*, Pope John Paul II wrote,

> The original source of all that is good is the very act of God, who created both the earth and man, and who gave the earth to man so that he might have dominion over it by his work and enjoy its fruits (Gen 1:28). . . . It is through work that man, using his intelligence and exercising his freedom, succeeds in dominating the earth and making it a fitting home. . . . Obviously, he also has the responsibility not to hinder others from having their own part of God's gift; indeed, he must cooperate with others so that together all can dominate the earth.[5]

Drawing heavily on the biblical language of domination, John Paul underscores the modern separation of humans from nature. He also emphasizes the dignity of cooperative human labor, however, as making something productive of God's gift of nature. Thus the traditional perspective of "dominion" in Genesis is balanced by a call for "stewardship" of nature. Although this teaching was a significant development of papal ecological teaching at the time, this view stands in marked contrast to his successors' more holistic view of nature.

Pope Benedict, for example, expanded Catholic thinking regarding the environment. His 2009 encyclical *Caritas in veritate* is focused on charity and our duty to the poor, as well as obligations to present and future generations.[6] He wrote of this responsibility arising from

> our relationship to the natural environment. The environment is God's gift to everyone, and in our use of it we have a

---

5. Pope John Paul II, *Centessimus annus* 31, May 1, 1991, *http://w2.vatican.va/content/john-paul-ii/en/encyclicals/documents/hf_jp-ii_enc_01051991_centesimus-annus.html.*

6. Pope Benedict XVI, *Caritas in veritate,* June 29, 2009, *http://w2.vatican.va/content/benedict-xvi/en/encyclicals/documents/hf_ben-xvi_enc_20090629_caritas-in-veritate.html.*

responsibility towards the poor, towards future generations and towards humanity as a whole. When nature, including the human being, is viewed as the result of mere chance or evolutionary determinism, our sense of responsibility wanes. In nature, the believer recognizes the wonderful result of God's creative activity, which we may *use responsibly* to satisfy our legitimate needs, material or otherwise, while respecting the intrinsic balance of creation. (*CV* 48, italics added)

Benedict moves away from language of domination over nature toward the protection of nature. Yet he conceives of creation as "in balance"; this differs from more contemporary perspectives of ecological science that see nature as in flux, with ecosystems in dynamic disequilibrium. Benedict also presents what he calls the "grammar of nature" which refers to the deeper cosmological structures of creation that evoke awe and reverence. He writes,

The natural environment is more than raw material to be manipulated at our pleasure; it is a wondrous work of the Creator containing a "grammar," which sets forth ends and criteria for its wise use, not its reckless exploitation. Today much harm is done to development precisely as a result of these distorted notions. Reducing nature merely to a collection of contingent data ends up doing violence to the environment and even encouraging activity that fails to respect human nature itself. (*CV* 48)

This emphasis on a "grammar of nature" by Pope Benedict echoes a well-known phrase of Berry: "The universe is not a collection of objects but a communion of subjects."[7] By this Berry means there is interiority not only in humans, but in species and in the ecosystem itself, which all consist of more than just physical matter. In this way Berry furthers the sense of patterning in nature suggested by "grammar of nature" to a straightforward emphasis on an interiority within the natural world. This interiority—also recognized by

---

7. Thomas Berry, *The Great Work: Our Way into the Future* (New York: Random House, 1999), 82.

Teilhard—is akin to the spirit and energy that religion and science respectively recognize as animating the universe.[8] For Berry, this interiority of all creation is what makes for a sacred universe that needs to be protected and revered accordingly.

Thomas Berry

Thomas Berry (1914–2009), a Roman Catholic priest of the Passionist order, "called for the articulation of a new story of evolution and the emergence of life. The work of Pierre Teilhard de Chardin was a major inspiration for [Berry] in developing his ideas for a universe story, especially Teilhard's feeling for the great sweep of evolution from lesser to greater complexity and consciousness."[9] As a result of his deep reflections on creation, Berry referred to himself as a "geologian."[10]

Benedict also wrote on the importance of justice for future generations, observing that global development "cannot ignore coming generations, but needs to be marked by solidarity and inter-generational justice, while taking into account a variety of contexts: ecological, juridical, economic, political and cultural."[11] There is a clear shift here from the narrower ecological vision of John Paul. Yet Benedict still relies on an anthropocentric (that is, human-centered) ethic of "wise use" of nature.

Pope Francis in *Laudato si'* frames an ecological vision in a new approach. Indeed, following Francis of Assisi, he invokes "Mother Earth" in the opening paragraph of the encyclical. This is

8. Pierre Teilhard de Chardin, *The Human Phenomenon*, trans. Sarah Appleton-Weber (East Sussex, UK: Sussex Academic Press, 2003), 22–32; Mary Evelyn Tucker, "Influences of Pierre Teilhard de Chardin on *Journey of the Universe*," in *Living Cosmology: Christian Responses to Journey of the Universe*, ed. Mary Evelyn Tucker and John Grim (Maryknoll, NY: Orbis, 2016), 62–72.

9. Mary Evelyn Tucker and John Grim, "Thomas Berry: Reflections on His Life and Thought," *Teilhard Studies* 61 (2010): 2.

10. For more on Berry, see The Thomas Berry Foundation, *http://www.thomasberry.org/*.

11. Pope Benedict XVI, *Caritas in veritate*, 48.

a perspective much more familiar to Latin American Catholics. His evocation of the "Canticle to Brother Sun and Sister Moon" similarly places the encyclical precisely in the tradition of Franciscan nature mysticism. In this case, the Franciscan spirit evokes awe that leads to action and reverence that leads to responsibility. It is a unique blending of cosmology and ecology.

Cosmology and Religious Cosmologies

Cosmology: the study of the nature of the universe. "In the humanities, cosmology refers to the myths of the origin and ongoing character of the universe, whereas in the physical sciences cosmology focuses primarily on the emergence of the early universe."[12]

Religious Cosmologies: "stories or understandings that orient humans to the unfolding of the cosmos in relationship to a larger context of life."[13]

Religious cosmology requires a broader ethical framework than the human context. It is why Daniel P. Scheid, a theologian at Duquesne University, and author of chapter 11 in this volume, calls for cosmological ethics for the cosmic common good in his new book of this title.[14] Such a broadened framework allows an evolutionary valuing of life throughout billions of years. It moves from an anthropocentric perspective to one that is anthropocosmic—that is, it recognizes humanity's uniqueness but "locates the human within the cosmos and with the community of life on Earth."[15] It is clear in the Christian context that religious cosmology draws on the many theological reflections on the Cosmic Christ in Saint Paul's epistles, and also in the opening of John's Gospel with the reference to *Logos* in all creation. Indeed, Pope Francis cites Dante's cosmological vision

12. Mary Evelyn Tucker and John Grim, *Ecology and Religion* (Washington, DC: Island, 2014), 178.

13. Ibid., 183.

14. Daniel P. Scheid, *Cosmic Common Good* (New York: Oxford, 2016).

15. Tucker and Grim, *Ecology and Religion*, 177.

of the scattered leaves of the universe gathered in the love that moves the Sun and stars.

Pope Francis draws not only from awe and wonder and evolution in *Laudato si'*. He also shifts the Church to a view of nature even more in line with environmental science. He calls for increased ecological literacy and understanding of environmental problems. He relies heavily on the scientific understanding of ecosystems and climate change, no doubt in part because of his own science studies and early teaching in chemistry. In all of this, Francis corrects the mistaken interpretation that the biblical call for humans to exercise "dominion" is license to exploitatively dominate creation. In its place, he lifts up an understanding of integral ecology that connects humans to their environment, and indeed to the whole evolutionary process.

Cosmological and Evolutionary Perspectives on Creation

In this respect, there are, as noted, echoes in the encyclical of the thought of Teilhard de Chardin and of Thomas Berry. Both saw something akin to Benedict's "grammar of nature" as reflecting an evolutionary unfolding of a deep patterning in Earth's ecosystems directly related to the larger evolution of the universe. This included an interiority that Teilhard called "consciousness" and an inner patterning of things he described as spirit-matter. Along with what Teilhard called his metaphysics, he was also prescient in seeing how emergent properties and self-organizing dynamics led to greater consciousness and complexification in evolution.

Teilhard's thinking about evolution led to his critique of the biblical Genesis story as explanatory of evolution. Teilhard explored ideas describing cosmogenesis, namely, an emerging universe expressing ever-new patternings of spirit-matter. When an early writing developing these ideas was submitted to conservative Vatican officials, Teilhard was urged to leave France for research in China in the early 1920s. This absence of tolerance for his cosmological thought led to his sustained exile from Europe to China beginning in the late 1920s. Teilhard's ideas were nevertheless influential, and of particular import is Teilhard's understanding of the human phenomenon as arising from and deeply connected to the dynamic, unfolding universe.[16] Teilhard felt that if we don't sense this connection, we lose our way and our purpose for living. In his words,

> Humans have every right to be anxious about their fate so long as they feel themselves to be lost and lonely in the midst of the mass of created things. For it will denote in them not a critical sense but a malady of the spirit if they were doubtful of the value and the hopes of an entire world. But let them once discover that their fate is bound up with the fate of nature itself and immediately, joyously, they will begin again their forward march.[17]

In *Laudato si'*, Pope Francis draws on the same notion to describe a dynamic cosmological and ecological relationship between humans and, indeed, all life:

> As part of the universe, called into being by one Father, all of us are linked by unseen bonds and together form a kind of universal family, a sublime communion which fills us with a sacred, affectionate, and humble respect. . . . God has joined us so closely to the world around us that we can feel the desertification of the soil almost as a physical ailment, and the extinction of a species as a painful disfigurement. (*LS* 89)

In this passage from Pope Francis, there are also echoes of Thomas Berry, who, following Teilhard, situated the human as arising from and dependent on this long evolutionary journey. He wrote that the loss of a species was the loss of a divine voice. He notes that "at such a moment [as the present], a new revolutionary experience is needed, an experience wherein human consciousness awakens to the grandeur and sacred quality of Earth processes. This awakening is our human participation in the dream of Earth."[18] From this cosmological perspective, Berry—like Pope Francis—calls on humans to participate in the "great work" of ecological transformation: building new ecological economics,

---

16. Teilhard de Chardin, *The Human Phenomenon*.

17. Pierre Teilhard de Chardin, *Hymn of the Universe* (New York: Harper & Row, 1965), 109.

18. Thomas Berry, "Reinventing the Human at the Species Level," in *The Christian Future and the Fate of Earth*, ed. M. E. Tucker and J. Grim (Maryknoll, NY: Orbis, 2009), 123.

educational and political systems, and religious and spiritual communities that are aligned with Earth's capacities and limits.

This evolutionary understanding of Earth's systems, so central to Teilhard and Berry, provides a broad context for Pope Francis's own revolutionary thinking. Indeed, this is the integrative perspective of *Journey of the Universe*, which narrates the epic story of evolution in film and book forms and, in light of *Laudato si'*, can complement and enrich study of the encyclical.[19] This integration resituates the human as part of the vast unfolding universe, and thus as responsible for the continuity of the life systems of the planet. As the *Journey of the Universe* "Conversations" education series indicates, this brings together new models for the wellbeing of the Earth community in cosmology, ecology, and justice.

This integrated perspective of a change of consciousness and conscience for humans could have a rippling effect on the contemporary climate debate. Without this integrated sense of mutually enhancing human–Earth relations in an evolving universe, climate discussions can become simply business as usual amid policy proposals, market-based schemes, and technological fixes. Animated by a broader cosmological spirit, *Laudato si'* calls on communities and individuals to awaken to the beauty of creation and engage in action for climate justice. This actively illustrates the heart of integral ecology, where people and planet are seen as "interconnected" (*LS* 70, 138, 240).

Social Justice and Ecological Justice in a Cosmological Context

What distinguishes Pope Francis's perspective from many others in society, then, is the linking of environmental and climate discussions with issues of social justice, poverty, and economic inequality. These are themes often missing from the United Nations' Intergovernmental Panel on Climate Change (IPCC) reports until fairly recently. Pope Francis's approach to ecology and climate change has the potential to transform the debate by connecting environmental science and policy with a century of social justice teachings from the

---

19. B. T. Swimme, and M. E. Tucker, *Journey of the Universe* (New Haven: Yale University Press, 2011); Journey of the Universe, "Conversations," 2011, *www.journey oftheuniverse.org.*

Christian churches. Ecology and equity are inextricably linked, says Pope Francis. That is what he communicates in *Laudato si'* to both Christians and "every person living on this planet" (*LS* 3)—and there are a number of resources that, along with *Journey of the Universe* and a study of Teilhard and Berry, can help persons better understand and respond to this message.

Ecology and Justice Series on Integral Ecology

For more than two decades the authors of this essay have been advisors to an Orbis Books series, Ecology and Justice, which seeks to enhance the dialogue on integral ecology.[20] There are some twenty books in the series, which has worked since its inception to build bridges between the perspectives of ecology and justice. Earlier, some theologians dismissed ecology as simply involving wilderness preservation or the rights of trees; conversely, environmentalists sometimes viewed poverty amelioration as secondary to preserving ecosystems. Yet these concerns are clearly linked, and are increasingly coming together in religious and environmental circles.

In this regard, it is worth noting that two of the other advisors in the Orbis series were major influences on the encyclical: Sean McDonagh, an Irish Columban priest who served many years among the T'boli people in the Philippines, and Leonardo Boff, a Brazilian liberation theologian who innovatively brought ecological concerns into dialogue with liberation theology.[21]

During the 1970s and 1980s, McDonagh's work in the Philippines provided him with first-hand experience of how the degradation of non-human creation injures humans, especially the poor and marginalized. Based on these experiences, McDonagh has drawn from Teilhard and Berry to argue that attention to modern ecological challenges requires a more "comprehensive *story of the universe*" that locates humans within the cosmos and is informed by both science and religion.[22]

20. For more on this series, see Orbis Books, Ecology & Justice, *http://www.orbis books.com/category-202/*.

21. For more on Boff, see chapter 6 in this volume, "Leonardo Boff's Franciscan Liberation Ecological Theology and 'Integral Ecology' in *Laudato si'*," by Dawn M. Nothwehr, OSF.

22. Sean McDonagh, *To Care for the Earth* (Santa Fe, NM: Bear, 1986), 12 (italics in original).

Like McDonagh, Boff was inspired by the work of Berry, especially the book *The Dream of the Earth*. Boff came to realize that there can be no liberation for humans from injury and oppression without liberation of Earth from exploitation.[23] Motivated by this insight, Boff wrote, among other books, *Cry of the Earth, Cry of the Poor*, which was published in the Orbis series; this title appears in *Laudato si'* (49). Additionally, Boff has woven the evolutionary insights articulated by Berry and Brian Swimme in *The Universe Story* into his other writings along with work on the *Earth Charter* movement, in which he has been active as a commissioner from Latin America.[24]

Earth Charter: Cosmology, Ecology, Justice, and Peace

Participants in the three-year drafting committee of the *Earth Charter*, which was released in 2000, tried to bring together these elements of cosmology, ecology, justice, and peace. The preamble to the charter intentionally points to cosmology: "Humanity is part of a vast evolving universe. Earth, our home, is alive with a unique community of life. . . . Earth has provided the conditions essential to life's evolution. The resilience of the community of life and the well-being of humanity depend upon preserving a healthy biosphere."[25]

Following this preamble, the charter outlines sixteen principles divided into four sections:

I. Respect and Care for the Community of Life

1. Respect Earth and life in all its diversity.

2. Care for the community of life with understanding, compassion, and love.

3. Build democratic societies that are just, participatory, sustainable, and peaceful.

---

23. Thomas Berry, *The Dream of the Earth* (San Francisco: Sierra Club, 1988).

24. Thomas Berry and Brian Swimme, *The Universe Story: From the Primordial Flaring Forth to the Ecozoic Era—A Celebration of the Unfolding of the Cosmos* (New York: HarperCollins, 1992).

25. Earth Charter Commission, *The Earth Charter*, 2000, *http://earthcharter.org /invent/images/uploads/echarter_english.pdf*.

4. Secure Earth's bounty and beauty for present and future generations.

II. Ecological Integrity

5. Protect and restore the integrity of Earth's ecological systems, with special concern for biological diversity and the natural processes that sustain life.

6. Prevent harm as the best method of environmental protection and, when knowledge is limited, apply a precautionary approach.

7. Adopt patterns of production, consumption, and reproduction that safeguard Earth's regenerative capacities, human rights, and community well-being.

8. Advance the study of ecological sustainability and promote the open exchange and wide application of the knowledge acquired.

III. Social and Economic Justice

9. Eradicate poverty as an ethical, social, and environmental imperative.

10. Ensure that economic activities and institutions at all levels promote human development in an equitable and sustainable manner.

11. Affirm gender equality and equity as prerequisites to sustainable development and ensure universal access to education, health care, and economic opportunity.

12. Uphold the right of all, without discrimination, to a natural and social environment supportive of human dignity, bodily health, and spiritual well-being, with special attention to the rights of indigenous peoples and minorities.

IV. Democracy, Nonviolence, and Peace

13. Strengthen democratic institutions at all levels, and provide transparency and accountability in governance, inclusive participation in decision making, and access to justice.

14. Integrate into formal education and life-long learning the knowledge, values, and skills needed for a sustainable way of life.
15. Treat all living beings with respect and consideration.
16. Promote a culture of tolerance, nonviolence, and peace.

These principles do not endorse any particular means by which to realize the specified ends. From a Catholic perspective, the principles should always be conscientiously pursued in ways consistent with the various levels of Church teaching.[26] Following these principles, the *Charter* concludes with a hopeful way forward that Pope Francis quotes in *Laudato si'*:

> As never before in history, common destiny beckons us to seek a new beginning. . . . Let ours be a time remembered for the awakening of a new reverence for life, the firm resolve to achieve sustainability, the quickening of the struggle for justice and peace, and the joyful celebration of life. (*LS* 207)

As such, the *Earth Charter* brings together cosmology, ecology, justice, and peace in a way that can help realize the vision of *Laudato si'*.

Conclusion

The publication of *Laudato si'* offers a unique opportunity to scale up and move forward the work to link cosmology and ecology by providing a renewed moral force and shared ethical commitment regarding environmental issues, especially climate change.[27] In particular, *Laudato si'* highlights the fact that humans have a special kinship with non-human nature and are responsible for its continuity

---

26. For more on the important topic of Church teaching authority, see Richard R. Gaillardetz, *By What Authority? Foundations for Understanding Authority in the Church* (Collegeville, MN: Liturgical Press, 2018). See especially Part Three: The Authority of the Magisterium and Part Four: The Authority of the Believing Community.

27. This is also the work of the Forum on Religion and Ecology at Yale University, *http://fore.yale.edu.*

for future generations. The flourishing of Earth, our common home, may well depend on how humans heed Pope Francis's call to "ecological conversion." The ability of *Laudato si'* to help us see ourselves as part of an earth community birthed out of deep time is a major step in this direction (*LS* 5, 217, 219–20).[28]

Review Questions

1. Define the term *cosmology*.
2. What are the elements of integral ecology as described by Cardinal Peter Turkson?
3. Explain the term *interiority*. How is it related to Pope Francis's notion of integral ecology?
4. Describe the relationship between evolution and cosmology.
5. How would you summarize the sixteen principles that make up the *Earth Charter*?

In-Depth Questions

1. Have you ever experienced the "interiority" of some non-human part of creation? If so, describe this experience. If not, are you open to the possibility of such an experience? Why or why not?
2. The authors claim that evolutionary and cosmological perspectives can have "a rippling effect on the contemporary climate debate." Do you agree or disagree with this assertion? Why or why not?
3. The authors quote Thomas Berry, who wrote that "a new revolutionary experience is needed, an experience wherein human consciousness awakens to the grandeur and sacred quality of Earth processes." What do you think would need to happen for society to embrace this new consciousness?
4. Do you think the *Earth Charter* principles are all consonant with Pope Francis's vision of integral ecology? If so, are you

28. It is important to highlight Francis's acknowledgement that his call for "ecological conversion" was first made by Pope John Paul II. See *LS* footnote 5, citing *Catechesis*, January 17, 2001.

more or less compelled by the additional presence of religious language in *Laudato si'*? If not, which *Earth Charter* principles do you see as in tension with the pope's teachings in *Laudato si'*?

5. Pick one principle from the *Earth Charter* and describe how you might uphold it through work in your discipline or field of studies.

Suggestions for Further Study

Scheid, Daniel P. *Cosmic Common Good.* New York: Oxford University Press, 2016.

Swimme, Brian Thomas, and Thomas Berry. *The Universe Story: From the Primordial Flaring Forth to the Ecozoic Era—A Celebration of the Unfolding of the Cosmos.* New York: HarperCollins, 1994.

Swimme, Brian Thomas, and Mary Evelyn Tucker. *Journey of the Universe.* New Haven: Yale University Press, 2011.

Teilhard de Chardin, Pierre. *The Divine Milieu.* New York: Harper Perrennial Modern Classics, 2001.

———. *The Human Phenomenon.* Translated by Sarah Appleton-Weber. East Sussex, UK: Sussex Academic Press, 2003.

Tucker, Mary Evelyn, and John Grim. *Ecology and Religion.* Washington, DC: Island, 2014.

———, eds. *Living Cosmology: Christian Responses to* Journey of the Universe. Maryknoll, NY: Orbis, 2016.

———, eds. *Thomas Berry: Selected Writings on the Earth Community.* Maryknoll, NY: Orbis, 2014.

CHAPTER 5

The Harmony of Nature in a Time of Technology: The Mystical Vision of *Laudato si'*[1]

DREW CHRISTIANSEN, SJ

Guided by Saint Francis's "Canticle of the Creatures," this chapter describes how Pope Francis's understanding of the cosmos is characterized by the dynamic interplay between particularity, diversity, unity, and harmony. Additionally, the chapter considers how technology can both sustain and damage the cosmos as Francis sees it. Finally, it suggests how mysticism and aesthetics can preserve Francis's cosmic vision in our technological age.

Particularity, Diversity, and Multiplicity

The particularity of every creature is a favorite theme of Pope Francis. Particularity, diversity, and multiplicity are terms that appear frequently in his teaching. Not since Blessed John Duns Scotus (1266–1308) has a major Catholic figure given such attention to the individuality, or what Scotus called the *haeceitas*, or "thisness," of creatures.[2]

---

1. This chapter was originally presented as the third of four talks to the seminarians and faculty of Theological College, Washington, DC, on November 20 and 21, 2015. All references to *Laudato si'* are taken from Pope Francis, *Laudato si': On Care for Our Common Home*, June 18, 2015, *http://w2.vatican.va/content/francesco/en/encyclicals/documents/papa-francesco_20150524_enciclica-laudato-si.html*.

2. On *haeceitas* (translated as "individual uniqueness)," see "Individuation," under "Duns Scotus," in *New Catholic Encyclopedia*, rev. ed. (Washington, DC: Catholic University of America, 2003), 4:936.

As religious poetry, the great appeal of Saint Francis's *Canticle* is precisely its particularity. Like Adam naming the animals in the garden, the three young men in the book of Daniel who summon creation to praise God after they are thrown into the fire, or the psalmists who often celebrate the particularities of God's creation, Saint Francis names each of the creatures through which he gives praise to God the Creator.[3] The beauty of the poem lies in its identification of each by name and function:

> Praised be you, my Lord, through
> Brother Wind,
> and through the air, cloudy and
> serene, and every kind of weather
> through whom you give
> sustenance to your creatures.
> Praised be you, my Lord, through Sister Water,
> who is very useful
> and humble and
> precious and chaste.
> Praised be you, my Lord,
> through Brother Fire,
> through whom you light the night,
> and he is beautiful
> and playful and robust and strong. (*LS* 87)

Each creature has its own place in creation and praises God in its own way.

In *Evangelii gaudium*, Pope Francis's exhortation on evangelization, and again in *Laudato si'*, Pope Francis appeals to Saint Thomas to justify this position.[4] He writes, "Saint Thomas Aquinas wisely noted that multiplicity and variety 'come from the intention of the

---

3. On Adam's naming the animals, see Gen. 2:18–23. For the Hymn of the Three Young Men, see Dan 3:24–45. Psalms of praise with that sense of particularity are 104, 147, 148.

4. Pope Francis, *Evangelii gaudium*, November 24, 2013, *http://w2.vatican.va/content /francesco/en/apost_exhortations/documents/papa-francesco_esortazione-ap_20131124 _evangelii-gaudium.html*.

first agent' who willed that 'what was wanting to one in the representation of the divine goodness' might be supplied by another," inasmuch as God's goodness "could not be represented fittingly by any one creature" (*LS* 87).[5] Hence thinking ecologically requires that we grasp the variety of things in their multiple relationships. Accordingly, to imagine the unity of creation Pope Francis proposes that we envisage the unity of creation not as a uniform sphere, but rather as a polyhedron of interlocking parts, like the pentagons and hexagons on a soccer ball, in which the distinctiveness of every part is recognizable (*EG* 36). It is a godlike vision in which each creature is loved for itself, just as parents love each of their children separately without comparison.

Drawing on a prayerful exercise in memory of the sort retreat directors often propose, Pope Francis asks us to evoke memories that will elicit our ties to the earth:

> The history of our friendship with God is always linked to particular places which take on an intensely personal meaning; we all remember places, and revisiting those memories does us much good. Anyone who has grown up in the hills or used to sit by the spring to drink, or played outdoors in the neighborhood square; going back to these places is a chance to recover something of their true selves. (*LS* 84)

Your Natural History

Do you associate certain places in your life with awareness of God? If so, are they found in nature? In human environments? In gatherings of people?

Have you ever worshipped in "a sacred landscape"? If so, how did it affect your prayer? Was your experience shared with others? Did the experience shape your life? Did it enhance your environmental awareness or commitment?

Religious mysticism is not found in flight to the general and the abstract, but rather in deep, affective appreciation of every

---

5. The pope is citing *Summa theologiae* I, 47.

creature—both its particularity and the cosmic web implicated in its existence.

Some religions, like Hinduism and Jainism, show profound respect for every living creature, exercising nonviolence (*ahimsa*) even in relation to flies and mosquitoes. They refrain from swatting or crushing them. Pope Francis does not ask an exaggerated respect for the creatures of the natural world, but he does suggest we need to pay attention to particular creatures, landscapes, and ecosystems. To be environmentally sensitive, we need to treasure what is different in creation and appreciate the costs of eliminating or modifying it. We need to show a degree of reticence before we intervene in nature and a readiness to let things just be. When we intervene, we need to do so in harmony with nature and awareness of "the genius of the place."

Christian Nature Mysticism

Pope Francis reminds us that true theology, as Baron von Hugel explained, includes not only doctrinal and institutional elements but a mystical component that, by extension, must be an integral element in a Christian theology of the environment.[6] Pope Francis notes how Saint Bonaventure, himself a member of the Franciscan religious order, reminds us that creatures in their individuality lead us to God. Citing Saint Bonaventure, he writes, we must find God in all things, not just in introspection but in appreciation of the natural world.[7]

The mysticism to which Francis invites his readers is far from the "oceanic experience," that is, a feeling of limitlessness as in being adrift on an ocean, which some mystics report and scholars describe. As Francis elaborates his creation mysticism, however, its primary form is an experience of harmony in diversity, of the unity of all in Christ, where our particularity contributes to the union of all things in God, which is the object of mystic perception.

---

6. See Friedrich von Hugel, "The Three Elements of Religion," chapter 2 of *The Mystical Element of Religion* (London: J. M. Dent and Sons; New York: E. P. Dutton and Co., 1923; repr. New York: Crossroad, 1999), 1:50–82.

7. See *LS* 233.

Dynamic Harmony: God in Creative Evolution

For Pope Francis, the harmony of nature is dynamic; the Holy Spirit is at work "renew[ing] the face of the earth" with each new day (Ps. 104:30). Keeping with the aesthetic metaphors of *Laudato si'*, one might say the Spirit is introducing new chords to the divine symphony, adding to the diversity and multiplicity that gives glory to God.

In August of 1919, during studies on the Isle of Jersey, Pierre Teilhard de Chardin, the French Jesuit scientist and spiritual writer who reconciled Catholicism with evolutionary theory, composed his "Hymn to Matter" modeled on the "Canticle of Creation."[8] "Matter" in his sense is the bare stuff of creation; in his work as a paleontologist it consisted of rocks, the ultimate in resisting nature. In the tension between humanity and matter, matter becomes the occasion for our growth in consciousness and our sanctification. In the style of the "Canticle of Creation," Teilhard wrote,

> Blessed be you, impenetrable matter: you who, interposed between our minds and the world of essences, cause us to languish with the desire to pierce through the seamless veil of phenomena.
>
> Blessed be you, mortal matter. . . .
>
> Without you, without your onslaughts, without your uprooting of us, we should remain all our lives inert, stagnant, puerile, ignorant both of ourselves and of God. You who batter us and then dress our wounds, you who resist us and yield to us, you who wreck and build, you who shackle and liberate, the sap of our souls, the hand of God, the flesh of Christ: it is you, matter, that I bless.[9]

And here is the main point: "I acclaim you as the *divine milieu*, charged with creative power, as the ocean stirred by the Spirit, as the clay molded and infused with life by the Incarnate Word."[10]

---

8. For more on Teilhard, see chapter 4 in this volume, "Cosmology and Ecology in *Laudato si'*" by Mary Evelyn Tucker and John Grim.

9. Pierre Teilhard de Chardin, *Hymn of the Universe* (New York: Harper, 1961), 69–70.

10. Ibid.

Evolution, as Teilhard envisaged it, embraces galactic, geological, and biological evolution, but for him what was most important was the evolution in which human science and creativity play a leading role, what some today call "the Anthropocene," the era of human-led evolution. As such, finding God in all things entails not just finding God in the natural world but also finding divinity present and working in the human world on the interface between humans and nature, including our technology.

As one example of how God might be found at the intersection of human and non-human creation, astronomer Aileen A. O'Donoghue describes how, when she fell mysteriously ill, she came to recognize the divine presence in medical technology. God was laboring for her in the diagnostic equipment that located her diseased cells and the treatment technology that helped heal the cause of her illness:

> As I lay beneath the hulk of the X-ray machine, I took comfort from it the way others find solace in a stuffed bear, a poem, a song or a phrase from Scripture. The sudden collapse of my body from anemia was frightening, but the machine represented the incredible wonders of the universe and of God, who had challenged me and comforted me along my journey with astronomers and monks.[11]

In beautiful prose, O'Donoghue testifies to the truth of Pope Francis's reflection on the positive elements of technology:

> Technology has remedied countless evils which used to harm and limit human beings. How can we not feel gratitude and appreciation for this progress, especially in the fields of medicine, engineering and communications? How could we not acknowledge the work of many scientists and engineers who have provided alternatives to make development sustainable? (*LS* 102)

In drafting *Laudato si'*, Pope Francis was properly concerned with correcting humanity's technological hubris; but he is no Luddite intent on condemning technology. He finds beauty in a skyscraper

---

11. Aileen A. O. Donaghue, "God in Machines," *America Magazine*, March 5, 2007, *http://americamagazine.org/issue/605/faith-focus/god-machines*.

or an airliner (*LS* 103). "Valuable works of art and music," he writes, "now make use of new technologies" (103). Think of synthesizers and electronica, for example. "So, in the beauty intended by the one who uses new technical instruments and in the contemplation of such beauty," he writes, "a quantum leap occurs, resulting in a fulfilment which is uniquely human" (103).

Citing Teilhard de Chardin, Francis affirms that "all creatures are moving forward with and through humanity towards a common point of arrival, which is God, in that transcendent fullness where the risen Christ embraces and illumines all things" (*LS* 83). The vision of the risen Christ embracing and illuminating all things is a clear reference to Teilhard's Cosmic Christ, an eschatological vision that was adopted by the Second Vatican Council in *Gaudium et spes*.[12] In a line that summarizes the spirituality of Teilhard's *Divine Milieu*, Francis writes, "Human beings, endowed with intelligence and love, and drawn by the fullness of Christ, are called to lead all creatures back to their Creator" (*LS* 68).

The Silent Rupture of Harmony in Technological Existence

In the latest phases of human and creation history, technology is intertwined with creation to an unprecedented degree. But, ironically, technology has also greatly augmented "the silent rupture" in the harmony of creation, the harmony of humans with one another and

---

12. For the Cosmic Christ, see Pierre Teilhard de Chardin, "The Nature of the Divine Milieu, the Universal Christ and the Great Communion," part 3.2 of *The Divine Milieu* (New York: Harper, 1960; New York: Perennial Classic, 2001), 93–102. The Second Vatican Council's use of this concept may be found in *Gaudium et spes*, 39, December 7, 1965, *http://www.vatican.va/archive/hist_councils/ii_vatican_council /documents/vat-ii_const_19651207_gaudium-et-spes_en.html*. For the papal acceptance of the "Cosmic Christ" imagery, see: *LS* note 53; Pope John Paul II, *Sollicitudo rei socialis*, 48, December 30, 1987, *http://w2.vatican.va/content/john-paul-ii/en/encyclicals/documents /hf_jp-ii_enc_30121987_sollicitudo-rei-socialis.html*; Pope Benedict XVI, *Caritas in veritate*, 7, June 29, 2009, *http://w2.vatican.va/content/benedict-xvi/en/encyclicals/documents /hf_ben-xvi_enc_20090629_caritas-in-veritate.html*; Pope Benedict XVI, "Homily of His Holiness Benedict XVI: Celebration of Vespers with the Faithful at Aosta," July 24, 2009, *http://w2.vatican.va/content/benedict-xvi/en/homilies/2009/documents/hf_ben-xvi_hom _20090724_vespri-aosta.html*; editors, "Teilhard at Vespers," *America Magazine*, August 17, 2009, *http://americamagazine.org/issue/705/editorial/teilhard-vespers*.

with the natural world, and ultimately with God. As Pope Francis points out, that rupture is sin: "The harmony between the Creator, humanity and creation as a whole was disrupted by our presuming to take the place of God and refusing to acknowledge our creaturely limitations" (*LS* 66).

For Francis, even the partial restoration of the harmony of creation depends on finding a more holistic view of life. Following his maxim "the whole is greater than the part" (*EG 237*), he argues for a holistic analysis of human, family, labor, urban, and environmental problems that responds to the complex interrelations of the various spheres of action. Accordingly, Pope Francis reasons, "Strategies for a solution demand an integrated approach to combating poverty, restoring dignity to the excluded, and at the same time protecting nature" (*LS* 139).

Restoring the harmony of creation, so far as it is in our power, requires approximation of that harmony in our science, our policy, and our lifestyles. Science and technology need not unsettle the harmony of creation. They can increase our appreciation of that harmony and enhance it as well.

In a famous lecture, "A Theology of the Earth," the ecologist Rene Dubos explained to his audience that preservation need not be the only policy of men and women who care for the earth; responsible, sensitive intervention is also possible.[13] "We cannot escape," he said, "an anthropocentric attitude which puts man at the summit of creation while still part of it." The first principle of an "enlightened anthropocentrism" he wrote, is that "man cannot effectively manipulate nature without loving nature for its own sake."

Dubos illustrates his case with the history of European monasticism, both Benedictine and Cistercian. Saint Benedict, he argued, equally merits standing with Saint Francis as a patron of the environment, especially for those who, like monks, transform the earth with sensitivity and a sense of place. For Dubos, a key example of the technological transformation of nature that reveals and enhances its beauty is the Taconic State Parkway in New York. "[The Taconic] is a product of technology," he observed, "which has transformed nature

---

13. Rene Dubos, "A Theology of the Earth," reposted from the Congressional Record, January 2, 1970, by Bates College, Archives and Special Collections: *http:// abacus.bates.edu/muskie-archives/ajcr/1970/Rene%20Dubos.shtml*.

by still respecting her character . . . a kind of creation which is in some ways the equivalent of a medieval cathedral." Dubos's vision of technology designed and operated in harmony with nature, exemplified in the Taconic Parkway, is consistent with Pope Francis's vision of integral ecology.

Harmony and Critique
of the Technological Paradigm

Pope Francis, though he sees the possibilities for integration of nature and technology, nonetheless recognizes the ambiguity of technology, its long-term downside as well as its benefits. Indeed, when it comes to Catholic social teaching, he is an innovator in his recognition that technology has become an enormously aggravating factor in disrupting the harmonious relations between humanity and nature and in relations among humans themselves. In particular, it is the nexus between technology and economics, or more precisely the too-little-regulated market, that is responsible for the depth of damage that humans have done to the planet. Together they share in our collective concupiscence—our unreasonable desires—since technology is always striving for greater control and markets are always looking to maximize profit. The drive for profit by the combination of techno-science and businesses magnifies humanity's sinfulness even more than our political collectivities. As Reinhold Niebuhr taught us, collective egoism gathers and greatly enlarges our private egoisms.[14]

The amplification of the negative impacts of the consumer economy by technology is further augmented by globalization and the abstraction from nature and from human relations it involves. Alienation from nature and society are opposed to the culture of encounter Pope Francis encourages and to the attention to particularity he believes is part of a prayerful and ecologically sensitive life. Globalization stimulates the illusion of unlimited growth among "economists, financiers and experts in technology," which in turn overtaxes the finite resources of the Earth (*LS* 103). Pope Francis's critique of technocracy consists in a social analysis of uncritical application of technology

---

14. Reinhold Niebuhr, *Moral Man and Immoral Society: A Study in Ethics and Politics* (Louisville: Westminster John Knox, 2013), 40–49.

and the cultural penetration of "the technocratic paradigm," in which everything human and natural is open to manipulation (*LS* 103–14).

Pope Francis concludes his criticism of the technocratic paradigm this way with a plea for people to slow down, look at the world with different eyes, appropriate sustainable technologies, and recover neglected values.

In Thomistic terms, he is asking us to limit the application of rationality (*ratio*), especially technocratic economic rationalism, with intelligence (*intellectus*), that is, a more aesthetic or intuitive understanding that embodies felt awareness of the whole web of relations in which we live.[15] For that reason he contends that a "kind of salvation" from such rationalistic reductionism comes "in beauty and those who behold it" (*LS* 112).

A Rupture in Creation

What do you think of Pope Francis's analysis that consumerism and globalization compound the destructive capacity of technology?

What might be the resources in human beings and in society to curb the destructive power of technology in our consumer economy?

Is restraint possible in a capitalist economy?

Is it possible to institutionalize restraint in the development and utilization of technology?

Beauty as a Way to Salvation

One of the less-noted themes found in *Laudato si'* is that of beauty, particularly the pedagogy of beauty as a remedy for the disharmonious technocracy of our time. Pope Francis writes, "By learning to see and appreciate beauty, we learn to reject self-interested pragmatism" (*LS* 112). Beauty also provides us with intimations of the divine

---

15. Pierre Rousselot, *The Intellectualism of Saint Thomas* (London: Sheed & Ward, 1935).

and the life to come. In Eastern spirituality, he tells us, "beauty is one of the best loved names" for the divine and for the transfigured or divinized human nature (*LS* 223). That beauty, he writes, is our eschatological hope: "At the end, we will find ourselves face to face with the infinite beauty of God (cf. 1 Cor. 13:12), and be able to read with admiration and happiness the mystery of the universe, which with us will share in unending plenitude" (*LS* 243).[16]

In the meantime, we are called to make this a beautiful world, in the preservation of nature, of course, but also in the beautification of human habitat, especially for those most deprived of beauty, namely, the poor. He writes, "More precious still is the service we offer to another kind of beauty: people's quality of life, their adaptation to the environment, encounter and mutual assistance" (*LS* 150).

Conclusion

Pope Francis's mystical vision of the universe as a harmony of creatures united in their particularity is an expression of the beauty that, according to Dostoyevsky, saves the world. It invites us to realize and enhance that harmony, preserving and appreciating the natural world around us as we give expression to human creativity and inventiveness in our technology, realizing in our lives and in our habitats an integral ecology that can only imperfectly mirror the cosmos we have received from the hand of the Creator.

Review Questions

1. How would you define "mysticism" after reading this chapter?
2. What is meant by "the harmony of diverse particulars?"
3. What are the central aspects of how Pope Francis criticizes the "technocratic paradigm"?
4. In what ways does Pope Francis think that greater appreciation of beauty can help humanity better care for our common home?

---

16. On beauty in scientific knowing, see Frank Wilczek, *A Beautiful Question* (New York: Penguin, 2015).

In-Depth Questions

1. Has a particular place ever awakened your environmental sensitivity? If so, did you experience something of the transcendent?

2. Have you experienced landscapes or environments enhanced by technological intervention, or landscapes or environments degraded by such intervention? If so, what was it about that particular use of technology that enhanced or degraded those spaces?

3. Why might Pope Francis's critics claim he is excessively critical of market capitalism, progress, and technology? After reading *Laudato si'*, what do you think of the pope's reflections on these topics?

4. Do you agree with Pope Francis that increased appreciation of beauty can lead people to better care for creation? If you disagree, explain why. If you agree, how can poor communities appreciate beauty in environments that are often degraded?

5. In our modern world, how can people come to a deeper appreciation of the harmony of creation and embrace the mystical vision of *Laudato si'*?

Suggestions for Further Study

Boff, Leonardo. *Francis of Assisi: A Model of Human Liberation*. Maryknoll, NY: Orbis, 1984.

Cunningham, Lawrence S. "Saint Francis and the Love of Nature." Chapter 6 of *Francis of Assisi: Performing the Gospel*, 92–106. Grand Rapids: Eerdmans, 2004.

DuBos, René. *A Theology of the Earth*. Washington, DC: Smithsonian Institution, 1969.

Ellul, Jacques. *The Technological Society*. Translated by John Wilkinson. New York: Knopf, 1964.

Saint Ignatius of Loyola. "Contemplation to Attain Divine Love." In *Ignatius Loyola: Spiritual Exercises and Selected Works*, edited by George Ganss, SJ, 176–77. Mahwah, NJ: Paulist, 1991.

Nash, James A. *Loving Nature: Ecological Integrity and Christian Responsibility*. Nashville: Abingdon, 1991.

Pavone, John. *Toward a Theology of Beauty.* Collegeville, MN: Liturgical Press, 1996.

Teilhard de Chardin, Pierre. *The Divine Milieu.* New York: Harper Torchbooks, 1965.

———. "The Mass on the World." In *Hymn of the Universe*, 13–37. New York: Harper, 1961.

Wilczek, Frank. *A Beautiful Question: Finding Nature's Deep Design.* New York: Penguin, 2015.

PART 3

Integral Ecology

Leonardo Boff's Franciscan Liberation Ecological Theology and "Integral Ecology" in *Laudato si'*

DAWN M. NOTHWEHR, OSF

A privileged few have seen the Earth from space. Those who have done so, like former NASA astronaut Russell Schweickart, have been forever changed:

> Viewed from outside, the Earth is so small that it could be covered with your thumb. Everything that has meaning for you, history, art, being born, death, love, happiness and tears, all these things are inside that small blue and white dot that could be covered with your thumb. Once you experience this, you feel that everything has changed; you have something new and things will not be as they were before.[1]

For founding liberation theologian Leonardo Boff, this outlook symbolizes "integral ecology." While retaining deep concern for oppressed peoples, Boff's reflections expanded to include the entire delicately balanced cosmos. He writes, "The Earth is ill. . . . Humans have shown they can commit not only homicide and ethnocide, but also biocide and geocide. . . . Humans must be liberated. . . . We are hostage to a paradigm that places us—against the thrust of the universe—*over* things instead of *with* them in the

---

1. Leonardo Boff, *Global Civilization: Challenges to Society and Christianity*, trans. Alexandre Guilherme (London: Equinox, 2005), 92. Schweickart piloted the Lunar Module of Apollo 9 in 1969.

great community."[2] Boff hopes that "a new paradigm is coming to birth—that of connectedness" between humans, non-human creation, and God.[3]

Leonardo Boff and Liberation Theology

Leonardo Boff, born December 14, 1938, in Córdoba, Santa Catarina, Brazil, and a Franciscan priest from 1964 until his resignation in 1992, was the first Latin American liberation theologian to link socio-political liberation with ecology. The *Earth Charter* and more than eighty books hold his Franciscan liberation ecological theology, sustaining his commitment to integral ecology.[4]

"Liberation theology" (from *liberare*, Latin for "to set free") refers to theology that upholds images of God as "justice" as its starting point and that seeks justice for all those oppressed in creation. Its method is "see, judge, act, and celebrate": *seeing* the reality of the poor firsthand; *judging* poverty and oppression as contradictory of God's plan; *acting* to eradicate causes of injustice; and *celebrating* life in light of the Gospel. Boff holding the same utilitarian logic of Enlightenment thinkers (Descartes, Newton, Bacon) connects causes of poverty and the exploitation of the earth. Out of this insight, a vigorous liberation eco-theology was born. Pope Francis follows this approach in his encyclical *Laudato si': On Care for Our Common Home*.

Boff's work on defining integral ecology influenced how the term is used in *Laudato si'*. This chapter opens with Franciscan perspectives on the Incarnation and Trinity that are foundational to Boff's development of integral ecology. Next it outlines Boff's appropriation of those teachings in his liberation ecological theology, especially his

---

2. Fazenda Sossego, preface, in Leonardo Boff, *Cry of the Earth, Cry of the Poor*, trans. Phillip Berryman (Maryknoll, NY: Orbis, 1997), xi–xii.

3. Ibid., xii.

4. Peter Hebblethwaite, "Boff Leaves the Priesthood and Order for the 'Periphery,'" *National Catholic Reporter*, July 17, 1992, 13.

integral ecology. Furthermore, the chapter reviews Boff's notion of integral ecology in *Laudato si'* and concludes by offering Saint Francis of Assisi as a model from whom we can learn to nurture integral ecology today.[5]

Franciscan Teachings That Undergird Boff's Integral Ecology

Scientists and theologians widely agree that a profound spiritual crisis underpins the ecological crisis.[6] In response, the Franciscan theological, spiritual, and environmental ethics traditions—rooted in Francis of Assisi's embodied religious experience of the natural world, Christian scriptures, and patristic sources—provide an alternative to the current malaise. In particular, attention to the Incarnation and Trinity can open a Franciscan ecological and moral vision for the world.

Incarnation

In the Christian tradition, the Incarnation refers to the total embodiment of God the Creator in the fully human person of Jesus Christ. Since Jesus "was in the beginning with God" and "all things came to be through him" (John 1:23), the Incarnation exposes commonalities between humans and all material reality, and shows an integral relation between the incarnate God and creation. This all-inclusive Franciscan vision of the cosmic community points incessantly to integral ecology.

SAINT FRANCIS OF ASSISI (1181/82–1226)

Francis, "the saint who loved animals," was no simplistic romantic. His famous animal encounters, which shaped his religious

---

5. Pope Francis, *Laudato si': On Care for Our Common Home*, June 18, 2015, *http:// w2.vatican.va/content/francesco/en/encyclicals/documents/papa-francesco_20150524 _enciclica-laudato-si.html*. The encyclical was promulgated on May 24, 2015 and released to the public on June 18, 2015.

6. The Forum on Religion and Ecology at Yale, "The Joint Appeal in Religion and Science: Statement by Religious Leaders at the Summit on Environment," June 3, 1991, *http://fore.yale.edu/publications/statements/joint-appeal/*.

conversion and drew him more deeply into God and devotion to the Incarnation, must be read in light of his religious interactions with various "others."[7] Saint Francis understood Psalm 22:7 as a Christological text, with implications for a Christian praxis of care for creation: "Even for worms he had a warm love, since he had read this text about the Savior: *I am a worm and not a man.* That is why he used to pick them up from the road, and put them in a safe place, so that they would not be crushed by the footsteps of passersby."[8] Through such perception of the incarnate Christ present in all of material reality, Saint Francis came to recognize the interconnectedness between humans and non-human creatures.

BLESSED JOHN DUNS SCOTUS (1265–1308)

John Duns Scotus reflected on New Testament texts (especially John 1:1–14; Eph. 1:3–10; Col. 1:15–17) to offer a provocative, penetrating meditation on the significance of the Incarnation.[9] For Scotus, creation was conceived by God, before the beginning of the world, to be capable of bearing Christ in human form. The act and process of creation was a prelude to a much fuller manifestation of divine love in the Incarnation. Because creation was fashioned to bear the Incarnation, every element, creature, and person gives material and outward expression of the Word of God (Christ). Because Jesus Christ became part of this material created universe, the entire cosmos is divinely affirmed. Understood in this way, we can say that the Incarnation is a paradigm for the goodness of creation and the human role as partners with God in the ongoing co-creation and co-redemption of the world.

---

7. Keith Warner, "Franciscan Environmental Ethics: Imagining Creation as a Community of Care," *Journal of the Society of Christian Ethics*, 31, no.1 (2011): 143–60, at 148. See Dawn M. Nothwehr, *Ecological Footprints: An Essential Guide for Faith and Sustainable Living* (Collegeville, MN: Liturgical Press, 2012).

8. Thomas of Celano, *The Life of Saint Francis by Thomas of Celano*, 29, in *Francis of Assisi: Early Documents*, vol. 1, *The Saint*, ed. and trans. Regis J. Armstrong, J. A. Wayne Hellmann, and William J. Short (New York: New City, 1999), 250–51.

9. Ilia Delio, "Revisiting the Franciscan Doctrine of Christ," *Theological Studies* 63 (2003): 3–25; Mary Beth Ingham, *Scotus for Dunces: An Introduction to the Subtle Doctor* (St. Bonaventure, NY: Franciscan Institute Publications, 2003), especially chapter 2.

Trinity

In the Christian tradition, the Trinity is the dogmatic proclamation that the one God exists in and through the relationship of three distinct yet interrelated Persons: Father, Son, and Spirit.[10] For Franciscans, the Trinity is a community-of-persons that symbolizes and deepens the relatedness of all things.[11] The Trinity is dynamic, creative, and self-diffusive in love, and from this viewpoint, the best image of God is a relationship.

SAINT FRANCIS OF ASSISI

"Francis reveled in the sun, gazed upon the stars, danced with the air, was drawn to the fire, marveled at water, and caressed the earth."[12] He named each of God's creatures a brother, sister, or mother in his "Canticle of the Creatures," and this prayer, which echoes Psalm 148 and Daniel 3:57–88 in celebrating God's love expressed in creation, reveals his Christian cosmological vision grounded in relationship.[13]

SAINT BONAVENTURE OF BAGNOREGIO (1217–1274)

Bonaventure's theology of the Trinity develops Saint Francis's intuitive, spiritual understanding of God's family, and advances the fourth-century Cappadocian patristic notion of Trinity as a community of divine persons.[14] From Pseudo-Dionysius (fifth–sixth century CE),[15] Bonaventure understood the Trinity as self-diffusive goodness and, grounded in Richard of Saint Victor's (1110–1173) notion, ultimate

---

10. See John C. Ford, "person, divine," in *Saint Mary's Press Glossary of Theological Terms* (Winona, MN: Saint Mary's Press, 2006), 143.

11. John C. Ford, "Trinity," in *Saint Mary's Press Glossary of Theological Terms*, 188.

12. Warner, "Franciscan Environmental Ethics," 151.

13. Francis of Assisi, "The Canticle of the Creatures" (1225), in *The Saint*, ed. Armstrong et al., 113–14.

14. Ilia Delio, *Christ in Evolution* (Maryknoll, NY: Orbis, 2008), 55; Catherine Mowry LaCugna, *God for Us: The Trinity and Christian Life* (New York: HarperCollins Publications, 1991), 53–81.

15. Kevin Corrigan and Michael L. Harrington, "Pseudo-Dionysius the Areopagite," in *The Stanford Encyclopedia of Philosophy*, http://plato.stanford.edu/archives/spr2015/entries/pseudo-dionysius-areopagite.

love.[16] The divine persons are intimately related to one another, mutually inhering in one another, and drawing life from each other.

Bonaventure's circle metaphor explains that all life comes from God, is sustained in relation with God, and will return to God. Like an artist, God created the cosmos by an act of divine self-expression, communicating something of God's-self to the world. Created in the divine image, humans are integrated spiritual and material beings, well-positioned to be the guardians of creation.[17] The Holy Spirit is the Creator Spirit who acts and moves through all things, giving life, sustaining, renewing the cosmos.[18]

In Bonaventure's view, the Word is the *inner self-expression* of God, and the created order is the *external expression* of the inner Word. The relationships of the divine persons of the Trinity provide a pattern for the relatedness of everything in creation to God the Creator. In fact, referencing Saint Augustine (*De civitatis dei*, book XVI), Bonaventure noted creation is "a kind of book" that reveals God.[19]

Other Influences on Boff's Work

Following the Second Vatican Council (1962–1965), with a renewed emphasis on Jesus as one like us in all ways but sin, use of the term "integral" became common in Catholic social thought.[20] Influenced

16. Zachary Hayes, "Introduction," in *Works of Saint Bonaventure*, vol. 3, *Disputed Questions on the Mystery of the Trinity* (St. Bonaventure, NY: The Franciscan Institute, 1979), 3–40.

17. Dawn M. Nothwehr, *The Franciscan View of the Human Person* (St. Bonaventure, NY: The Franciscan Institute, 2005), 38–39; Alexander Schaefer, "The Position and Function of Man in the Created World According to Bonaventure," *Franciscan Studies* 21 (1961): 320; Ewert Cousins, *Christ of the 21st Century* (Rockport, MA: Element, 1992), 152–55.

18. Leonardo Boff, *Ecology and Liberation: A New Paradigm* (Maryknoll, NY: Orbis, 1995), 49–50.

19. Zachary Hayes, "The Cosmos: A Symbol of the Divine," in *Franciscan Theology of the Environment: An Introductory Reader*, ed. Dawn M. Nothwehr (Quincy, IL: Franciscan Press, 2002), 252–55.

20. Jacques Maritain, *Integral Humanism: Temporal and Spiritual Problems of a New Christendom* (New York: Scribner, 1968); Pope Paul VI, *Populorum progressio*, March 26, 1967, *http://w2.vatican.va/content/paul-vi/en/encyclicals/documents/hf_p-vi _enc_26031967_populorum.html*, especially paragraphs 20–21; Pope Benedict XVI, *Caritas in veritate*, June 29, 2009, *http://w2.vatican.va/content/benedict-xvi/en/encyclicals /documents/hf_ben-xvi_enc_20090629_caritas-in-veritate.html*.

by this current, as well as the work of the German biologist and philosopher Ernest Haeckel (1834–1919), the French psychotherapist and philosopher Felix Guattari (1930–1992), and the "new sciences," Boff engaged Christian humanism with Franciscan theological perspectives as his ultimate interpretive lens.[21] In particular, Boff developed his integral ecology within a distinct liberation ecological theology synthesis. He held that humanity needs a living and vital *cosmology*, an understanding of the universe:

> This cosmovision challenges the very way we understand the dynamics of change. . . . Transformation is seen within a new framework that uproots our assumptions about both linear causality and blind chance. The importance of intuition, spirituality, and ancient wisdom traditions becomes apparent. Instead of passive consumers and spectators in a blind game of chance, we come to see ourselves as actual participants in the subtle mystery of unfolding cosmic purpose.[22]

Etymology of *Integral*

The word *integral* comes from the Latin *integer*, meaning a "whole" or "complete entity." For Leonardo Boff, becoming integral with the Earth community suggests that humans would understand themselves as members of one single yet multiform community that includes all of the planet's habitats and inhabitants, ideas and societies, humans and nonhumans.[23] However, "the prefix of the word *integral (in-)* has a negative or privative force (like *un-* in English), and the *-teg-* shares the

Continued

---

21. Mathai Kadavil, *The World as Sacrament: Sacramentality of Creation from the Perspectives of Leonardo Boff, Alexander Schmemann and St. Ephrem* (Leuven, Belgium: Peeters-Luven, 2005), 90–97.

22. Mark Hathaway and Leonardo Boff, *The Tao of Liberation: Exploring the Ecology of Transformation* (Maryknoll, NY: Orbis, 2009), 10.

23. Sam Mickey, *On the Verge of a Planetary Civilization: A Philosophy of Integral Ecology* (New York: Rowman & Littlefield, 2014), 17.

Etymology of *Integral* Continued

same derivation as the Latin *tangere* ("to touch")."[24] As such, Mickey points out,

> Etymologically, the word *integral* could be defined as "untouched" or "intact," like an undivided whole. This does not mean that integral ecology is simply holism. Nor does it mean that integral ecology calls for humans to stop touching the natural world and let it return to some pristine or original state (as if that were even possible). The untouched is the limit of touch, where touch makes contact with something else, something different. Integral ecology calls for a touch that attends to its limits, its contacts. It calls for humans to reinvent themselves so that their touch is tactful, so that their practices enhance ecological relations instead of dulling and destroying them.[25]

Boff's Development of Integral Ecology

In 1995, Boff, along with Thomas Berry (1914–2009), used the term "integral" to link ecology and Christian cosmology.[26] In particular, four of Boff's publications available in English illustrate the evolution of his thought concerning what he termed "integral ecology."

Ecology and Poverty: Cry of the Earth, Cry of the Poor

In the *Concilium* editorial, "Ecology and Poverty: Cry of the Earth, Cry of the Poor,"[27] Leonardo Boff and Virgilio Elizondo wrote,

---

24. Ibid., 39, note 51.

25. Ibid., 18–19.

26. For more on Berry, see chapter 4 in this volume, "Cosmology and Ecology in *Laudato si'*" by Mary Evelyn Tucker and John Grim.

27. Leonardo Boff and Virgil Elizondo, "Ecology and Poverty: Cry of the Earth, Cry of the Poor—Editorial," *Concilium* 5 (1995): ix–xii. Available online at *http://www.bijbel.net/concilium/?b=25976*.

The quest today is increasingly for an *integral ecology* that can articulate . . . a new alliance between societies and nature, which will result in the conservation of the patrimony of the earth, socio-cosmic well-being, and the maintenance of conditions that will allow evolution to continue on the course it has now been following for some fifteen thousand million years. For an integral ecology, society and culture also belong to the ecological complex. Ecology is, then, the relationship that all bodies, animate and inanimate, natural and cultural, establish and maintain among themselves and with their surroundings. In this holistic perspective, economic, political, social, military, educational, urban, agricultural and other questions are all subject to ecological consideration.[28]

This reflection on integral ecology stressed the interdependent moral and socially ethical obligations of all to care for creation as a common good, not merely conserve it for the wealthy or as a laboratory for science.

Ecology and Liberation: A New Paradigm

Boff opened *Ecology and Liberation* with a sweeping claim:

Ecology has to do with the relations, interactions, and dialogue of all living creatures (whether alive or not) among themselves and with all that exists. This includes not only "nature" (natural ecology) but culture and society (human ecology, social ecology, and so on). From an ecological viewpoint, everything that exists, co-exists. Everything that co-exists, pre-exists. And everything that co-exists and pre-exists subsists by means of an infinite web of all-inclusive relations. Nothing exists outside of relationships. Ecology reaffirms the interdependence of beings, interprets all hierarchies as a matter of function, and repudiates the so-called right of the strongest. All creatures manifest and possess their own relative autonomy; nothing is superfluous or marginal. All being constitutes a link in the vast cosmic

---

28. Ibid.

chain. As Christians, we may say that it comes from God and returns to God.[29]

Utilizing the "new sciences," Boff extended Ernest Haeckel's 1866 definition of ecology, focusing on Felix Guattari's (*ecosophy*)— mental ecology, social ecology, and environmental ecology.[30] More complex notions of ecological relationships require humans to shift to "interdisciplinary understandings of things," such as planetary evolution, mental and spiritual development, ethical solidarity across generations, and a vision of "the whole" understood from the organic interdependence of everything with everything else.[31] Humans need to attend to several specific projects and practices to align our living more holistically to planetary and, ultimately, human needs.[32]

Cry of the Earth, Cry of the Poor

In *Cry of the Earth, Cry of the Poor*, Boff broadens the gaze of liberation theology to include the natural environment and close breaches between and within liberation theology and environmentalism. His in-depth analysis of the ecological crisis using contemporary sciences shows the deep interdependencies and interrelatedness of everything with everything else. Boff's key word is "connectedness," and he believes that human amnesia about the interconnectedness of the whole of creation—particularly the responsibility to protect creation—has produced ecological crisis. Boff reasserts that humans' place is *within* creation and their moral obligation is to be its guardian.

Boff presents an evolutionary view of creation, linking humans and other-kind, thus relativizing human lordship over the universe. The relationships of the Persons of the Trinity model the dynamics for liberation from ecological degradation:

> They are what they are by their essential and intrinsic communion and inter(retro)relating. . . . 'Each of the Divine

---

29. Boff, *Ecology and Liberation*, 7–8.

30. Ibid., 24–29, 32–36; Felix Guattari, *The Three Ecologies*, trans. Ian Pinder and Paul Sutton (London: Ahtlone, 2000), 27.

31. Boff, *Ecology and Liberation*, 10–11.

32. Ibid., 19–43.

Persons is in each of the others, and all are in each one, and each one is in all, and all are in all and all are only one.' The modern ecologist could hardly express better this interplay of relationships, inasmuch as it constitutes the basic logic of cosmogenesis.[33] If God is communion and relationship, then the entire universe lives in its relationship and all is in communion with all points at all moments. . . . For this is what quantum physicists, those working in earth sciences, including ecologists, continually repeat.[34]

Boff constructs a revolutionary ecotheological synthesis, within which the poor remain central:

Liberation theology and ecological discourse have something in common: they start from two bleeding wounds. The wound of poverty breaks the social fabric of millions and millions of poor people around the world. The other wound, systematic assault on the earth, breaks down the balance of the planet, which is under threat from the plundering of development as practiced by contemporary global societies. Both lines of reflection and practice have as their starting point a cry: the cry of the poor for life, freedom, and beauty (cf. Ex 3:7), and the cry of the Earth groaning under oppression (cf. Rom 8:22–23).[35]

For Boff, then, the same logic drives dominant populations to oppress the marginalized and plunder the earth, while a strong interconnection binds the ecological, human, social, and spiritual aspects of life. The poor must thus be "the point from which one attempts to conceive of God, Christ, grace, history, the mission of the churches, the meaning of the economy, politics, and the future of societies and of the human being."[36]

---

33. That is, the origin or evolution of the universe.

34. Boff, *Cry of the Earth, Cry of the Poor*, 156. Boff cites Saint Augustine, *De Trinitate* 10, 12.

35. Boff, *Cry of the Earth, Cry of the Poor*, 104.

36. Michael Schut, *Money and Faith: The Search for Enough* (Denver: Morehouse, 2008), 135.

The Tao of Liberation

The Tao of Liberation is one of Boff's more complex texts, and in it integral ecology is defined as a holistic evolutionary vision that is practically expressed in the *Earth Charter*—"an ethical framework for building a just, sustainable, and peaceful global society in the 21st century" supported by individuals and institutions around the world.[37] Additionally, integral ecology coordinates and incorporates three other ecologies. The "environmental vision" explores the exteriors of the members and the whole of the Earth community.[38] "Social ecology" addresses socioeconomic and political issues, implications of justice, democracy, violence, and consumerism.[39] "Deep ecology" considers different kinds of interiority and mentality, as well as ethical and religious issues of responsibility and reverence for the natural world.[40]

Guided by this synthetic understanding of integral ecology, Boff reasserts the connections between liberation theology and ecology: liberation involves personal salvation *and* social justice, which both "seek liberation" from the "bleeding wounds" of social oppression and environmental degradation.[41] Additionally, Boff's notion of integral ecology interacts with his related concept of "integral liberation," which necessarily includes transformation of the economic, political, cultural, pedagogical, and religious sources that oppress the poor and privilege the rich while allowing the privileged to remain ignorant of their role as oppressors.[42] In particular, Boff's integral ecology asks of integral liberation, "How can we move forward toward

---

37. Hathaway and Boff, *The Tao of Liberation*, 300. Earth Charter Initiative, *Earth Charter*, Earth Charter Associates, Ltd., June 29, 2000, *http://earthcharter.org/discover/*. Boff was a board member and author of the *Charter*.

38. Hathaway and Boff, *Tao of Liberation*, 298–306.

39. Ibid.

40. Ibid., 301.

41. Ibid., 304, 320, 334–36; Boff, *Cry of the Earth, Cry of the Poor*, 104.

42. Leonardo Boff and Clodovis Boff, *Liberation Theology: From Confrontation to Dialogue*, trans. Robert R. Barr (San Francisco: Harper & Row, 1986), 30; Leonardo Boff, *Jesus Christ Liberator: A Critical Christology for Our Time*, trans. Patrick Hughes (Maryknoll, NY: Orbis, 1978), 267; Leonardo Boff, *When Theology Listens to the Poor*, trans. Robert Barr (San Francisco: Harper & Row, 1988), 19–21; Leonardo Boff, "What Are Third World Theologies?," in *Convergences and Differences*, ed. Leonardo Boff and Virgil Elizondo, trans. Paul Burns (Edinburgh: T&T Clark, 1988), 3–4.

an integral liberation for humanity and the Earth itself?"[43] Integral liberation includes the personal, spiritual, and collective social justice senses of liberation and situates them "in a wider, ecological—and even cosmological—context."[44] In its cosmological context, the process of integral liberation is the "conscious participation of humanity" in the cosmogenetic processes of differentiation, subjectivity, and communion.[45]

Boff's Definitions: Four Ecologies

In view of these works, Boff has developed a rich taxonomy of ecologies. *Environmental ecology* involves ecological issues through scientific and technological development. Humans are seen as outside of nature, either as caretakers and conservationists or consumers and destroyers. People manage endangered species and use technological solutions to correct damage caused by various human interventions or industrialization.

Social ecology addresses issues of social justice and genuine sustainability of social institutions at a socio-cosmic level.[46] "It must attend to the needs of the other beings in nature, the plants, the animals, the microorganisms, because all together they constitute the planetary community, in which we are inserted and without whom we ourselves could not exist."[47] Humans stand within nature, and justice among them is the necessary prior step to environmental justice.[48]

Mental ecology (deep or profound) focuses on consciousness and indicates that ecological problems call for healthier processes of subjectivity, processes that revitalize socio-cosmic well-being by renewing vital engagements with the natural world, cultures, gender roles, religious world views, and unconscious desires. Simply put,

---

43. Hathaway and Boff, *Tao of Liberation*, 61.

44. Ibid., xxv.

45. Ibid., 292.

46. Boff, *Cry of the Earth, Cry of the Poor*, 105.

47. Boff and Elizondo, "Ecology and Poverty," ix. 2. See also Boff, *Cry of the Earth, Cry of the Poor*, 112.

48. Boff, *Cry of the Earth, Cry of the Poor*, 113.

changing the state of the world requires a revolution in consciousness that involves the participation of entire global societies.[49] Relationship and care are true ontological states for healthy people and whole societies.[50] Sustainability's prerequisite is sound mental ecology.[51]

These three ecologies, which are ways of studying phenomena—*environmental* (differentiation), *mental* (consciousness), and *social* (relation)—are parallel to his three aspects of cosmogenesis: (1) "complexity and differentiation," which structures the objective or exterior facets of things; (2) "self-organization and consciousness," which structures the subjective depth or interior facets of things; and (3) "reconnection and relation," which structures the ways things come together not merely as a collection of different objects but as communicating agents, communing subjects to dimensions of real processes of becoming.[52] Understood in this way, integral ecology for Boff includes three ecologies and presents a new vision of Earth wherein humans and Earth are situated in processes of *cosmogenesis* and *anthropogenesis*—that is, the evolution or genesis of humankind.

Boff: Conveyer of Integral Ecology from Saint Francis to Pope Francis

As *Laudato si'* was being drafted, Pope Francis invited Boff, once condemned by Rome to "obsequious silence" for his liberationist writings, to a private meeting and requested his corpus of publications on liberation ecotheolgy.[53] Thus it is unsurprising that, "although Boff and his work are nowhere acknowledged in the encyclical's text or footnotes, his presence seems to hover like a ghost."[54]

---

49. Hathaway and Boff, *The Tao of Liberation*, 63–67.

50. Boff, *Ecology and Liberation*, 36, 58.

51. Ibid., 78.

52. Hathaway and Boff, *Tao of Liberation*, 281–89.

53. Paul Vallely, "Pope Francis: Has His Revolution Even Started?" *The Guardian*, March 11, 2014, *http://www.theguardian.com/world/2014/mar/11/pope-francis-revolution-even-started-catholic-church-vatican.*

54. Wen Stephenson, "How Pope Francis Came to Embrace Not Just Climate Justice but Liberation Theology," *The Nation*, September 9, 2015, *http://www.thenation.com/article/how-pope-francis-came-to-embrace-not-just-climate-justice-but-liberation-theology/.*

Laudato si' uses "integral ecology" ten times, including as the title of chapter 4, which is an extensive discussion of the concept.[55] Similarly, "relationship" is used sixty-one times.[56] Indeed—"everything is connected."[57] Though the influence of Boff on Pope Francis's use of integral ecology is discernible at several places in *Laudato si'*, paragraph 49 arguably provides one of the most obvious examples: "Today, however, we have to realize that a true ecological approach *always* becomes a social approach; it must integrate questions of justice in debates on the environment, so as to hear *both the cry of the earth and the cry of the poor*"—a clear reference to Boff's work.

For his part, Boff has downplayed involvement in the development of *Laudato si'*. When asked what kind of suggestions he sent the pope and which contributions were incorporated into the encyclical, Boff replied,

> This question causes me embarrassment. The Pope has his body of experts and he consulted many people. The encyclical is his and not the collaborators'. With regard to Pope Francis' request, I sent through the Argentine ambassador to the Vatican—otherwise there's the risk that it doesn't get there—various materials and books, as I'd already been working intensely for 30 years on this integral ecology issue. . . . Whether the Pope made use of these materials or not is not for me to say. I did my part as a simple useless servant, as the gospel says.[58]

Additionally, Boff emphasizes how Pope Francis's identity uniquely colors the use of integral ecology in *Laudato si'*. This is especially true of the "wording and tone of the encyclical," the liberation method of "see, judge, act, and celebrate," and "the themes of the 'common

55. See *LS* 10, 11, 62, 124, 137, 156, 159, 225, 230.

56. *LS* 11, 15, 16, 47, 65, 66, 67, 68, 70, 71, 79, 81, 86, 88, 92, 96, 100, 106, 110, 116, 118, 119, 125, 126, 128, 138, 139, 142, 143, 148, 150, 155, 215, 217, 218, 221, 231, 232, 237, 240.

57. *LS* 90, 117.

58. Patricia Fachin and João Vitor Santos, "Integral Ecology: The Big News of *Laudato si'*: A Special Interview with Leonardo Boff," trans. Rebel Girl, *Iglesia Descalza Blog*, June 23, 2015, *http://iglesiadescalza.blogspot.com/2015/06/integral-ecology-big-news-of-laudato-si.html*.

home,' of 'Mother Earth,' the 'cry of the Earth and the cry of the poor,' the 'care' of the 'interdependence of all beings,' of the 'poor and vulnerable,' the 'paradigm shift,' the 'human being as Earth' that feels, thinks, loves and reveres, [and] 'integral ecology.'"[59] Furthermore, Boff says that Pope Francis's encyclical places ecology "systematically within a bold new systems approach under the new paradigm, building, for almost a century now, from the life and Earth sciences, from the new cosmology, quantum physics and the new biology. In this, the Pope is absolutely innovative."[60]

Nevertheless, Boff implicitly acknowledges that Pope Francis's use of integral ecology in *Laudato si'* is consistent with his own understanding of this concept:

> [Pope Francis] sees the world as orders open to each other, all interconnected, which implies an evolutionary view of the universe. . . . In his integral ecology, he is looking at all the interconnected facts and phenomena. Hurting the Earth is hurting the human being who is also Earth, as the Pope says, citing Genesis. Productivist and consumerist greed produces two types of injustice—one ecological, degrading ecosystems, and the other social, throwing millions of people into poverty and destitution. The Pope denounces this causal connection. So he proposes a paradigm shift in the relationship between all, which is more benevolent to nature and more just to humans and all other beings that inhabit the common home.[61]

Given how Boff's influence on the integral ecology of *Laudato si'* is not difficult to recognize, it is unfortunate that Boff is not explicitly referenced in the encyclical. No doubt this was good political strategy on Pope Francis's part: in 1984 and 1991, Boff was silenced by the Vatican for his writings on ecclesiology and the priesthood, respectively. Although the first silence was lifted in 1986, Boff saw the second silencing as evidence of, in his words, "ecclesiastical power

---

59. Leonardo Boff, "The Magna Carta of Integral Ecology: Cry of the Earth— Cry of the Poor," leonardoBOFF.com, June 18, 2016, *https://leonardoboff.wordpress.com/2015/06/18/the-magna-carta-of-integral-ecology-cry-of-the-earth-cry-of-the-poor/*.

60. Fachin and Santos, "Integral Ecology."

61. Ibid.

[that] is cruel and merciless" and resigned from the priesthood.[62] Against this background, Pope Francis likely recognized that explicit reference to Boff in *Laudato si'* would have made some in the Church less likely to receive the message of the encyclical. Yet by his reconciling gesture and reliance on Boff, Pope Francis embodied what Boff proposes as central for transition to the "new paradigm" of ecology—namely, following the principle of responsibility and the principle of compassion.[63] As such, and in light of how his life's work on integral ecology permeates *Laudato si'*, it seems right to call Boff "the most important contributor" to the encyclical.[64]

Conclusion: Saint Francis of Assisi as Exemplar of Integral Ecology

As a way to advance the vision of integral ecology, Boff urges living the "cardinal ecological virtues," which can be summarized as obedience, love, humility, and poverty, and which were exemplified by Saint Francis of Assisi.[65] Prayer was Saint Francis's entrée to his self-understanding as an ontological poet-mystic, one able to grasp the origin and sacramentality of all things. He reveled in religious erotic enchantment, wonder, fascination, and desire for and with all things in the universe (love). Francis's insight that God is radically relational compels humanity to care for their kin in all creation as God cares for them (obedience). Francis experienced his own dignity bound up with all creation insofar as everything originates in One Creator (humility). From this stance, Francis encountered all relationships as one utterly available to the need of others (poverty). Through penance, poverty, and prayer, Francis lived securely and passionately, grounded in his relationship with God and all creation—especially with the poor.

---

62. Jim Rice, "Leonardo Boff Resigns Priesthood," *Sojourners*, October 1992, *https://sojo.net/magazine/october-1992/leonardo-boff-resigns-priesthood*.

63. Boff, *Cry of the Earth, Cry of the Poor*, 135–36.

64. Evelyn Finger, "Catholic Climate Change: Pope Francis's Ecology Encyclical," *Transatlantic Academy*, June 11, 2015, *http://www.transatlanticacademy.org/node/821*.

65. Boff, *Cry of the Earth, Cry of the Poor*, 213–20; Boff, *Ecology and Liberation*, 30, 38, 45–46, 138, 152; Leonardo Boff, *Francis of Assisi: Model for Human Liberation*, trans. John W. Diercksmeier (Maryknoll, NY: Orbis, 2006).

In Saint Francis of Assisi, Boff sees the exemplar of "ecological conversion." Francis lived an ecologically virtuous life, ever mindful that everything and everyone is connected (integral ecology). With this—as with many other ideas of Boff—Pope Francis agrees: "I believe that Saint Francis is the example par excellence of care for the vulnerable and of an integral ecology lived out joyfully and authentically. . . . Francis helps us to see that an integral ecology calls for openness to categories which transcend the language of mathematics and biology, and take us to the heart of what it is to be human" (*LS* 10, 11). In sum, Saint Francis can help us learn to cultivate integral ecology in our modern world and so enable us all to care for our common home.

Review Questions

1. In what way does Saint Francis's *Canticle of the Creatures* inform integral ecology?
2. What characteristics describe today's environmental global paradigm?
3. What are the main contributions from Boff's four publications treated in this chapter to his understanding of integral ecology?
4. How does an evolutionary worldview of creation contribute to integral ecology?
5. Compare the way quantum physicists explain the relationships among the elements of creation and how a theologian explains the relations of the Persons of the Trinity.
6. What are the "two bleeding wounds" Boff discusses? In what way do they inform his understanding of integral ecology?
7. Explain the four kinds of ecology and their relationship to one another.

In-Depth Questions

1. Read "Care for Our Common Home," chapter 4 of *Laudato si'* (137–62) and compare what it says about integral ecology with Boff's notion of this concept. What similarities do you notice?

2. In what way does the Incarnation call humans to care for creation? How does that understanding support the idea of integral ecology?

3. Research Thomas Kuhn's concept of a paradigm. Then compare and contrast today's global social, political, economic, and ecological patterns with what Boff proposes for a new paradigm characterized by integral ecology.

4. Research Jacques Maritain's notion of "integral humanism" and Pope Paul VI's concept of "integral human development." Compare the meaning of these terms with integral ecology. What is distinct about each? What is common? What is complementary?

Suggestions for Further Study

Boff, Leonardo. *Cry of the Earth, Cry of the Poor.* Maryknoll, NY: Orbis, 1997.

———. "Earth as Gaia: An Ethical and Spiritual Challenge." *Concilium* (2009, no. 3): 24–32.

———. *Ecology and Liberation: A New Paradigm.* Maryknoll, NY: Orbis, 1995.

———. *Francis of Assisi: A Model for Human Liberation.* Maryknoll, NY: Orbis, 2006.

———. *Holy Trinity, Holy Community.* Maryknoll, NY: Orbis, 1998.

Castillo, Daniel P. "Integral Ecology as a Liberationist Concept," *Theological Studies* 77, no. 2 (June 2016): 353–76.

Nothwehr, Dawn M. *Ecological Footprints: An Essential Franciscan Guide for Faith and Sustainable Living.* Collegeville, MN: Liturgical Press, 2012.

CHAPTER 7

The Cry of the Earth: The Scientific Background of *Laudato si'*

RICHARD W. MILLER

Laudato si' addresses both "the cry of the earth and the cry of the poor" (*LS* 49). The cry of the earth and the cry of the poor are inter-related and cannot be separated, for "nature cannot be regarded as something separate from ourselves or as a mere setting in which we live. We are part of nature, included in it and thus in constant inter-action with it" (*LS* 139). As such, "all of us as living creatures are dependent on one another" (*LS* 42). The cry of the earth and the cry of the poor, then, are not two crises, but rather "one complex crisis which is both social and environmental" (*LS* 139). As a result, "strat-egies for a solution demand an integrated approach to combating poverty, restoring dignity to the excluded, and at the same time pro-tecting nature" (*LS* 139). Since ecological systems and social systems are not separate from each other but exist in a dynamic relationship, Pope Francis develops an integral ecology that articulates the rela-tion of the human being with God, with other human beings, and with the rest of creation.

While the cry of the earth and the cry of the poor cannot be separated, this chapter will focus on the cry of the earth, providing the scientific background for the urgency that permeates *Laudato si'*.[1]

---

1. The Vatican's Pontifical Academy of Sciences, which is made up of a distin
guished group of scientists, including several Nobel Laureates that advise the Pope on
science, began studying scientific issues related to ecology in the early 1970s. "In 1983
the Academy carried out a specific study on the damage done to the environment
by the increase in carbon dioxide and by the thinning of the ozone layer ('Chemical
Events in the Atmosphere and their impact on the Environment')." Marcelo Sánchez

The description of the cry of the earth also reveals how ecological degradation and the destabilizing of planetary systems can destabilize social systems threatening all of civilization, especially the poor. This treatment of the scientific background will draw upon leading studies in the peer-reviewed literature to describe the implications of the science to help internalize our ecological crisis in accord with the action-oriented aims of *Laudato si'*. As Pope Francis writes, "our goal is not to amass information or to satisfy curiosity, but rather to become painfully aware, to dare to turn what is happening to the world into our own personal suffering and thus to discover what each of us can do about it" (*LS* 19).

"What Is Happening to Our Common Home?"

In chapter 1 of *Laudato si'*, Pope Francis asks, "What is happening to our common home?" In response he describes the present situation typified by environmental degradation and indifference to the poor.[2] In terms of the environmental problem, the primary focus here, Pope Francis identifies, classifies, and presents a host of environmental problems and then treats the effects of environmental degradation on the human community, especially the poor. When he treats pollution, in section I, he addresses pollution of the atmosphere, soil, and water and then discusses how toxic and radioactive pollutants build up in the environment and negatively affect organisms, including human beings. He then mentions reducing, reusing, and recycling, and argues that we need to model ourselves on nature, where waste is reused so as to provide conditions for new life. He gives a fuller treatment to climate change, which he singles

---

Sorondo, "Introduction," in *Papal Addresses to the Pontifical Academy of Sciences 1917–2002 and to the Pontifical Academy of Social Sciences 1994–2002, http://www.casinapioiv.va/content/dam/accademia/pdf/sv100.pdf,* xlvii. In 2011, the Pontifical Academy of Sciences published a report entitled "Fate of Mountain Glaciers in the Anthropocene," as part of the scientific consultation with Pope Francis leading up to the writing of *Laudato si'*. See *http://www.pas.va/content/accademia/en/events/2011/glaciers.html.*

2. For example, the study by Oxfam international maintains that "in 2015, just 62 individuals had the same wealth as 3.6 billion people—the bottom half of humanity." Deborah Hardoon, Sophia Ayele, and Ricardo Fuentes-Nieva, "An Economy for the 1%," Oxfam Briefing Paper 201 (Oxford: Oxfam International, Jan. 2016), 2.

The Cry of the Earth 115

out as "one of the principal challenges facing humanity in our day" (*LS* 25). In section II, he turns to fresh water scarcity and declares, "*Access to safe drinking water is a basic and universal human right*" (*LS* 30, italics in original). In section III, he examines biodiversity loss and the extinction of species, both on land and in the oceans, and repeats at the end of that section one of the central themes of the encyclical: "All of us as living creatures are dependent on one another" (*LS* 42).

Planetary Boundaries and *Laudato si'*

It is possible to further explicate and provide scientific background for the environmental problems that are treated in *Laudato si'* by drawing upon the planetary boundaries framework and its emphasis on the dynamic interrelationship of nine aspects of the earth system.[3] The planetary boundaries approach can enrich one's reading of *Laudato si'* for several reasons. First, the framework confirms Pope Francis's concept of "integral ecology," in which "everything is interconnected" (*LS* 70, 138, 240). Second, the framework aids the "see, judge, act" model of Catholic social action that seems to inform *Laudato si'*.[4]

The planetary boundary framework is particularly helpful for this threefold process, or any similar process, because it allows us to see the scale of the ecological problems and the scientific soundness of Pope Francis's concept of integral ecology. Furthermore, the planetary boundary framework supports the moments of judgment and action by enabling us to distinguish and prioritize responses to

---

3. This framework was introduced in a highly influential paper in 2009 by a group of scientific researchers and experts led by Johan Rockström and Will Steffen. The framework is now being updated throughout the earth science community based on a new paper in 2015. Johan Rockström et al., "Planetary Boundaries: Exploring the Safe Operating Space for Humanity," *Ecology and Society* 14, no. 2, art. 32 (2009): 1; J. Rockström et al., "A Safe Operating Space for Humanity," *Nature* 461 (September 24, 2009): 472–75; Will Steffen et al., "Planetary Boundaries: Guiding Human Development on a Changing Planet," *Science* 347, no. 6223 (February 13, 2015): 1259855-1–1259855-10.

4. David Cloutier, *Reading, Praying, Living Pope Francis's Laudato Si': A Faith Formation Guide* (Collegeville, MN: Liturgical Press, 2015).

"See, Judge, Act"

Pope John XXIII described the process of seeing, judging, and acting in his 1961 encyclical, *Mater et magistra*:

> There are three stages which should normally be followed in the reduction of social principles into practice. First, one reviews the concrete situation; secondly, one forms a judgment on it in the light of these same principles; thirdly, one decides what in the circumstances can and should be done to implement these principles. These are the three stages that are usually expressed in the three terms: look, judge, act.[5]

---

particular ecological problems so that people can determine how to act socially and politically[6] to avoid unimaginable ecological impacts and manage unavoidable impacts,[7] some of which represent, as we will see, catastrophic impacts for the human community.

---

5. Pope John XXIII, *Mater et magistra*, May 15, 1961, *http://w2.vatican.va/content /john-xxiii/en/encyclicals/documents/hf_j-xxiii_enc_15051961_mater.html*.

6. For instance, university students will recognize that if their university gives attention to sustainability the starting point is often recycling programs with some attention paid to reducing (the often overlooked, crucial first step) and reusing. As such, for those who are not reading the literature on ecological degradation, environmental issues are understood in terms of recycling and in terms of conservation of a finite resource; we only have so much of a resource so we must recycle it when we are finished using it. Without further study, the environmental problems and responses never advance much beyond recycling. We need, however, to see ecological systems as dynamic and as dynamically related to other systems and to recognize that campus recycling programs do not even remotely address the scale of the problem. See Richard W. Miller, "Rethinking the Social Role of Universities in Response to the Planetary Emergency," in *The Urgency of Climate Change: Pivotal Perspectives*, ed. Gerry Magill and Kiarash Aramesh (Newcastle upon Tyne, UK: Cambridge Scholars Publishing, 2017), 313–51.

7. This comes from the title of the report prepared for the United Nations Commission on Sustainable Development—Scientific Expert Group on Climate Change. See Rosina M. Bierbaum, John P. Holdren, Michael C. MacCracken, Richard H. Moss, and Peter H. Raven, eds., *Confronting Climate Change: Avoiding the Unmanageable and Managing the Unavoidable* (Washington, DC: United Nations Foundation), 2007.

The Planetary Boundaries

There is not only a dynamic interrelationship between systems, but also these systems can operate in non-linear ways. That is, a system can be pushed out of balance and cross a threshold beyond which the system produces large changes far past the initial conditions that destabilized it. This goes to the heart of the planetary boundaries concept and the scale of changes:

> Anthropogenic pressures on the Earth System have reached a scale where abrupt global environmental change can no longer be excluded. . . . Transgressing one or more planetary boundaries may be deleterious or even catastrophic due to the risk of crossing thresholds that will trigger non-linear, abrupt environmental change within continental-to planetary-scale systems.[8]

The human community is generating such large, negative changes that if we do not profoundly change our social, political, and economic systems, we will push the earth system to a new state less hospitable for human civilization, which emerged during the past 11,700 years of the Holocene Epoch, where biophysical processes "stayed within a relatively narrow range."[9]

The planetary boundaries approach adopts the precautionary principle and as such understands the boundaries not as the threshold beyond which there is the possibility of non-linear abrupt change, but as the guard rail within which the human community can likely safely flourish.[10] The nine interlinked "biophysical processes that regulate the stability of the Earth system"[11] are climate change, change in biosphere integrity, stratospheric ozone depletion, ocean acidification, biogeochemical flows, land system change, freshwater use, atmospheric aerosol loading, and introduction of novel entities.

---

8. J. Rockström et al., "Planetary Boundaries," 1.

9. J. Rockström et al., "A Safe Operating Space for Humanity," 472.

10. Pope Francis also adopts the precautionary principle: "If objective information suggests that serious and irreversible damage may result, a project should be halted or modified, even in the absence of indisputable proof" (*LS* 186).

11. W. Steffen et al, "Planetary Boundaries," 1259855-1.

In order to utilize the planetary boundaries framework to better understand the reality to which *Laudato si'* points, it is important to review each of the biophysical processes. Since climate change is a pivotal boundary that merits an extended discussion, it will be discussed after the other eight boundaries. Where appropriate, some of the ways that boundaries interact with each other will be noted.

Biosphere Integrity

Biosphere integrity is concerned with genetic biodiversity, "which provides the long term capacity of the biosphere to persist under and adapt to abrupt and gradual . . . change."[12] The current indicator of that genetic biodiversity is the global species extinction rate. The extinction rate for several million years prior to the Holocene was one per million species per year. The group of experts that identified planetary boundaries proposes, as an aspiration, returning to this level of background extinction, but allows for a boundary of ten species per million species per year. The current rate of loss is one hundred to one thousand species per million, with some research suggesting that "the rate of extinction of species and races is conservatively estimated to be 877 times above that prevailing before the origin of humanity."[13]

Stratospheric Ozone Depletion

Ozone in the stratosphere acts as the earth's sunscreen because it absorbs most of the ultraviolet sunlight (UV-B), which is damaging to organisms. Stratospheric ozone depletion, which came to be known as "the hole in the ozone layer," is caused by chlorofluorocarbons (CFCs), which are "long-lived chemicals that had been used in refrigerators and aerosols sprays since the 1930s" and break down in the atmosphere through a chemical process that destroys molecules of ozone.[14] This boundary has not been transgressed

---

12. Ibid., 1259855-5.

13. Edward O. Wilson, *Half-Earth: Our Planet's Fight for Life* (New York: Liveright, 2016), 39.

14. NASA Earth Observatory, "World of Change: Antarctic Ozone Hole," *http://earthobservatory.nasa.gov/Features/WorldOfChange/ozone.php*.

because of the implementation in 1989 of the Montreal Protocol, which mitigated the production of ozone-depleting chemicals. This is an example of international success in dealing with a critical planetary system. Subsequent modeling suggests that had the world not acted quickly, the ozone layer, which is "essential for terrestrial life and a constant feature of the biosphere for two billion years, would have been largely destroyed by humanity in just a few decades."[15]

Ocean Acidification

This boundary is linked to the prime driver of climate change; namely, the rise in atmospheric carbon dioxide (CO_2) that comes from the burning of fossil fuels and the felling of forests. The absorption by the oceans of around 30 percent of our CO_2 emissions[16] alters ocean chemistry (increasing acidity) making it difficult and at some point impossible for organisms to make their calcium carbonate skeletons. This is especially true of coral reefs, which support 25 percent of the biodiversity in the oceans, and some phytoplankton.

Although the ocean acidification boundary has not yet been exceeded, evidence indicates that this transgression will likely occur if global atmospheric concentrations of carbon dioxide are not stabilized at 350 parts per million (ppm).[17] According to the National Oceanic and Atmospheric Administration, the global mean atmospheric CO_2 concentration in August 2016 was 401 ppm.[18] A temporary overshoot of 350 ppm is possible as long as there is a rapid return of atmospheric CO_2 to less than 350 ppm.

---

15. Mark Lynas, *The God Species: Saving the Planet in the Age of Humans* (Washington, DC: National Geographic Society, 2011), 220; cf. Michael Carlowicz, "The World We Avoided by Protecting the Ozone Layer," National Aeronautics and Space Administration, May 13, 2009, *http://earthobservatory.nasa.gov/Features/World WithoutOzone/.*

16. J. E. N. Veron, "The Coral Reef Crisis: The Critical Importance of <350 ppm CO_2," *Marine Pollution Bulletin* 58 (2009): 1428–36, at 1430.

17. Steffen et al., "Planetary Boundaries," 1259855–56.

18. Earth System Research Laboratory, "Recent Global CO_2," National Oceanic and Atmospheric Administration, September 6, 2016, *http://www.esrl.noaa.gov/gmd /ccgg/trends/global.html.*

Biogeochemical Flows

This boundary focuses on the increasing levels of nitrogen and phosphorus (though planetary boundaries may need to be developed for other elements) that humanity is introducing into the environment through the fertilization of crops in agricultural production. Excessive nitrogen and phosphorus that make their way from fertilized crop fields to ocean and freshwater ecosystems stimulate the overgrowth of algae. When that algae dies, the ensuing decomposition draws down oxygen levels in the water, a process that produces so-called "dead zones" of oxygen-depleted ocean. The second largest global dead zone is in the Gulf of Mexico, which in 2015 encompassed "an area about the size of Connecticut and Rhode Island combined."[19]

Since many organisms cannot live in oxygen-starved areas, excessive nitrogen also leads to "slow but chronic loss of biological diversity."[20] Thus this boundary is closely linked with the biosphere integrity and the freshwater boundaries. It is also linked with the climate change boundary because reactive nitrogen can be converted into the powerful greenhouse gas nitrous oxide (N_2O). N_2O is nearly three hundred times more potent than carbon dioxide in trapping the sun's heat and it remains in the atmosphere for a century. The biogeochemical flows boundary, in particular nitrogen and phosphorus, has already been transgressed.[21]

Land System Change

Human beings are converting large sections of ice-free land—including forests, grasslands, and wetlands—for a variety of uses,

---

19. National Oceanic and Atmospheric Association, "2015 Gulf of Mexico Dead Zone 'Above Average,'" August 4, 2015, *http://www.noaanews.noaa.gov/stories 2015/080415-gulf-of-mexico-dead-zone-above-average.html*.

20. Christopher M. Clark and David Tilman, "Loss of Plant Species after Chronic Low-Level Nitrogen Deposition to Prairie Grasslands," *Nature* 451 (February 7, 2008): 712–15.

21. The planetary boundary research group proposes a boundary of 11 teragrams or 11 million metric tons per year of phosphorus flowing from freshwater systems into the ocean (current amounts are 22 teragrams per year) with regional phosphorus flows at 6.2 teragrams per year (current value is 14 teragrams per year). For nitrogen the planetary boundary group recommends 62–82 teragrams per year (current value is 150 teragrams per year). See Steffen et al., "Planetary Boundaries," 1259855–54.

most especially agriculture. This conversion of land leads to species extinction and biodiversity loss, which impares biosphere integrity and disrupts fresh water flows and freshwater habitats that are part of the freshwater boundary. As more land becomes farmland, more nitrogen and phosphorus enter into the environment and affect the biogeochemical boundary. Finally, since land conversion often levels trees that remove CO_2 from the atmosphere, activities that endanger the land system change boundary also endanger the climate change boundary.

Freshwater Use

All living organisms need water. As human beings destroy wetlands, dam rivers, and pump freshwater from lakes, reservoirs, and renewable groundwater stores, they damage freshwater ecosystems. Wetlands provide habitat for plants, animals, and a host of ecosystems and, as such, are places of concentrated biodiversity. According to a report by the International Union for the Conservation of Nature, "while freshwater habitats cover less than 1% of the world's surface[22] they provide a home for 7% (126,000 species) of the estimated 1.8 million described species,[23] including a quarter of the estimated 60,000 vertebrates."[24] In addition, "the extinction rate for freshwater species is five times higher than for terrestrial species, and according to the latest IUCN [International Union for Conservation of Nature] Red List survey, 37 percent of assessed species are counted as threatened."[25] This demonstrates that the freshwater boundary interacts with the biosphere integrity boundary.

Additionally, the freshwater boundary is related to the climate boundary in terms of resilience to climate impacts since dammed

---

22. P. H. Gleick, "Water Resources," in *Encyclopaedia of Climate and Weather*, ed. S. H. Schneider (New York: Oxford University Press, 1996), 817–23.

23. E. V. Balian, H. Segers, C. Lévêque, and K. Martens, "The Freshwater Animal Diversity Assessment: An Overview of the Results," *Hydrobiologia* 595 (2008): 627–37.

24. W. Darwall et al., "Freshwater Biodiversity: A Hidden Resource under Threat," in *The 2008 Review of The IUCN Red List of Threatened Species*, ed. J.-C. Vié, C. Hilton-Taylor, and S. N. Stuart (Gland, Switzerland: International Union for the Conservation of Nature, 2008), 1.

25. Lynas, *God Species*, 143.

rivers no longer provide sediments to river deltas—a reality that, in turn, causes these deltas to sink and makes cities located on them even more vulnerable to global warming-induced sea level rise. This is happening to some of the world's most populated cities that are built on delta plains, including "Shanghai on the Yangtze Delta, Calcutta and Dhaka on the Ganges–Brahmaputra, Lagos on the Niger, and Ho Chi Minh City on the Mekong Delta."[26]

Atmospheric Aerosol Loading

Aerosols are minute airborne particles generated primarily from polluting human activities like combustion of fossil fuels, wood, and biomass. The resultant air pollution has staggering consequences for human health. A World Health Organization study estimates that in 2012 around seven million people died as a result of air pollution exposure.[27] In addition, it also affects the earth system. These particles can have a warming effect or cooling effect depending on their characteristics and their location in the atmosphere. Black soot, which comes from coal, diesel, and biomass combustion, has a warming effect by virtue of its dark color, which absorbs more of the sun's heat. When it falls out of the atmosphere and is deposited on mountain glaciers, the Greenland ice sheet, and arctic sea ice, its relatively dark color increases their melt rates. Sulfate particles, on the other hand, have a cooling effect because they reflect solar radiation to space. Though there is a large degree of uncertainty concerning aerosols, some leading researchers argue that aerosols could be cooling the planet as much as 1.2°C.[28] This means that if we stopped all polluting today, then in about five days atmospheric pollution would

---

26. Ibid., 145.

27. World Health Organization, "Burden of Disease from the Joint Effects of Household and Ambient Air Pollution for 2012," *http://www.who.int/phe/health_topics /outdoorair/databases/AP_jointeffect_BoD_results_March2014.pdf.* See also World Health Organization, "7 Million Premature Deaths Annually Linked to Air Pollution," *http:// www.who.int/mediacentre/news/releases/2014/air-pollution/en/.*

28. There is great uncertainty around aerosols. Hansen et al. estimate that the aerosol forcing is -1.6 ± 0.3 watts per sq. m. See James Hansen, Pushker Kharecha, and Makiko Sato, "Climate Forcing Growth Rates: Doubling Down on Our Faustian Bargain," *Environmental Research Letters* 8, no. 1 (2013): 1–9, at 5. This level of forcing translates into around 1.2°C.

drift to earth and temperatures could more than double from 1°C, relative to the 1880–1920 mean, to 2.2°C.

In the context of global warming this cooling effect is positive, but it also has negative consequences like disrupting the African and Asian monsoons. Indeed, published studies argue that aerosols have "darkened the atmosphere above the North Atlantic Ocean [and] pulled life-giving rains away from North Africa, allowing the desert to spread south as precipitation levels declined by 40 percent."[29] With the implementation of pollution controls, rainfall over the Sahel has recovered. In addition, aerosols over Asia (the Asian brown cloud) have disrupted the circulation patterns of the Indian monsoon that sustains "the food production and livelihoods of over a billion people across the subcontinent."[30] The east Asian monsoon has also been disrupted such that the north of China has experienced more frequent droughts while the south of China has experienced more flooding.[31] Here we see that the aerosol boundary interacts with the climate change boundary, the freshwater boundary, and by extension the biosphere integrity boundary.

Introduction of Novel Entities

Novel entities are "new substances, new forms of existing substances, and modified life forms that have the potential for unwanted geophysical and/or biological effects."[32] These include chemicals and other new materials and organisms that are alien to the history of life on earth. They also include naturally occurring elements like heavy metals (such as mercury and cadmium) that are increased through human activity and distributed around the planet. For instance, the mining and burning of coal takes naturally occurring toxic elements (including lead, mercury, cadmium, nickel, tin, and arsenic) and releases them into the atmosphere and waterways. Coal burning is one of the major reasons that it is no longer advisable to eat tuna fish frequently because tuna has relatively high concentrations of mercury.

---

29. Lynas, *God Species*, 186.

30. Ibid.

31. Ibid.

32. Steffen et al., "Planetary Boundaries," 1259855–57.

Among the tens of thousands of chemicals introduced into the environment, some persist for a long time, including agricultural pesticides like DDT, which is now heavily regulated, herbicides like atrazine, and multi-use chemicals like polychlorinated biphenyls (PCBs) that are used in electric equipment, lubricants, paints, and flame retardants. Many of these chemicals, along with phthalates and bisphenol–A (BPA) that are found in polycarbonate plastics, are endocrine disrupters that have very deleterious effects on the reproductive system of animals including human beings.

Plastics are ubiquitous in our environment, even extending to areas far away from human habitation. For instance, there are several ocean areas, most notably in the North Pacific, that contain large concentrations of broken down plastics called *microplastics*. On the Midway Atoll, which is roughly equidistant between North America and Asia (approximately 1,500 miles west of Hawaii), "albatrosses are estimated to feed their chicks a combined 5 tonnes of plastic each year, and 200,000 out of the half-million chicks die each year as a result because of dehydration, perforated stomachs or starvation."[33] The scale of the areas affected is staggering. The National Oceanic Atmospheric Association estimates that it would take sixty-seven ships working for a year to clean up less than 1 percent of the areas affected in the North Pacific Ocean.[34]

The planetary boundary of novel entities is not yet quantified because of its complexity and high levels of uncertainty. Nevertheless, we recognize general ways in which this boundary is connected with others. This boundary interacts with the freshwater and biosphere integrity boundaries because novel entities pollute freshwater ecosystems and stress animal and plant life. It also interacts with the climate change boundary because reduction in the use of fossil fuels, most immediately coal, is necessary to meet the climate change boundary. Finally, the novel entities boundary interacts with the stratospheric ozone boundary because chlorofluorocarbons (CFCs) are considered novel entities.

33. Lynas, *God Species*, 157.

34. NOAA Office of Response and Restoration, "How Much Would It Cost to Clean Up the Pacific Garbage Patches?," July 19, 2012, *http://response.restoration.noaa.gov/about/media/how-much-would-it-cost-clean-pacific-garbage-patches.html*.

Climate Change[35]

The experts that identified the planetary boundaries have not only provided a framework for properly classifying and distinguishing environmental problems (those that have an effect on the earth system), but they have also provided guidance in prioritizing them. In this framework, climate change and biosphere integrity are considered "core planetary boundaries through which the other boundaries operate."[36]

> They operate at the level of the whole Earth System, and have co-evolved for nearly 4 billion years. They are regulated by the other boundaries and, on the other hand, provide the planetary-level overarching systems within which the other boundary processes operate. Furthermore, large changes in the climate or in biosphere integrity would likely, on their own, push the Earth System out of the Holocene state. In fact, transitions between time periods in Earth history have often been delineated by significant shifts in climate, the biosphere, or both.[37]

For many experts, climate change is the most immediately pressing boundary. Because of the long life of carbon dioxide and the thermal inertia of the oceans, we can lock in cascading impacts that will profoundly affect all of the other boundaries. Transgressing the climate change boundary will lead to species extinction and biodiversity loss both for terrestrial ecosystems, including freshwater ecosystems, and ocean ecosystems. As such the climate change boundary is crucial for the other core boundary, the biosphere integrity boundary. The rise in carbon dioxide, which is the primary driver of climate change, is the cause of ocean acidification (the ocean acidification boundary) and this together with the warming of the oceans from climate change can cause a mass extinction of ocean ecosystems.

---

35. Some of the scientific evidence from this section is reiterated in Richard W. Miller, "Thinking the Unthinkable: The Theologian and the Planetary Emergency," in *Turning to the Heavens and the Earth: Theological Reflections on a Cosmological Conversion: Essays in Honor of Elizabeth A. Johnson*, ed. Julia Brumbaugh and Natalia Imperatori-Lee (Collegeville, MN: Liturgical Press, 2016), 235–55, especially 235–38.

36. Steffen et al., "Planetary Boundaries," 1259855–58.

37. Ibid.

Climate change-induced droughts will severely affect the freshwater boundary. In addition, immediate unprecedented reductions in greenhouse gas emissions are necessary to avoid locking in impacts that are irreversible for millennia to millions of years.[38] Because of the crucial importance of the climate change boundary, this section takes a relatively in-depth look at this boundary.

To understand why climate change is a uniquely urgent threat, it is necessary to briefly describe the science behind it. The atmosphere is composed of a host of gases that trap heat radiated from the earth's surface (the so-called greenhouse gases) and have kept earth from becoming locked in a deep freeze. The relatively stable climate over

---

38. Jim Hansen argues that meeting the 350 ppm CO_2 boundary by the end of the century requires a rapid reduction in fossil fuel use and the removal of a 100 GtC (i.e., 367 billion metric tons of CO_2) from the atmosphere over the next ninety years through improved forestry and agricultural practices. Because of the long life of greenhouse gases, especially carbon dioxide (CO_2), it is not enough to reduce the level of carbon dioxide emissions; rather, there is only a certain amount of carbon dioxide we can put into the atmosphere. If we assume that we will draw the prescribed CO_2 from the atmosphere through improved forestry and agricultural practices, then we must reduce emissions by 6 percent per year (the starting point in his paper being 2013). If we delay emission reductions until 2020, then we need to reduce emissions globally at a rate of 15 percent per year. See James Hansen, "Assessing 'Dangerous Climate Change': Required Reduction of Carbon Emissions to Protect Young People, Future Generations and Nature," *PlosOne* 8, no. 12 (2013): 1–26, at 10. To have an idea of the staggering scale of this carbon reduction challenge, it is important to recall that the only time that emission reductions over a ten-year period have been more than 1 percent per year was during the economic collapse (i.e., a halving of the economy) of the former Soviet Union after the fall of the Berlin Wall, when emissions declined 5.2 percent per year. See Nicholas Stern, *The Economics of Climate Change: The Stern Review* (Cambridge, UK: Cambridge University Press, 2007), 231–32. It is also important to note that we have the technology to do this, but we lack political and social will. The distinguished Stanford researcher Mark Jacobsen argues that we have enough wind and solar in developable locations to power the world fifty times over. See Mark Z. Jacobsen and Mark A Delucchi, "Providing All Global Energy with Wind, Water, and Solar Power, Part 1: Technologies, Energy Resources, Quantities and Areas of Infrastructure, and Materials," *Energy Policy* 39 (2011): 1154–69; Mark Z. Jacobsen and Mark A Delucchi, "Providing All Global Energy with Wind, Water, and Solar Power, Part 2: Reliability, System and Transmission Costs, and Policies, *Energy Policy* 39 (2011): 1170–90. Jacobsen argues that we could move the entire world to renewables by 2030, and if we take into account the huge health costs from burning fossil fuels, the cost would be relative to the cost of our present fossil fuel energy mix. See also Louis Bergeron, "The World Can Be Powered by Alternative Energy, Using Today's Technology, in 20–40 Years, Says Stanford Researcher Mark Z. Jacobson," *Stanford News*, January 26, 2011, *http://news.stanford.edu/news/2011/january/jacobson-world-energy-012611.html*.

the past 11,700 of the Holocene Epoch, which has allowed for the growth of civilization, is due to the relative stability of both the amount and location of solar radiation reaching the earth and the concentration of greenhouse gases. A host of greenhouse gases are warming the planet, including carbon dioxide, methane, nitrous oxide, ozone, and water vapor, but carbon dioxide is the main driver of the climate change problem.[39]

Through the burning of fossil fuels and the felling of forests, which take in CO_2 and release oxygen, CO_2 levels are increasing in the atmosphere. While CO_2 levels have been much higher than they are now at different times in the earth's history, the increase in CO_2 from 280 ppm to 400 ppm since the industrial revolution is destabilizing the Holocene, which is typified, among other things, by stable sea level. The terrible truth of this destabilization is being revealed through scientific research, perhaps most notably by two studies from leading researchers who maintain that six glaciers on the West Antarctic ice sheet are now in a phase of unstoppable melt that will lead to a sea level rise of 1.2 meters (4 feet). If these studies hold up, this means that we have already condemned to destruction Charleston, New Orleans, Fort Lauderdale, Tampa, Saint Petersburg, and Miami. These estimates do not factor in storm surge damage, which will likely ravage our coasts much earlier. One study suggests that a five-foot sea level rise, which could be inevitable in view of contributions from Greenland, would bring Superstorm Sandy-style surges every other year along the East Coast, putting our cities under siege.[40]

A four-foot sea level rise also condemns much of the rice-growing regions of Asia to destruction, including 50 percent of the rice fields in Bangladesh (home to 160 million people with projections of 250 million by 2050) and more than half of those in Vietnam (the world's second largest rice exporter). This will lead to large scale movements of people, which will likely lead to conflict; note that the drought in Darfur led to nearly 300,000 deaths from malnutrition, disease, and conflict, and the most intense drought in the history of Syria led to

---

39. For simplicity sake, this study will focus on carbon dioxide.

40. Mark Fischetti, "Sea Level Rise 5 Feet in New York City by 2100," *Scientific American* (June 1, 2013), *https://www.scientificamerican.com/article/fischetti-sea-level-could-rise-five-feet-new-york-city-nyc-2100/*.

mass migrations of farmers into the cities, contributing to the destabilization of Syria and its descent into civil war.[41]

According to NASA scientist Eric Rignot, the aforementioned
melting of West Antarctic glaciers is likely to trigger "the collapse of
the rest of the West Antarctic ice sheet, which comes with a sea level
rise of between three and five meters [10 to 16 feet]."[42] A sixteen-foot
rise would flood Boston and Houston and reduce San Diego, Seat-
tle, and New York to remnants of their former selves. While Rignot
states conservatively that this collapse could take centuries, a subsequent study has shown that over the past five years the ice mass loss
on Greenland and West Antarctica has doubled.[43] While it is too
early to see if this trend will continue, Jim Hansen, one of the most
influential climate scientists of the past forty years, has argued that
three to four feet of sea level rise is possible, on our current path, in
fifty years (that is, by about 2065), when college students of the class
of 2020 will be in their sixties.[44]

Drought, however, will be arriving earlier. Indeed, the transition
to a more arid climate in the southwestern part of the United States
might already be under way.[45] As we continue on our present path
there is an increasing likelihood of mega-droughts,[46] the kind that
led to the destruction of past civilizations. On our current path, in
2050, when college students today are in their fifties, CO_2 levels will

41. C. P. Kelley, S. Mohtadi, M. A. Cane, R. Seager, and Y. Kushnir, "Climate
Change in the Fertile Crescent and Implications of the Recent Syrian Drought," *Proceedings of the National Academy of Sciences* 112, no.11 (March 17, 2015): 3241–46.

42. Eric Rignot, "Global Warming: It's a Point of No Return in West Antarctica.
What Happens Next?," *Guardian* (May 17, 2014).

43. Robin McKie, "'Incredible' Rate of Polar Ice Loss Alarms Scientists," *Guardian*
(August 23, 2014). The *Guardian* report is based on V. Helm, A. Humbert, and H.
Miller, "Elevation and Elevation Change of Greenland and Antarctica Derived from
CryoSat-2," *The Cryosphere* 8 (2014): 1539–59.

44. James Hansen et al., "Ice Melt, Sea Level Rise and Superstorms: Evidence
from Paleoclimate Data, Climate Modeling, and Modern Observations That 2°C
Global Warming Could Be Dangerous," *Atmospheric Chemistry and Physics Discussions*
16 (2016): 3761–812.

45. Richard Seager et al., "Model Projections of an Imminent Transition to a More
Arid Climate in Southwestern North America," *Science* 316 (April 5, 2007): 1181–84.

46. "NASA Study Finds Carbon Emissions Could Dramatically Increase Risk
of U.S. Megadroughts" NASA, February 12, 2015, *http://www.nasa.gov/press/2015
/february/nasa-study-finds-carbon-emissions-could-dramatically-increase-risk-of-us.*

reach 560 ppm and many of the world's mountain glaciers, which feed the rivers that provide the fresh water for half the world's population, will be substantially diminished or gone. This includes glaciers in the Hindu-Kush-Himalayan-Tibetan plateau, which will create water problems for hundreds of millions to a billion people in Asia.[47] By this time the Sierra Nevada snowpack could be committed to a 30 percent to 70 percent decline, greatly impairing California's agriculture,[48] which today produces nearly half of the fruits and vegetables grown in the United States. Corn and soy yields in the United States could drop by 30 percent to 46 percent.[49] Forests throughout the Western part of the United States will burn; California could lose 50 percent to 70 percent of its forests.[50]

Should we continue on our current path, CO_2 levels could reach 600 ppm by the 2060s, when today's college students are in their sixties. If positive feedbacks[51] are strong, the world could be 4°C warmer[52] and 40 percent to 70 percent of assessed species could be committed to eventual extinction.[53] A 600 ppm world[54] with rates of

47. Baiqing Xu et al., "Black Soot and the Survival of Tibetan Glaciers," *Proceedings of the National Academy of Sciences* 106, no. 2 (December 29, 2009): 22114–18, at 22114.

48. Katharine Hayhoe et al., "Emissions Pathways, Climate Change, and Impacts on California," *Proceedings of the National Academy of Sciences* 101, no. 34 (August 24, 2004): 12422–27, at 12422.

49. Wolfram Schlenker and Michael J. Roberts, "Nonlinear Temperature Effects Indicate Severe Damages to U.S. Crop Yields under Climate Change," *Proceedings of the National Academy of Sciences* 106, no. 37 (September 15, 2009): 15594–98 at 15594. The United States currently produces 41 percent of the world's corn and 38 percent of the world's soybeans.

50. Hayhoe et al., "Emissions Pathways," 12422.

51. A positive feedback is a process in which an initial warming will bring about additional warming. For instance, the loss of arctic sea ice exposes a dark ocean that absorbs more of the sun's energy, which in turn leads to more warming and the loss of more sea ice. Because of such feedback loops, scientists warn that there are "tipping points" in the system that could push the world into much more severe impacts that will unfold over millennia.

52. Richard A. Betts et al., "When Could Global Warming Reach 4°C?" *Philosophical Transactions of the Royal Society A*, 369 (2011): 67–84.

53. R.K. Pachauri and A. Reisinger eds., *Climate Change 2007: Synthesis Report. Contribution of Working Groups I, II and III to the Fourth Assessment Report of the Intergovernmental Panel on Climate Change*, (Geneva, Switzerland: IPCC), 13–14.

54. Veron, "The Coral Reef Crisis," 1428.

change that we have seen over the past decades (that is, one hundred times faster than the Paleocene/Eocene extinction event fifty-six million years ago)[55] will commit the Earth "to a trajectory from which there will be no escape."[56] The warming and acidification of the oceans will likely lead to a collapse of the world's coral reefs and the extinction of organisms that need calcium carbonate to build their shells, including a large part of the plankton in the southern ocean (the coccolithophorids). This will likely cause a domino effect that will lead to a mass extinction of ocean ecosystems.[57]

In the 2090s, today's college students would be in their nineties. They will live in a world where sea levels could be higher by 3 feet[58] to 16.5 feet.[59] The abandonment of many of the world's great cities will be underway, with large-scale population migration. Corn and soy yields from the US could be reduced between 60 percent and 83 percent, and if the snow pack in the Sierras declines 73 percent to 90 percent this would likely lead to the collapse of California agriculture. The forests of the American West would be ablaze; according to one of the world's leading fire ecologists, Tom Swetnam, half of the forests in the American Southwest,[60] and possibly the whole of the West,[61] could be destroyed by bark beetle infestation and fires.

The negative effects will escalate post 2100 and will probably continue for millennia. Based on what is known of the earth's history, if current atmospheric CO_2 concentrations are not reduced we will set in motion unimaginable impacts. CO_2 levels were this high

55. Noah S. Diffenbaugh and Christopher B. Field, "Changes in Critical Terrestrial Climate Conditions, *Science* 341 (2013): 486–92, at 490.

56. J. E. N. Veron, "Mass Extinctions and Ocean Acidification: Biological Constraints on Geological Dilemmas," *Coral Reefs* 27 (2008): 459–72, at 470.

57. Ibid.

58. T. F. Stocker, D. Qin, G.-K. Plattner, M. Tignor, S. K. Allen, J. Boschung, A. Nauels, Y. Xia, V. Bex, and P. M. Midgley, eds., *Climate Change 2013: The Physical Science Basis; IPCC Working Group I Contribution to AR5* (Cambridge, UK: Cambridge University Press, 2013).

59. Hansen et al., "Ice Melt, Sea Level Rise and Superstorms," 3761–812.

60. A. Park Williams et al., "Forest Responses to Increasing Aridity and Warmth in the Southwestern United States," *Proceedings of the National Academy of Sciences* 107, no. 50 (2010): 21289–94, at 21293.

61. William deBuys, "The West in Flames," *The Nation* (July 24, 2012).

(400 ppm) three million years ago,[62] when sea levels were between fifty and eighty feet higher than today,[63] and fifteen million years ago, when sea levels were between eighty and 130 feet higher than today.[64] Unless we reduce CO_2 levels from their current 400 ppm levels to below 350 ppm, it is likely that seas will continue to rise for centuries to millennia. This is one reason the planetary boundaries group maintains that CO_2 levels should be less than 350 ppm to ensure a safe operating space for humanity. In terms of mass extinctions, the effects will be felt for millions of years for terrestrial[65] and ocean ecosystems, for the five preceding great mass extinctions "left the Earth without living reefs for at least four million years"[66]

This description of the possible future explains why twenty past winners of the Blue Planet Prize[67] have declared, "In the face of an absolutely unprecedented emergency society has no choice but

---

62. M. E. Raymo, B. Grant, M. Horowitz, and G. H. Rau, "Mid-Pliocene Warmth: Stronger Greenhouse and Stronger Conveyor," *Marine Micropaleontology* 27 (1996): 313–26, at 323.

63. Hansen, "Assessing 'Dangerous Climate Change,'" 6.

64. Aradhna K. Tripati, Christopher D. Roberts, Robert A. Eagle, "Coupling of CO_2 and Ice Sheet Stability over Major Climate Transitions of the Last 20 Million Years," *Science* 326, no. 5958 (2009): 1394–97, at 1394.

65. As a reference point, complex ecosystems likely did not return for eight to nine million years after the greatest mass extinction, at the end of the Permian. See Zhong-Qiang Chen and Michael J. Benton, "The Timing and Pattern of Biotic Recovery Following the End-Permian Mass Extinction," *Nature Geoscience* 5 (2012): 375–83.

66. Veron, "Mass Extinctions," 459.

67. The Blue Planet Prize, often described as the Nobel for environmental sciences, is awarded to scientists whose scientific research contributes to solving global environmental problems. See the Blue Planet Prize Laureates, *Environment and Development Challenges: The Imperative to Act*, The Asahi Glass Foundation, February 20, 2012, *http://www.af-info.or.jp/en/bpplaureates/doc/2012jp_fp_en.pdf*. Authors for this synthesis paper included global leaders in climate science and climate economics: Dr. James Hansen (former director of NASA's Goddard Institute for Space Studies and one of the most important climate scientists over the past forty years); Dr. Susan Solomon (Senior Scientist, U.S. National Oceanic and Atmospheric Association and Chair of the National Academy of Sciences Committee that produced the 2010 Climate Science Report); Professor Sir Bob Watson (Chief Scientific Advisor in the U.K. and Chair of the Intergovernmental Panel on Climate Change [IPCC] from 1997 to 2002); Lord Robert May of Oxford (former Chief Scientific Adviser to the U.K. Government and President of the Royal Society of London); and Lord Nicholas Stern (professor at the London School of Economics, former Chief Economist and Senior Vice-President of the World Bank from 2000 to 2003, and author of the most influential work in climate economics, *The Economics of Climate Change: The Stern Review*.

to take dramatic action to avert a collapse of civilization. Either we will change our ways and build an entirely new kind of global society, or they will be changed for us."[68] It is why Pope Francis speaks with such urgency in *Laudato si'*: "Things are now reaching a breaking point" (*LS* 61), "contemporary lifestyle, unsustainable as it is, can only precipitate catastrophes" (*LS* 161). He speaks of "the spiral of self-destruction which currently engulfs us" (*LS* 163) and the need for "radical change" (*LS* 171), including "progressively replacing coal, oil, and natural gas without delay" (*LS* 165).

Conclusion

Pope Francis, especially in chapter 1 of *Laudato si'*, soberly recognizes the reality and scope of the challenges that constitute the modern ecological crisis. In conjunction with his concept of integral ecology, and its understanding of human dependence upon and responsibility to protect the natural world, Pope Francis underscores the urgent need to reform how humanity interacts with non-human nature.

This chapter provided the scientific basis for Pope Francis's understanding of the interconnectedness of all things in his integral ecology through the analysis of the dynamic relationship between nine different aspects of the earth system that constitute the planetary boundaries within which humanity can safely flourish. In light of the current transgression of several of these boundaries, humanity cannot afford to downplay or dismiss the gravity of our present situation. Rather, as Pope Francis says, we must "dare to turn what is happening to the world into our own personal suffering and thus to discover what each of us can do about it" (*LS* 19).

Review Questions

1. Why does Pope Francis say that "the cry of the earth and the cry of the poor" cannot ultimately be separated?
2. What are the nine systems that make up the planetary boundaries framework and how do they interact?

---

68. Blue Planet Prize Laureates, *Environment and Development Challenges*, 7.

3. How does the planetary boundaries framework enable us to distinguish and prioritize responses to ecological problems? How could this inform university sustainability efforts?

4. Explain the "see, judge, act" model of Catholic social action.

5. Why does the author argue that climate change is the most important planetary boundary?

6. What is a "positive feedback" in the context of climate change? What are the implications of positive feedbacks in the climate system?

In-Depth Questions

1. The author provides the scientific basis for the urgent language in *Laudato si'* and maintains, drawing on Pope Francis, that the purpose of describing the impacts of ecological degradation is "to become painfully aware, to dare to turn what is happening to the world into our own personal suffering and thus to discover what each of us can do about it" (*LS* 19). From what you read, do you think this urgency is warranted? What is your reaction to the material presented in this chapter?

2. Pope Francis and the authors of the planetary boundaries framework appeal to the precautionary principle. What is this principle? What are the implications of this principle for our political and economic systems?

3. Guided by the "see, judge, act" model of Catholic social action, how would you address one of the planetary boundaries discussed in this chapter?

4. The author argues that climate change is the most important planetary boundary. Do you agree? Why or why not?

5. Pick one planetary boundary, and describe one action you can take to better care for creation and one way you can advocate for systemic change in this area.

Suggestions for Further Study

Alley, Richard B. *The Two-Mile Time Machine: Ice Cores, Abrupt Climate Change, and Our Future.* Princeton: Princeton University Press, 2014.

Allison, I., et al. *The Copenhagen Diagnosis: Updating the World on the Latest Climate Science.* Sydney, Australia: The University of New South Wales Climate Change Research Centre, 2009.

Brown, Lester R. *Plan B 4.0: Mobilizing to Save Civilization.* New York: Norton, 2009.

Hansen, James. *Storms of My Grandchildren: The Truth about the Coming Climate Catastrophe and Our Last Chance to Save Humanity.* New York: Bloomsbury USA, 2009.

Jacobson, Mark Z., and Mark A. Delucchi. "A Path to Sustainable Energy by 2030." *Scientific American* 301, no. 5 (November, 2009): 58–65.

Kolbert, Elizabeth. *The Sixth Extinction: An Unnatural History.* New York: Henry Holt, 2014.

Lynas, Mark. *The God Species: Saving the Planet in the Age of Humans.* Washington, DC: National Geographic Society, 2011.

Mann, Michael E., and Lee R. Kump. *Dire Predictions: Understanding Global Warming.* 2nd ed. New York: DK Publishing, 2015.

Norgaard, Kari Marie. *Living in Denial: Climate Change, Emotions, and Everyday Life.* Cambridge, MA: MIT Press, 2011.

Oreskes, Naomi, and Eric Conway. *Merchants of Doubt: How a Handful of Scientists Obscured the Truth on Issues from Tobacco Smoke to Global Warming.* New York: Bloomsbury, 2011.

Till, Charles, and Yoon Il Chang. *Plentiful Energy: The Story of the Integral Fast Reactor: The Complex History of a Simple Reactor Technology, with Emphasis on Its Scientific Bases for Non-Specialists.* CreateSpace Independent Publishing Platform, December 6, 2011.

Veron, J. E. N. *A Reef in Time: The Great Barrier Reef from Beginning to End.* Cambridge, MA: Belknap, 2008.

Ward, Peter D. *Under a Green Sky: Global Warming, the Mass Extinctions of the Past, and What They Can Tell Us about the Future.* New York: Smithsonian Books, 2007.

Weart, Spencer R. *The Discovery of Global Warming.* Rev. and expanded ed. Cambridge, MA: Harvard University Press, 2008.

PART 4

Ecological Conversion

CHAPTER 8

Converting to and Nurturing Ecological Consciousness— Individually, Collectively, Actively

JAME SCHAEFER

During Pope Francis's first homily as the 266th leader of the Roman Catholic Church, he urged all people to be "'protectors' of creation, protectors of God's plan inscribed in nature, protectors of one another and of the environment."[1] He frequented this imperative on many occasions over the next two years of his pontificate and signed on May 24, 2015, the first encyclical dedicated to the ecological crisis, *Laudato si': On Care for Our Common Home*.[2]

In this epochal encyclical, Pope Francis explains the need to convert from attitudes and actions that are causing the ecological crisis to attitudes and actions that can be responsive to its many ominous manifestations. His discussion yields positive characteristics of the human person, some of which resonate with moral virtues that are valued in the Catholic theological tradition and variously within other world religions. Because ecological problems encompass many multi-faceted, local-to-global, and future-oriented challenges that require collective action, religious communities can nurture these

---

1. Pope Francis, "Homily of Pope Francis: Mass, Imposition of the Pallium and Bestowal of the Fisherman's Ring for the Beginning of the Petrine Ministry of the Bishop of Rome, Saint Peter's Square," March 19, 2013, *http://w2.vatican.va/content /francesco/en/homilies/2013/documents/papa-francesco_20130319_omelia-inizio -pontificato.html*.

2. Pope Francis, *Laudato si': On Care for Our Common Home*, June 18, 2015, *http:// w2.vatican.va/content/francesco/en/encyclicals/documents/papa-francesco_20150524 _enciclica-laudato-si.html*. All parenthetical citations in this chapter refer to *Laudato si'*.

characteristics among their members and act collectively in the public square.

Converting to Ecological Consciousness

Pope Francis was well aware of his predecessors' increasing concerns about the need to care about and for God's creation.[3] Building on Pope John Paul II's encouragement and support in 2001 for the "ecological conversion" that was occurring among some people and groups,[4] Pope Francis appealed in *Laudato si'* to all people throughout the world to engage in dialogue on the "immensity and urgency" of ecological problems (15) and to convert to ways of living harmoniously with other people, species, and systems of Earth—our common home.[5]

The conversion Pope Francis envisions is transitioning from negative attitudes and actions that are causing the ecological

---

3. Especially see Pope Paul VI, *Octogesima adveniens*, May 14, 1971, *http:// w2.vatican.va/content/paul-vi/en/apost_letters/documents/hf_p-vi_apl_19710514 _octogesima-adveniens.html*, where the environment is identified among the new social problems that need addressing; Pope John Paul II, *Peace with God the Creator, Peace with All of Creation: Message of His Holiness Pope John Paul II for the Celebration of the World Day of Peace*, January 1, 1990, *http://w2.vatican.va/content/john-paul-ii /en/messages/peace/documents/hf_jp-ii_mes_19891208_xxiii-world-day-for-peace.html*, the first papal statement dedicated to the ecological crisis as a moral responsibility; and Pope Benedict XVI, *If You Want to Cultivate Peace, Protect Creation: Message of His Holiness Pope Benedict XVI for the Celebration of the World Day of Peace*, January 1, 2010, *http://w2.vatican.va/content/benedict-xvi/en/messages/peace/documents/hf_ben-xvi _mes_20091208_xliii-world-day-peace.html*, where he underscores "creation as God's gift to humanity" and encourages "contemplating the beauty of creation [which] inspires us to recognize the love of the Creator," no. 2.

4. Pope John Paul II, "God Made Man the Steward of Creation," General Audience, January 17, 2001, *http://w2.vatican.va/content/john-paul-ii/en/audiences/2001 /documents/hf_jp-ii_aud_20010117.html*.

5. Air pollution forcing changes in the global climate, accumulation of wastes requiring disposition, decline in the quality and availability of potable water, and loss of biological diversity that exacerbate social problems including decline in the quality of human life and breakdown of society, inequalities between rich and poor individuals and countries, adverse effects especially on poor and vulnerable people, and threats to future generations (17–42). As Pope Francis stated at the United Nations General Assembly in September 2015: "Any harm done to the environment is harm done to humans" ("Address of the Holy Father: Meeting with the Members of the General Assembly of the United Nations Organization," September 25, 2015, *http://w2.vatican.va/content/francesco/en/speeches/2015/september/documents/papa -francesco_20150925_onu-visita.html*).

crisis[6] to positive attitudes and actions that prompt caring for Earth (216–21).[7] Though he does not explicitly identify characteristics that manifest a person's ecological conversion, they surface implicitly in *Laudato si'*.[8] Drawing these manifestations to the forefront is the task to which this study now turns.

Characteristics of an Ecologically Conscious Person

A close reading of *Laudato si'* yields characteristics of the ecologically conscious person that Pope Francis envisions: open to awe and wonder, grateful, humble, respectful, cooperative, protective, compassionate, responsible, courageous, and contemplative. Each characteristic is probed briefly with reference to the encyclical.

Open to Awe and Wonder

An ecologically conscious person approaches with awe and wonder all aspects of Earth from the smallest types of life to panoramic vistas (85).[9] Openness to them leads to recognizing the human connectedness with all creatures, realizing that they manifest God's presence and loving character, and seeking knowledge about them.

---

6. These attitudes and actions include thinking about humans as separate from other species and as objects to be dominated, making decisions based on our short-term economic desires, over-consuming and wasting the natural goods of the earth, deferring to technology as the source of solutions, and failing to care about other people whose suffering is exacerbated by the many manifestations of ecological degradation (102–36).

7. Positive attitudes include recognizing the earth as the common home of human and all other living and inanimate creatures, valuing them intrinsically for their natures and functioning in relation to one another, respecting human interconnections and interdependence with them, and exercising the unique intellectual and spiritual capacities of human creatures to interpret reality as "a kind of universal family" that God calls into existence (89).

8. An examination of Pope Francis's writings, speeches, interviews, and actions epitomize the characteristics of an ecologically conscious person that are explored in this essay.

9. Canadian Conference of Catholic Bishops, Social Affairs Commission, *You Love All That Exists . . . All Things Are Yours, God, Lover of Life*, October 4, 2003, *http://www.cccb.ca/site/Files/pastoralenvironment.html*, p. 1.

AWED BY INTERRELATIONSHIPS

In the introduction to *Laudato si'*, Pope Francis urges our opening to the awe and wonder of the "beauty in our relationship with the world" whereby "we feel intimately united with all that exists" (11). We recognize our interrelations and interconnections as "bonds" that God has "linked us to all beings" (220). Quoting from the *Catechism of the Catholic Church*, he emphasizes the divinely willed interdependence of creatures and their need for one another (86).[10] Through awe and wonder about the connectedness and interdependence of humans with other creatures, ecologically conscious persons view them as constituting a "family" (42, 89) for which they care. The ecologically conscious never approach the family of creatures as "masters, consumers, [and] ruthless exploiters" who turn these creatures into objects "simply to be used and controlled" (11). Awareness of the human interconnections with other creatures is a "loving" awareness that leads the ecologically conscious to think about themselves as "joined in a splendid universal communion" and inspires them to "greater creativity and enthusiasm in resolving the world's problems" (220).

OPEN TO GOD'S SELF-MANIFESTATION

Openness to the awe and wonder of Earth and her constituents has another meaning for faith-filled people who are ecologically conscious: the visible world is revelatory of God's character. In sync with *Laudato si'* and the *Catechism of the Catholic Church*, the ecologically conscious recognize that "each creature possesses its own particular goodness and perfection" and that each "reflects in its own way a ray of God's infinite wisdom and goodness" (69).[11] With Pope Francis and the Canadian bishops, the ecologically conscious approach other species and vistas as "a constant source of wonder and awe," and no creature is excluded from this "continuing revelation of the divine" (85).[12] They

---

10. *Catechism of the Catholic Church* (Washington DC: United States Catholic Conference, 1994), no. 340, p. 88.

11. Ibid., no. 339, p. 88: "Man must therefore respect the particular goodness of every creature, to avoid any disordered use of things which would be in contempt of the Creator and would bring disastrous consequences for human beings and their environment."

12. Canadian Conference of Catholic Bishops, *You Love All That Exists*, p. 1.

embrace the understanding of patristic and medieval theologians that God is the writer of "a precious book . . . whose letters are the multitude of created things present in the universe" (85).[13] The ecologically conscious accept Saint Francis of Assisi's invitation "to see nature as a magnificent book in which God speaks to us and grants us a glimpse of his infinite beauty and goodness" (12).[14] They understand with Saint Thomas Aquinas that the many diverse creatures constituting the universe represent "the divine goodness" (86),[15] and they grasp with Pope Francis "the importance and meaning of each creature" that is best contemplated "within the entirety of God's plan" (86).

Wondering about Scientific Findings

The ecologically conscious are also open to discovering scientific knowledge about a problem in order to make informed decisions about responding (183). In his encyclical, Pope Francis demonstrates a broad understanding of scientific findings and those upon which the other bishops based their pastoral statements on problems occurring in and near their dioceses.[16] He recognizes Earth as the common home of human and all other living and inanimate creatures, the human connectedness with them, their interdependence within ecological systems and the larger biosphere, and human reliance on clean water to drink, clean air to breathe, and a climate within which to survive (17–42). An ecologically conscious person nurtures the sense of wonder that prompts searching for scientific knowledge that is indispensable for deciding how to function within the home humans share with one another, other species, and systems that constitute Earth.

---

13. For a historical overview of theological discourse on the sacramentality of creation, see Jame Schaefer, "Acting Reverently in God's Sacramental World," in *Ethical Dilemmas in the New Millennium II*, ed. Francis A. Eigo (Villanova, PA: Villanova University Press, 2001), 37–90.

14. "For from the greatness and beauty of created things comes a corresponding perception of their Creator" (Wis. 13:5); "His eternal power and divine nature, invisible though they are, have been understood and seen through the things he has made" (Rom. 1:20).

15. *Summa theologiae* 1:47:1.

16. See especially 20–42, wherein Pope Francis demonstrates his understanding of scientific facts when discussing the four major ecological problems, all of which have societal ramifications: pollution and wastefulness, climate change, availability of potable water, and loss of biological diversity. The importance of recognizing the locales in which these problems occur and their local ramifications cannot be overstated.

Grateful for Earth—God's Gift to All

The ecological conversion that Pope Francis envisions calls for recognizing the world as "God's loving gift" and for expressing gratitude to God by imitating God's "generosity" through "self-sacrifice and good works" (220). From the pope's perspective, God's gift of the world must be received as a gift *for all*, to be shared *by all*, and to be preserved and protected *by all* for their common good (67, 95, 159). Ecologically conscious persons accept these restrictions and responsibilities, and they express their gratitude to God through demonstrations of justice that are aimed at assuring the flourishing of people in the present and a life-flourishing planetary home for future generations. They also express their gratitude through self-restraint when encountering and using the goods of Earth.

Intra-Generationally Just

Following the pope's teachings, the ecologically conscious demonstrate justice among current generations by being open to the plights of materially poor and vulnerable people and nations that are plagued with ecological, economic, and political impediments to sustaining themselves and by acknowledging that these impediments are erected primarily by materially-developed nations. Ecologically conscious people recognize this injustice and strive to challenge and correct it. They are not self-seeking or self-centered. Nor do they engage in the destructive culture of "instant gratification" and "impulsive and wasteful consumption" (162).[17] They limit themselves to consuming the goods of Earth for the *necessities* of life (67),[18] and they avoid wasteful practices that are detrimental to other species, ecological systems, and the biosphere of Earth (22). They are aware of the suffering of the poor and vulnerable, see themselves in solidarity with them (162), and seek to mitigate their suffering individually and collaboratively with others in caring, sensitive, respectful, and creative ways. Following Pope Francis, ecologically conscious people

---

17. See also 95.

18. Pope Francis interprets the Genesis 2 story of creation and supportive scriptures as meaning that "each community can take from the bounty of the earth whatever it needs for subsistence, but it also has the duty to protect the earth and to ensure its fruitfulness for coming generations" (67).

also engage the poor and vulnerable in determining how their suffering can and should be mitigated (183).

Inter-Generationally Just

Demonstrating justice toward generations in the future is a responsibility that ecologically conscious people take seriously. They know that the long-honored principle of seeking the common good also extends to future generations, as Pope Francis underscores (159). They are committed to inter-generational solidarity because they know they are dealing with "a basic question of justice, since the world we have received also belongs to those who will follow us" (159). They think about the general direction in which they want to leave Earth, our common home. They ask deep questions: "What is the purpose of our life in this world? Why are we here? What is the goal of our work and all our efforts? What need does the earth have of us?" (160).

Ecologically conscious people know that leaving an inhabitable planet to future generations is warranted, and how they act gives "ultimate meaning" to their lives (160). They orient their actions toward eliminating the current perils to a life-sustaining planet. They recognize as a positive step in that direction the Paris Agreement made by 195 nations in December 2015 to "hold the increase in the global average temperature to well below 2°C above pre-industrial levels" and to pursue "efforts to limit the temperature increase to 1.5°C above pre-industrial levels."[19] They also recognize the need to contribute generously to the Green Climate Fund that was created to help poor nations mitigate and adapt to changes in the global climate.

Self-Restraining

Closely connected with the intra- and inter-generational justices to which the ecologically conscious are committed is the characteristic of self-restraint. Pope Francis prefers the term "sobriety" (11, 126, 223–24) to contrast the consumerism and wastefulness to which many people are addicted today. Ecologically conscious people restrict themselves to consuming what they *need* to sustain their lives

---

19. United Nations, *Paris Agreement*, 2015, article 2.1.a, *http://unfccc.int/files/essential_background/convention/application/pdf/english_paris_agreement.pdf.*

(67), using the goods of Earth efficiently, and minimizing wastes (22). They are convinced that "less is more," and they believe that adopting a simpler lifestyle liberates them "to stop and appreciate small things, to be grateful for the opportunities which life affords us, to be spiritually detached from what we possess, and not to succumb to sadness for what we lack" (222). They set limits to economic growth for themselves and their families, and they redefine "progress" from exclusively economic and materialistic categories to more inclusive categories such as the quality of life, a healthful environment, social relationships, and recreational opportunities (47, 78, 112).

Humble

What does Pope Francis mean when urging everyone to express a "healthy humility" (224)? From his perspective, humility becomes a characteristic of ecologically conscious persons who have shed "the possibility of limitless mastery over everything," avoid viewing themselves as "autonomous" to the exclusion of God, and refuse to replace God with their "own egos" (224). Conversion to ecological consciousness is characterized by persons who humbly acknowledge their interconnectedness with and dependence upon other species and abiota[20] that constitute Earth (68, 139).[21] They also acknowledge that they are not God and recognize their responsibility to God for how they function within God's wondrous creation (69). Finally, they realize that our species, *Homo sapiens*, is a relatively late

---

20. The inanimate constituents of Earth: air, land, and water.

21. Pope Francis advanced his thinking in *Laudato si'* when addressing the members of the General Assembly of the United Nations on September 25, 2015. There he proffered a "right of the environment" for two reasons: (1) Humans are "part of the environment," "live in communion with it, since the environment itself entails ethical limits which human activity must acknowledge and respect," possess bodies "shaped by physical, chemical and biological elements, and can only survive and develop if the ecological environment is favourable. Any harm done to the environment, therefore, is harm done to humanity"; and, (2) "every creature, particularly a living creature, has an intrinsic value, in its existence, its life, its beauty and its interdependence with other creatures." He continued from his faith perspective: "We Christians, together with the other monotheistic religions, believe that the universe is the fruit of a loving decision by the Creator, who permits man respectfully to use creation for the good of his fellow men and for the glory of the Creator; he is not authorized to abuse it, much less to destroy it."

arrival within the 13.8 billion year history of the universe.[22] Their humility is prompted by the realization that our species emerged from earlier hominins in the biological evolutionary process approximately 400,000 years ago,[23] share more than 99 percent of our DNA sequence with African chimpanzees and modern gorillas,[24] and, like all species of organic life, consist of elements that were manufactured in the furnace of stars.[25] Acceptance of these scientific findings leads the ecologically conscious to resist the temptation of assuming any sense of mastery over or management of other species, systems, or Earth. Instead, ecologically conscious persons think humbly about how to *manage themselves* by exercising their unique capabilities.[26]

Respectful

In *Laudato si'*, respectfulness takes several forms that are compelling for people who are ecologically conscious. They respect the "paternal relationship God has with all" creatures (96) and God's love for all creatures (93, 228). "Because all creatures are connected," Pope Francis teaches, "each must be cherished with love and respect, for all of us as living creatures are dependent on one another" (42). The

---

22. The history of the universe is well documented in the scientific literature and reflected in popular literature. For one helpful example, see Nora Taylor Redd, "How Old Is the Universe?" Space.com, December 30, 2013, *http://www.space.com/24054 -how-old-is-the-universe.html*.

23. See, e.g., Francisco Ayala, "Evolution and the Uniqueness of Humankind," *Origins* 27, no. 34 (1998): 565–80, at 565–68, and Ian Tattersall, "Human Evolution: An Overview," in *An Evolving Dialogue: Theological and Scientific Perspectives on Evolution*, ed. James B. Miller (Harrisburg, PA: Trinity, 2001), 197–209, at 197.

24. Edward O. Wilson, *Biophilia* (Cambridge, MA: Harvard University Press, 1984), 130. See also Ian Barbour's supportive discussion in *Religion and Science: Historical and Contemporary Issues* (San Francisco: HarperSanFrancisco, 1997), 253–55.

25. E.g., Harold Morowitz, "The First 2 Billion Years of Life," *Origins* 27, no. 34 (1998): 577–80, at 579: "The atoms of every living thing, including each one of us, were at one time in the history of the universe cooked up deep in the core of some unbelievably hot star."

26. The term "stewardship" conveys a sense of management over other species and systems of Earth that is inappropriate to use as a model of the human person. Among alternates is the "virtuous cooperator" model as explained in Jame Schaefer, "The Virtuous Cooperator: Modeling the Human in an Age of Ecological Degradation," *Worldviews: Environment, Culture, Religion* 7, no. 1–2 (2003): 171–95.

ecologically conscious respect the natural environment (126, 143) and the "laws of nature" (66) within which all constituents of Earth function. They also respect the "unique place" of humans in the world (15) and live respectfully in relation to other living and inanimate constituents of our common home.

Key to living respectfully is valuing other species and systems *intrinsically* for themselves and their interactions with other species as well as *instrumentally* for their usefulness to humans. This requires following Pope Francis's teachings about God's love for and intrinsic valuing of species, ecosystems, and the biosphere of Earth. The ecologically conscious person values other species, ecosystems, and Earth intrinsically (115, 118, 140), recognizes that each has its own particular goodness and perfection (69), significance (76), and purpose (84) apart from its usefulness to humans, and respects the natural capacity of other species, ecosystems, and Earth to flourish (44, 69).

The ecologically conscious share Pope Francis's end-of-time perspective from which to consider valuing other species, systems, and Earth. With him and Teilhard de Chardin, SJ, ecologically conscious Christians believe animals and systems proceed "with us and through us" toward the end of time where all will be embraced and illuminated by the risen Christ (83). The ecologically conscious respect all creatures as intrinsically valuable by recognizing their participation in this ongoing journey, knowing about them, loving them, and cooperating with them for their mutual flourishing in this life in anticipation of a glorious culmination in the presence of God.[27]

Cooperative

Following the Catholic theological tradition, Pope Francis teaches that God counts on our cooperation to "bring good out of the evil we have done" (80). Harming the life-sustaining capacity of the Earth community is evil within the context of *Laudato si'*. Ecologically conscious people view their cooperation with one another, other species, and systems of Earth as a way of cooperating with God. With the

---

27. The pope's end-of-time (eschatological) perspective has significance for his theology of hope that all people will convert to an ecological consciousness and act accordingly (61, 65, 71, 74, 142, 154, 165, 190, 198), a perspective that warrants in-depth development as encouraged by one reviewer of this essay.

pope, they understand that God "wishes to work with us" and draws us into "the act of cooperation" in the work of creation within which God is continuously present without impinging on creation's autonomy (80). The ecologically conscious cooperate with God by limiting and directing technology to a constructive type of progress that resolves problems and promotes human dignity (112), assessing and mitigating human-caused harm to other species, *abiota*, and systems of Earth (117), and thinking about themselves as cooperators who seek their mutual flourishing.[28]

Cooperation is also demonstrated collectively by the ecologically conscious at increasing levels of governance when the need for action exceeds prior levels. Cooperation becomes essential at the international level when problems exceed the capability of countries to resolve.[29] Among the examples to which Pope Francis points is the Earth Summit that was held in 1992 in Rio de Janeiro, where the nations proclaimed that "human beings are at the centre of concerns for sustainable development"[30] and enshrined principles for "international cooperation to care for the ecosystem of the entire earth" (167).[31] Pope Francis laments the many "ill-advised delays" in acting

---

28. For further exploration of the concept of cooperation, see Jame Schaefer, "Grateful Cooperation: Cistercian Inspiration for Ecological Ethics," *Cistercian Studies Quarterly* 37, no. 2 (2002): 187–203; also Jame Schaefer, "The Virtuous Cooperator: Modeling the Human in an Age of Ecological Degradation," *Worldviews: Environment, Culture, Religion* 7, no. 1–2 (2003): 171–95. Scientific evidence of cooperation among biota and abiota has prompted many publications; see, for example, essays in *Cooperation and Its Evolution*, ed. Kim Sterelny, Richard Joyce, Brett Calcott, and Ben Fraser (Cambridge: MIT Press, 2013).

29. Pontifical Council for Justice and Peace, *Compendium of the Social Doctrine of the Church* (Washington, DC: United States Conference of Catholic Bishops, 2004), nos. 81–83. For an exploration of subsidiarity and extension to bio-regional decision-making, see Jame Schaefer, "Solidarity, Subsidiarity, and Preference for the Poor," in *Confronting the Climate Crisis: Catholic Theological Perspectives*, ed. Jame Schaefer (Milwaukee, WI: Marquette University Press, 2011), 389–425, especially at 396–401 and 413–15.

30. *Rio Declaration on Environment and Development*, June 14, 1992, Principle 1, http://www.unesco.org/education/nfsunesco/pdf/RIO_E.PDF; also accessible in *Report of the United Nations Conference on Environment and Development*, United Nations General Assembly, Annex 1, August 12, 1992, http://www.un.org/documents/ga/conf151/aconf15126-1annex1.htm.

31. Among other principles enshrined at the Earth Summit in Rio that Pope Francis mentions are the obligation of those who cause pollution to assume its costs, the duty to assess the environmental impact of proposed projects, and limitations on greenhouse gas emissions (167).

cooperatively at the international level as envisioned at the Earth Summit and subsequent international gatherings. He attributes these delays to positions taken by countries that "place their national interests above the global common good" (167). Clearly, an international ecological consciousness is warranted in which nations recognize that the global common good is essential for mutual flourishing.

Protective

As previously mentioned, Pope Francis lauded Saint Joseph's protectiveness of Mary and Jesus during the first homily of his pontificate and urged all people to be "protectors" of God's creation.[32] He expressed the model of protector in *Laudato si'* in several ways that ecologically conscious people demonstrate. They follow his interpretation of the Genesis 2 story of creation and supportive scriptures that humans are duty-bound "to protect the earth and to ensure its fruitfulness for coming generations" (67). They promote the development of strategies aimed at protecting species that are endangered and on the verge of becoming extinct (42). They receive God's gift of the world to be preserved and protected by all for their common good (67, 95, 159). And, they encourage the implementation of ecologically protective laws on appropriate levels—from local to international (38).

Compassionate

Pope Francis's words and actions throughout his pontificate epitomize compassion for the poor and vulnerable, including endangered species, degraded ecological systems, and Earth (2, 34–42).[33] When describing in *Laudato si'* the "deep sense of communion" humans have with other species and systems, he cautions that this sense "cannot be real if our hearts lack tenderness, compassion and concern for

---

32. Pope Francis, "Homily of Pope Francis: Mass, Imposition of the Pallium and Bestowal of the Fisherman's Ring."

33. "Mother Earth" and "like . . . a beautiful mother" when quoting and paraphrasing from Saint Francis of Assisi's *Canticle of the Creatures* (1); "mother earth" when paraphrasing *Canticle* (92).

our fellow human beings" (91). Thus, ecologically conscious people express their compassion for poor and vulnerable humans by offering to work with them in identifying actions that should be taken to eliminate the environmental injustices that are occurring in their blighted neighborhoods, assuring the availability of fresh foods for their families, and providing green spaces in which their children can experience other animals and breathe fresher air through the cleansing action of trees.

Broadening the goals of environmental education is key to bringing about the deep sense of compassion that Pope Francis urges. In addition to promoting scientific information about ecological problems and raising consciousness about them, he encourages educational efforts that include "developing an ethics of ecology, and helping people, through effective pedagogy, to grow in solidarity, responsibility and compassionate care" (10). One impressive example that meets his criteria is *Healing Earth*, the environmental science textbook commissioned by the Higher Education Secretariat of the Society of Jesus in which scientific knowledge about major ecological problems are reflected upon from spiritual and ethical perspectives.[34]

Responsible

Pope Francis's calling upon all people to recognize and respond to ecological problems persists throughout *Laudato si'*.[35] Though he recognizes that people are motivated variously to respond to ecological degradation and that some may by motivated by the fact that they are "a part" of the environment, Christians realize that "their responsibility within creation, and their duty towards nature and the Creator, are an essential part of their faith" (64). He focuses an entire chapter of his encyclical on the "ample motivation" that the Christian tradition provides for responding to ongoing ecological perils

---

34. *Healing Earth*, International Jesuit Ecology Project, 2016, *http://healingearth .ijep.net*. This project is administered by biologist Nancy Tuchman, PhD, and theologian Michael Schuck, PhD, at Loyola University Chicago.

35. "Responsibility" or a variant thereof occurs fifty-five times in reference to humans becoming aware of and addressing ecological concerns.

(62–100), and he encourages people of other faiths to return to the sources of their traditions for inspiration (200).

Unique to humans who are endowed with intellectual abilities to reason, develop arguments, interpret reality, and engage in meaningful relationships with others and with God (81, 119), an engrained sense of responsibility propels ecologically conscious people to dialogue with one another about their relationships with other creatures, their habitats, and the biosphere of Earth and to make and execute decisions for their mutual flourishing (68). According to Pope Francis, failing to be responsible ruins the person's relationships with others, with God, and with Earth (70).

Ecologically conscious people recognize their responsibility to care for Earth through "little daily activities of environmental responsibility" (211), correcting irresponsible use and abuse of God's creation (2, 6), inventorying and safeguarding species (42), and advocating the passage and implementation of protective laws (38). Committed to living up to their dignity as responsible persons, the ecologically conscious are described by Pope Francis as "selfless" (181).

Courageous

Responding effectively to the ecological crisis requires courage to make the ecological conversion that Pope Francis envisions and to remain ecologically conscious of problems that are occurring and assiduously predicted (160, 169, 181). People who are ecologically conscious are persistent. They consistently think of the common good before their own interests. They face challenges with conviction. They are not deterred from their convictions and commitments by "undue pressure and bureaucratic inertia" (181). They are able to persist because they are open to and draw upon God's grace (200, 205) that motivates and strengthens them to remain steadfastly courageous when seeking the common good of the Earth community.[36]

---

36. Highly instructive for understanding how God's grace works in people collectively is Robert M. Doran, "Social Grace," *Journal of Lonergan Studies* 2, no. 2 (2011): 131–42.

Contemplative

Pope Francis's discussion of God's self-manifestation in and through the world leads to recognizing the benefits of contemplating each creature for its meaning "within the entirety of God's plan" (86). One benefit is discovering "a teaching which God wishes to hand on to us" and another is seeing "ourselves in relation to all other creatures" (85). Both benefits help the ecologically conscious live more cooperatively with all creatures for their mutual good.

Contemplation of God's creation can also prompt praise for God. Not surprisingly, the pope points to Saint Francis of Assisi's *Canticle of the Creatures* as a "magnificent expression" of praise for God (87).[37] Praising God in unison with other creatures by interrelating with them for their common good resonates with Pope Francis's understanding that God calls all into "universal communion" (76).

Pope Francis also encourages contemplating God's creation through a "Trinitarian key" of humans, other creatures, and Earth (239). Taking this approach stimulates in-depth probing of their interconnection in a way that parallels exploring the interconnection of the three persons in the Blessed Trinity: Father, Son, and Holy Spirit.[38] In this way, the ecologically conscious "discover a key to [their] own fulfilment" as creatures who are intimately connected with other creatures (240).[39]

---

37. Grounded in Ps. 148 and Dan. 3:57–81, theological reflection on creatures' praise for God according to their "voices" and humans joining voices with those of other creatures in a grand chorus is explored in the fourth chapter of Jame Schaefer, *Theological Foundations for Environmental Ethics* (Washington, DC: Georgetown University Press, 2009), 103–20.

38. See Augustine's Trinitarian sacramental discourse, discussed in Jame Schaefer, "Augustine's Trinitarian Sacramental Sensibilities, Influence, and Significance for Our Imperiled Planet," in *Augustine and the Natural Environment*, ed. Kim Pattenroth, John Doody, and Mark Smillie, 141–63 (Lanham, MD: Lexington Books, 2016).

39. Pope Francis explains (240) why using the human-other creatures-Earth lens helps us "discover a key to our own fulfilment": "The human person grows more, matures more and is sanctified more to the extent that he or she enters into relationships, going out from themselves to live in communion with God, with others and with all creatures. In this way, they make their own that trinitarian dynamism which God imprinted in them when they were created."

Nurturing Ecological Consciousness within Religious Communities

Families, parishes, and other religious communities can help facilitate the ecological conversion of members by encouraging them to reflect on the sources of their faith as a basis from which to discern problems and identify actions for mitigating them (200). Families, parishes, and other religious communities are also vital for nurturing and advancing the characteristics of ecological consciousness in a person who has converted but needs support and encouragement to remain steadfast.

For Pope Francis, the family is "the primary social group" (142), the "basic cell of society" (189), the starting place for facilitating an ecological conversion and nurturing an ecological consciousness (213). Families provide indispensable settings for identifying, developing, and nurturing the characteristics that exemplify an ecological consciousness. Parents and guardians serve as key examples for their children.

Religious communities can support, advance, and enrich family efforts to facilitate and nurture ecological conversions. Priests, ministers, rabbis, imams, monks, and gurus can teach about their religious traditions that have meaning for ecological-societal concerns.[40] Catechetical directors and leaders of educational programs can provide prolonged opportunities for youths and adults to study ecological statements issued by their leaders, deepen their understanding of traditions that are promising for addressing the ecological crisis, and apply them to problems in their communities. Parish councils can establish teams of parishioners who are dedicated to acting on *Laudato si'* within their parishes,[41] working with other parishes, and collaborating with other religious communities to constitute an effective ecologically conscious voice in the public square.

---

40. As already noted, Pope Francis is confident that the Christian faith is sufficient for motivating the ecological conversion of the faithful (64), and he encourages people of other faiths to return to the sources of their traditions for inspiration and motivation (200).

41. Among immediate possibilities for parish councils is assessing their buildings and grounds to identify ways of functioning that reflect the ecological consciousness Pope Francis proffers. Catholic Climate Covenant provides some thoughtful and constructive ideas for establishing "Creation Care Teams" in parishes. See *http://www .catholicclimatecovenant.org/cct*.

Bishops and parallel regional leaders of religious communities can encourage and facilitate activities aimed at mitigating impediments to the flourishing of ecological systems in their regions. One impressive example of episcopal leadership is an action plan motivated by *Laudato si'* that was written by faculty and staff at the University of Georgia in consultation with the Archbishop of Atlanta.[42]

Conclusions

Pope Francis calls all people to an ecological conversion that is aimed at assuring the life-flourishing capacity of Earth. Maintaining this conversion requires an ecological consciousness that is manifested by key characteristics that can be discerned in *Laudato si'*: *openness to awe, wonder, and discovery* of scientific facts about other species and systems of Earth; *gratitude* for God's gift of Earth to all through self-restraint, intra-generational justice, and inter-generational justice; *humility* in relation to other species and systems of which humans are an integral part; *respectfulness* of the natures and interrelationships of human and other creatures; *protection* of other humans, species, habitats, and Earth's systems; *cooperation* with other species within systems of Earth for their mutual well-being and flourishing; *compassion* toward vulnerable people and species; *responsibility* to others and ultimately to God for addressing ecological problems; *courage* by steadfastly maintaining and advancing their ecological conversion; and *contemplation* of their role in relation to others within Earth that God made possible.

Developing these characteristics begins within the family. Local religious communities can help nurture and deepen these characteristics through educational and service programs. Bishops and area leaders of larger religious communities are vital for promoting, encouraging, and facilitating local efforts. Religious communities can network with one another to advocate action at appropriate governmental levels. As Pope Francis underscores, God's grace is readily available to all people for strengthening their efforts.

---

42. Archdiocese of Atlanta, *Laudato si'—On Care for Our Common Home: An Action Plan for The Roman Catholic Archdiocese of Atlanta,* November 2015, *http://www.dio .org/uploads/files/Missions/Resources/UGA-Action-Plan-2015-11-24-10am.pdf.*

Review Questions

1. What does the phrase "ecological conversion" mean?
2. Name and explain three characteristics of an "ecologically conscious" person.
3. Why is humility a characteristic of a person who is ecologically conscious?

In-Depth Questions

1. What characteristic of an ecologically conscious person do you think would be most difficult to embrace and demonstrate?
2. How can a family best nurture an ecological consciousness in young children and in teenagers?
3. What activity would you want your religious community to begin that best reflects Pope Francis's teachings in *Laudato si'*?

Suggestions for Further Study

Healing Earth. International Jesuit Ecology Project. Loyola University, Chicago. *http://healingearth.ijep.net*.

Schaefer, Jame. "Environmental Degradation, Social Sin, and the Common Good." In *God, Creation, and Climate Change*, edited by Richard W. Miller, 69–94. Maryknoll, NY: Orbis, 2010.

Schaefer, Jame. "Solidarity, Subsidiarity, and Preference for the Poor." In *Confronting the Climate Crisis: Catholic Theological Perspectives*, edited by Jame Schaefer, 389–425. Milwaukee: Marquette University Press, 2011.

Schaefer, Jame. *Theological Foundations for Environmental Ethics: Reconstructing Patristic and Medieval Concepts*. Washington, DC: Georgetown University Press, 2009.

CHAPTER 9

Calling Forth the Invisible, Spreading Goodness: Virtue Ethics in *Laudato si'*

NANCY M. ROURKE

On the surface, Pope Francis's *Laudato si'* does not look like a call for an ecological virtue ethics.[1] Large-scale social change seems to be the main point. In two hundred and forty-six paragraphs, the word "virtue" appears only five times. The word "vice" appears once. Yet virtue ethics is the fuel that powers this encyclical. The call for an integral ecology and its repeated reminders that "everything is connected" are rooted in the particular wisdom specific to virtue theory. This chapter will explore the role of virtue ethics in *Laudato si'*.

Virtue Ethics

Virtue ethics is a moral theory concerned with moral character. Its main focus is not social systems or the morality of actions (although both are nevertheless important). Instead its main concern is us. It examines what we (human beings) are like, the sorts of people we should strive to be, and the ways we can realize this anthropological vision.[2] Virtue theorists imagine the "parts" of a person's moral character, looking for things like virtues and vices. Virtues and vices are

---

1. Pope Francis, *Laudato si': On Care for Our Common Home*, June 18, 2015, http://w2.vatican.va/content/francesco/en/encyclicals/documents/papa-francesco_20150524_enciclica-laudato-si.html.

2. Alasdair MacIntyre, *After Virtue* (Notre Dame, IN: University of Notre Dame Press, 2007).

habits of being in certain ways. Because they are habits, virtues and vices are formed by practicing them. Virtues are good traits or tendencies. Traditionally, virtue ethics calls each virtue a specific "excellence." Virtues are like well-balanced habits. Imagine a kind person as a person who has a habit of being kind and who tends to be good at being kind. This means, of course, a kind person also has other virtues (like patience, frugality, or attentiveness). All these virtues work together to make up a person's moral character.

A moral character has vices. Vices are habits or tendencies that are out of balance, like greed, apathy, or wastefulness. This means a trait that is either too weak or too powerful. For example, one person might have developed the virtue of temperance, which means a tendency to enjoy good things in good amounts and for good reasons.[3] Another person who never practiced being temperate could have a tendency to go overboard with sensory pleasures. That person could have developed a vice like gluttony. A third person might not understand that balanced enjoyment is actually good and, having failed to practice balanced enjoyment, now has a vice like stinginess, or a sour suspicion of all good experiences. A good moral character is made up of many well-balanced traits, or virtues, all working in a well-balanced way together.

The Cardinal Virtues

Catholic virtue ethics often focuses on four specific virtues called the cardinal virtues: prudence, temperance, fortitude, and justice. These are the virtues that organize and keep all the other moral virtues balanced. Prudence (or practical wisdom) in particular does many things for a moral character. According to Catholic virtue ethics, prudence helps persons to see how best to do the things they know are right to do, helps them see what virtues need more development, coordinates persons' moral and intellectual work when they are making decisions, and connects all of one's moral virtues to the theological virtues through the virtue of charity.

---

3. Diana Fritz Cates, "The Virtue of Temperance," in *The Ethics of Aquinas*, edited by Stephen Pope (Washington, DC: Georgetown University Press, 2002), 321–39.

The explanation of virtue ethics offered above uses hypothetical people to explain what virtues and vices are. This says something else about virtue ethics: it relies on role models, actual and fictional, to help us direct our moral growth in good directions. Think about it: can you imagine any moral virtue or vice without imagining an example of it, embodied in a person? Role models help anyone who is interested in becoming a better person to identify what virtues they need to practice and what these embodied habits look like.

Virtue theory's best insight is that we (humans) can better ourselves. We shape ourselves through practice. Practice means both participating in large-scale actions (like joining a school's efforts to get solar energy) and doing small actions (like growing a tomato plant for food). According to virtue theories, people become who they want to be by practicing being that way, in big ways and small. Even before governments and organizations offer the programs and structures that help people to live gently on earth, persons and communities can practice participating in the integral ecology vision of Pope Francis's *Laudato si'* (see especially *LS* 180–81).

Laudato si' shows why systemic changes are needed but it also demonstrates that small actions are important. Our actions have the power to change *us* as people. What we do can change our hearts. Practicing ecologically sustainable habits is the way to sustainable and ecologically aware lifestyles. There are many kinds of virtue theories (Catholic, philosophical, Buddhist) and all of them help to demonstrate that persons' actions all have a way of seeping inwardly into their selves and, in turn, shaping future actions.

Littering and Morality

Sometimes my environmental ethics students choose the topic of littering when asked to write a speech about an environmental ethics issue. These students' motivations are good but I used to find this topic choice frustrating for two reasons.

First, while many students dislike seeing garbage in places it does not belong, few students recognize the connections between that garbage and the larger systems that create and store waste. They rarely think to ask where properly-disposed garbage goes after it gets tossed into trash cans. More importantly, what does garbage *do* when it gets to those places? Very few students ask why garbage exists in the first place.

Second, the students' focus on littering frustrated me because I thought such a small act is unimportant compared to larger ecological issues, like climate change, refugees forced to flee areas because of resource conflicts, soil death, water shortages, and premature deaths from air pollution. In the face of such macro-level issues, moral indignation about littering seemed petty. It is like arguing over which brand of automotive paint is least harmful to the environment, while in fact it would be better to stop owning cars altogether. Why, I wondered, do students not take on bigger environmental problems? Eventually I realized that there are good reasons for this.

Students want to speak out against littering because they can see the action of littering and the consequences of this action. Larger environmental problems are not as visible. For many of my students, water shortage is not apparent. "Soil death" does not even make sense, because dirt does not appear to be "alive." Climate instability is still, for some, disputed, too uncertain to be treated as a fact. Refugees flee their homes because of politics or evil regimes, not because they do not like the weather where they live. Air pollution is certainly a problem but that is mostly in other countries, like China, where factory regulations do not exist "like they do here." The bigger problems are invisible or uncertain. Littering is visible, obvious, and it bothers students because it is irresponsible and because it disturbs the natural beauty of their surroundings.

The moral failures of littering are visible in a way my students are accustomed to recognizing. They notice cigarette butts on sidewalks, crushed chip bags in parks, and water bottles abandoned in classrooms. They respect the duty to keep our common areas neat. They easily see that people who fail to clean up after themselves are in the wrong.

They do not as easily see the human duty to avoid creating waste. They understand that visible garbage is a problem but they do not so easily see that *hidden* garbage is a bigger problem. In effect, they have been taught that their responsibility ends when they place their trash in the right receptacles. Garbage cans are everywhere, demonstrating that humans are *expected* to create garbage. The small actions of disposing of garbage trains us well to continue to generate trash with every meal, snack, purchase, and drink and to do so while keeping the waste hidden. Our communal practice of supplying receptacles just for garbage in all kinds of spaces reinforces this. Because we practice hiding this problem, we are now less able to see it.

Our world needs a humanity that recognizes effortlessly that the most important problems of garbage are that it both symptomizes and perpetuates consumerism and its "throwaway culture," that it leeches hazards into water and air even when it is discarded "properly," and that many economies are actually structured around creating garbage. We humans need better recognition. We need to see better. We need to change our beliefs about what deserves our attention. Many ecological ethicists have said this, including Pope Francis (*LS* 209–15).[4] Human beings ought simply and easily to be able to recognize the ways they affect their environments and the ways environments affect them. Many humans can do so. In the industrialized, wealthy, socially privileged culture of the globe's economic North, most people do not practice noticing this, and so as a result they are less able to see.

Laudato si' has made this argument. In this encyclical, Pope Francis notes that effective efforts to resist the "technocratic paradigm" will require "a distinctive way of looking at things, a way of thinking, policies, an educational programme, a lifestyle and a spirituality" (*LS* 111). This way of seeing supports an "integral ecology," which in turn helps us think better. The "integral ecology" is an awareness that can end the "fragmentation of knowledge and the isolation of bits of information" that "backfire into becoming ignorance instead" (*LS* 138). He is saying that, with practice, human beings can learn to see themselves in a way that is attuned to environments, to ecosystems, and to their interrelationality with ecosystems. The conversion to this viewpoint can come through small steps; the moral approach that attends to moral growth on the scale of small steps is virtue ethics. Ecological virtue ethicists in philosophy have argued that this overlooked approach helps people practice the virtues necessary to

---

4. See Steven Bouma-Prediger, *For the Beauty of the Earth: A Christian Vision for Creation Care*, 2nd ed. (Grand Rapids: Baker Academic, 2010) for an excellent theological description of this problem. See Christiana Z. Peppard, *Just Water: Theology, Ethics and the Global Water Crisis* (Maryknoll, NY: Orbis, 2014) for an illustration of how ecological literacy improves theology and ethics.

sustain healthy lives on a healthy planet: ecological awareness and attunement.[5]

The virtue thought driving *Laudato si'* appears in its attention to things that are small. The smaller scales of moral concern are important to this encyclical's argument. The encyclical trusts small practices to be a source of good habits and therefore of moral growth.

Laudato si' on Cultures and Habits

At many points the thinking behind Pope Francis's *Laudato si'* can be understood as an expression of virtue ethics. How do you see virtue ethics at work in the following quotation?

> An awareness of the gravity of today's cultural and ecological crisis must be translated into new habits. Many people know that our current progress and the mere amassing of things and pleasures are not enough to give meaning and joy to the human heart, yet they feel unable to give up what the market sets before them. In those countries which should be making the greatest changes in consumer habits, young people have a new ecological sensitivity and a generous spirit, and some of them are making admirable efforts to protect the environment. At the same time, they have grown up in a milieu of extreme consumerism and affluence which makes it difficult to develop other habits. We are faced with an educational challenge. (*LS* 209)

---

5. See, for example, Louke Van Wensveen, *Dirty Virtues: The Emergence of Ecological Virtue Ethics* (Amherst, NY: Humanity, 1999). Some history and analysis can be read in Robert Hull, "All about EVE: A Report on Environmental Virtue Ethics Today," *Ethics & the Environment* 10, no. 1 (June 13, 2005): 89–110. Works by Phillip Cafaro, Ronald Sandler, Geoffrey Frasz, Thomas Hill Jr., and Bill Shaw are also useful.

On the centrality of the virtues of awareness and attunement see Nancy M. Rourke, "Prudence Gone Wild," *Environmental Ethics: An Interdisciplinary Journal Dedicated to the Philosophical Aspects of Environmental Problems* 33 (Fall 2011), 249–66. For a related point focusing on the virtue of integrity see Nancy M. Rourke, "Good Chaos, Bad Chaos, and the Meaning of Integrity in Both," in *An Unexpected Wilderness: Christianity and the Natural World*, ed. Colleen Carpenter, College Theology Society Annual Volumes 61 (Maryknoll, NY: Orbis, 2016), 79–89.

Here is one example. In a paragraph describing the sort of spirituality that comes with a well-established integral ecology, *Laudato si'* notes that a person's "obsession with consumption" can keep him or her from experiencing deeper enjoyment and peace (*LS* 222). In the same paragraph, the encyclical notes, "A constant flood of new consumer goods can baffle the heart and prevent us from cherishing each thing and each moment." The encyclical adds that noticing the birth of each new moment might be small but it "opens us to much greater horizons of understanding and personal fulfillment." The practice of noticing new moments nurtures growth toward a simplicity, or an ability "to be happy with little." Looking for small changes and even practicing an awareness of littleness itself can heal people's "baffled" hearts.

In Francis's reflection about Saint Thérèse of Lisieux, he praises "simple daily gestures," like smiles given freely and other small actions or practices as a way to "break with the logic of violence, exploitation and selfishness" (*LS* 230). He is not saying that giving a smile to a stranger every day can end violence. As he says elsewhere, "We must not think that these efforts[6] are not going to change the world. They benefit society, often unbeknown to us, for they call forth a goodness which, albeit unseen, inevitably tends to spread" (*LS* 212). This is a virtue-style observation. Small actions grow us in certain directions. Coercive or murderous intention is harder to maintain when one gives a (genuine) smile. The encyclical adds that "such actions can restore our sense of self-esteem; they can enable us to live more fully and to feel that life on earth is worthwhile" (*LS* 212). There is a contagiousness to the goodness of a simple smile. The spirit shared spreads.

Small actions are efficacious in ways that heal people. This kind of healing is humanity's best hope for creating societies that are not centered around consumption. How does this happen? Small actions shape awareness and awareness shapes everything: hopes, motives, fears, tastes, preferences—all that we choose to do and even which decisions we recognize as choices. Renewed awareness is at the heart of the integral ecology Francis seeks.

---

6. The "efforts" referred to here (from the preceding paragraph) might mean the small acts of daily creation care, and they might mean efforts to increase ecological education.

Awareness itself can be a small thing. Awareness is not like the gasp of a shocking revelation. It is not the sudden start of eyes opened from sleep into full wakefulness. It is not the dramatic double-take that follows when one sees something unexpected. Awareness is not melodramatic. It is constant and continual. Its most significant feature is that it is at work exactly when we are not trying to engage in it. It is smaller even than "noticing" but it is powerful because it defines the area within which our "noticing" happens. Awareness is also a significant ecological virtue.[7]

Virtue and Vice in *Laudato si'*

The significance of small actions in *Laudato si'* opens many virtue theory-like observations. More become apparent when one examines the encyclical's explicit references to virtue or vice.[8]

Laudato si' mentions "vices" in paragraph 59 while describing the connection between obliviousness about humanity's ecological impacts and self-destructive tendencies. This paragraph explains connections between willed ignorance, fearfulness, and recklessness. The observation is astute: a tendency to think that the earth's condition is not very serious "serves as a license to carrying on with our present lifestyles and models of production and consumption" (*LS* 59). Persons who are overwhelmed willingly allow self-deception. In other words, a habit of denying what they are actually doing allows people to continue as before. Fears about making changes are pacified. This is an important reminder that vices, like virtues, support and enhance one another. Everything is connected, including people's fears and hopes, human habits, and what humans are willing and able to notice.

Paragraph 224 mentions the imbalances created by failing to practice virtues like sobriety and humility. To heal these imbalances, people now must learn to think of the integrity of all human life. This is a major theme in the document. Here Francis elaborates on the need to "promote and unify all the great values" (*LS* 224). Our

---

7. See the argument in Rourke, "Prudence Gone Wild."

8. The word "character" also appears only once, and there it is used as a synonym for "quality" (*LS* 5).

lack of humility and sobriety, our disintegrating ecosystems, and the fragmented state of our values are all interconnected.

Of course, values are not virtues. It is not exactly clear what is meant by "values" in this paragraph, but the examples named (a "happy sobriety" and a "healthy humility") are actually virtues. There is a close connection between virtues and values—after all, the habits people form both reflect and grow from that which they truly value. Values in practice are the practices that shape virtue.

Paragraph 217 explains that when it comes to Christians, a person's "encounter with Jesus Christ" becomes evident and visible in his or her "relationship with the world around." This marks an "ecological conversion" for believers and it is "essential to a life of virtue." This encounter, which the Church sees as being at the heart of Christian life, relates to morality, but what is described here is not exactly moral deliberation or any kind of an action. It is about *relationship*. Relationship (in contrast with action) is constant and has no clear beginning point. It is not an act one does or even the sum of many acts. Relationship is more like an attitude than an action, or a way of moving among, between, and within. The relationship described here is like what post-colonial Christian ethicist Hannah Ka calls a "graceful sharing of (our) indebted life."[9] Relationship exists even when it is not consciously on one's mind. Relationship nurtures all the virtues. Relationship fed by an "encounter with Christ" works with the theological virtues, connecting a person's moral self with God.[10]

Paragraph 211 discusses "ecological education," one of the recommendations with which the encyclical concludes. Here *Laudato si'* notes that an education that only conveys information and laws cannot bring about the change needed. Virtue alone can support sustainable change. "Only by cultivating sound virtues will people be able to make a selfless ecological commitment" (*LS* 211). Laws and

---

9. Hannah Ka, "Environment," in *Asian American Christian Ethics*, ed. Grace Y. Kao and Ilsup Ahn (Waco, TX: Baylor University Press, 2016), 203–23, at 220.

10. For more on theological virtues see Nancy M. Rourke, "The Environment Within: Virtue Ethics" in *Green Discipleship: Catholic Theological Ethics and the Environment*, ed. Tobias L Winright (Winona, MN: Anselm Academic, 2011), 163–82, or Stephen Pope, *The Ethics of Aquinas* (Washington, DC: Georgetown University Press, 2002).

enforcement will not help if people lack the internal motivation and character to live well with all of life. To help persons cultivate such habits, *Laudato si'* praises the "nobility" of "little daily actions" (*LS* 211). Ecological education is not valuable only because more people understand how life works but also because such an education encourages certain "ways of acting." These "ways" are small actions and *habits* that "reflect a generous and worthy creativity" (*LS* 211). How does this work? Small actions and habits "call forth a goodness which . . . tends to spread" (*LS* 212). Small actions have contagious effects. The goodness spreads without and within. Here is one of the clearest and most powerful examples of how virtue ethics supports an integral ecology: the virtues are fecund. They tend to multiply. One well-balanced "part" of a moral character tends to help balance other areas of that character. Virtues also cultivate new ecological conversions and awareness of the interconnectedness of all creation spreads.

In paragraph 88, the document mentions "ecological virtues." This phrase comes from a 1992 Brazilian bishops' conference statement on the Church and ecology.[11] Here *Laudato si'* notes that "the Spirit of life dwells in every living creature." This is one way in which God "calls us to enter into relationship" with God's own self. Of course, just being alive means being in relationship with all other forms of life because ecological relationality is what allows life to be. *Laudato si'* explains that those who notice that God's presence is in these living beings become motivated "to cultivate the 'ecological virtues'"[12] (*LS* 88). Believers who look for God in creation get better at noticing, looking, searching, and finding God and life itself. They become more aware of ecological interrelationality and that awareness becomes more ecological in nature.

In a fifth mention of virtue, *Laudato si'* says explicitly that people must "cultivate virtues," and that this cultivating work is

---

11. National Conference of the Bishops of Brazil, *A Igreja e a Questão Ecológica* (Sao Paulo, Brazil: Edicoes Paulinas, 1992).

12. Kevin Irwin comments further on this concept, noting that it is a new idea and that it refers as support to the Brazilian bishops conference. See Kevin W. Irwin, *A Commentary on Laudato Si': Examining the Background, Contributions, Implementation and Future of Pope Francis's Encyclical* (Mahwah, NJ: Paulist Press, 2016), note 117 (see chapter 1, part IV, "Recent Episcopal Conference Teaching on the Environment," in the section titled "Episcopal Conference Documents Quoted in *Laudato si'*").

central to Christian life (*LS* 217). The document notes, "Living our vocation to be protectors of God's handiwork is essential to a life of virtue; it is not an optional or a secondary aspect of our Christian experience" (*LS* 217). Ecological virtue development characterizes the life of faith. The encyclical encourages us to make a habit of "assessing the impact of our every action and personal decision on the world around us" (*LS* 208). This habit of noticing is the virtue of attentiveness or awareness; it is central to ecological virtue ethics.[13]

Attitudes and Modeling

There is a lot to learn from mention of virtues in *Laudato si'*, but the encyclical nods to virtue theory in many other ways as well. Two examples will be considered here: reflections on "attitude" and the presentation of Jesus as an ecological role model.

Laudato si' frequently lifts up "attitudes" like honesty, responsibility, sobriety, humility, innocence, self-control, willingness to learn, and gratitude. In Christian ethics, these are often identified as virtues. The encyclical gives no technical definition of "attitude" but nontechnical definitions seem suitable.[14] An attitude is a trait, disposition, behavior style, or inclination. It is somewhat imperceptible as it influences one's way of interpreting the world. On the other hand, it is quite visible in the responses one gives to what one encounters. Attitude appears in the "gut reaction," the first assumption, the default response prior to further deliberation. It is a tendency that may—or may not—be checked or overridden by further thought or a second look. Even when it is not acted upon, attitude is still present as a baseline. Attitudes are habitual, just

---

13. Attunement is a necessary ecological virtue; the virtue formed after attentiveness develops. See Rourke, "Prudence Gone Wild."

14. According to online dictionaries, "attitude" refers to a "manner, disposition, feeling, position," or a "position or posture of the body" ("attitude," *Random House Dictionary*, Random House, Dictionary.com, *http://dictionary.reference.com/browse /attitude*). It is also "the way a person views something or tends to behave towards it, often in an evaluative way" ("attitude," *Collins English Dictionary—Complete & Unabridged 2012 Digital Edition*, HarperCollins, Dictionary.com, *http://dictionary .reference.com/browse/attitude*).

like virtues. Pope Francis says people must cultivate an attitude that "approaches life with serene attentiveness" (*LS* 226). Attentiveness is the virtue of being "fully present" and aware. Attitude may not be a virtue, exactly, but it does seem to be an essential character trait.

As noted earlier, virtue ethics uses role models. *Laudato si'* also uses this method. For example, *Laudato si'* presents Jesus' gaze as a model of "attentiveness to the beauty of the world" (*LS* 97).[15] The Gospels indicate that Jesus Christ noticed his environment habitually. It appears in his stories and as a focus of his attentions. An overtly virtue ethics document might speak to how Jesus' virtue of attentiveness was shaped—and *Laudato si'* does too, imagining that Jesus' vocational practice of carpentry helped him develop this awareness (*LS* 98). We can thus conclude that work with one's hands, cooperation with materials in order to make something new with them, is a practice that shapes ecologically important virtues. Collaboration with one's environment requires and enhances ecological awareness.

Conclusion

Laudato si' models virtue ethics. It does not preach it, but it does presume it. The encyclical does not say that virtue ethics will help our ecological problems and it never lists the virtues one must cultivate. It does assume virtue theory's understanding of morality and it uses that to help change human attitude and character (*LS* 107).

Attitudes and other character traits like virtues are the narrow, deep, and quiet streams that feed human action and lifestyles. They come from a less carefully monitored source than the intention or the will, which are the traditional foci of much of Catholic ethics. But as *Laudato si'* shows, we ride the surge of these unwatched tributaries and we *always* carry with us the quality of their water. The things we do when we are not acting deliberately are important

---

15. Notice this recurrence of attentiveness. For more on the topic of Jesus and virtue ethics, see Daniel Harrington and James Keenan, *Jesus and Virtue Ethics: Building Bridges Between New Testament Studies and Moral Theology* (Lanham, MD: Sheed & Ward, 2002).

because they have consequences[16] and because, through them, we practice being a certain kind of people. This is the very soul of virtue thought. It is also exactly what *Laudato si'* means when it speaks of an integral ecology.

Review Questions

1. What is virtue ethics' main focus and what does it say about morality?
2. Is littering a significant moral problem? Explain your answer.
3. Where does *Laudato si'* mention virtue or virtues and what does it say about them?

In-Depth Questions

1. Do you agree with virtue ethics' way of thinking about morality? Explain one way in which it seems right and one way in which it seems to miss the mark.
2. What does it mean to "notice a new moment"?
3. What virtues seem to you to be important for environmental sustainability?
4. What exactly is an "integral ecology" and how is it related to virtue ethics?

Suggestions for Further Study

Boff, Leonardo. *Cry of the Earth, Cry of the Poor.* Maryknoll, NY: Orbis, 1997.

---

16. Habitual and routine actions often have a greater ecological impact than the kinds of actions people carry out after careful deliberation. For example, people may spend several minutes and research carefully while choosing an herbicide for their lawn. But all available herbicides pollute water runoff. This environmental damage is habitually inflicted simply for the purpose of complying with a morally dubious aesthetic—a purpose that does not merit the damage caused. See David Cloutier, *Walking God's Earth: The Environment and Catholic Faith* (Collegeville, MN: Liturgical Press, 2014) and Rachel Carson, *Silent Spring* (Boston: Houghton Mifflin, 1962).

Bouma-Prediger, Steven. *For the Beauty of the Earth: A Christian Vision for Creation Care.* 2nd ed. Grand Rapids: Baker Academic, 2010.

Keenan, James. *Virtues for Ordinary Christians.* Lanham, MD: Rowman & Littlefield, 1996.

Rourke, Nancy M. "A Catholic Virtues Ecology." In *Just Sustainability: Ecology, Technology, and Resource Extraction*, edited by Christiana Z. Peppard and Andrea Vicini, 194–204. Maryknoll, NY: Orbis, 2015.

Van Wensveen, Louke. *Dirty Virtues: The Emergence of Ecological Virtue Ethics.* Amherst, NY: Humanity, 1999.

10

Personal Conversion and Civic Love: Individual and Social Change in *Laudato si'*

DAVID CLOUTIER

I recently moved in order to take a new job. My previous job was at a rural college with little housing in the immediate vicinity, and so I had a twenty-mile each-way commute from the nearest city. My new job is at an urban university, well served by public transportation. I rented an apartment on direct bus and rail routes to work. I also downsized, going from a one-thousand-two-hundred square-foot row house to a five-hundred-square-foot apartment. The jobs were close enough that I, like many, could have made the commute into the city, but that would have been about a forty-five-mile trip each way. Or I could have ridden a commuter train, which would have entailed a two to three mile drive to the station, but the train only runs a few times each day and takes more than ninety minutes to reach the city.

   This story illustrates the complex relationship of personal choices and social structures involved in making the ecologically responsible choices for which Pope Francis calls in *Laudato si'*.[1] Most people of good will do not want to wreck the earth's environment. Nevertheless, the pope is right that we face a "spiral of self-destruction which currently engulfs us" (*LS* 163). It is always tempting to try to identify dark villains who can be held responsible for the crisis

---

1. Pope Francis, *Laudato si': On Care for Our Common Home*, June 18, 2015, *http://w2.vatican.va/content/francesco/en/encyclicals/documents/papa-francesco_20150524_enciclica-laudato-si.html*.

lurking behind the scenes. But in fact there is no Darth Vader in the environmental tale. Instead, mostly without intending to do so, human beings have built up ways of living and trading that put unsustainable pressures on the planet. Because of this, the pope is right to say at the start of his final chapter, "Many things have to change course, but it is we human beings above all who need to change" (*LS* 202).

This essay introduces some of the key relationships between the personal and the structural that are most important in *Laudato si'*. As the pope says repeatedly, "Everything is connected" (*LS* 91, 117). This is both the most daunting and the most hopeful aspect of the environmental problem. On the one hand, because everything is connected, there is no magic bullet solution. But on the other hand, the interconnectedness of creation affords endless ways to live more ecologically-sensitive lives that enable believers to better love God, self, and neighbor (cf. *LS* 66).

Individual Actions, Social Structures

How do individual actions and social structures relate to one another? More than ever in human history, individual daily lives now depend upon ongoing social structures. For basic everyday food and transportation, people often rely on far-flung and complex networks of systems and organizations that produce, store, transport, and sell the needed resources and discard the waste. At the same time, these large structures are sustained by smaller ones, such as a particular store or a local police department. Finally, these "social structures" both enable and are enabled by individual choices: the decision to buy a product supports the company and industry that makes it, while the sales taxes fund public services.

It is tempting to make overly-tidy distinctions—over-simplifications—in understanding these systems, putting personal choices in one category and social structures in another. In theological terms, one distinguishes between acts of individual charity that protect human life and dignity, especially the human life and dignity of the poor (for example, bringing food items to a local pantry or cooking a meal at a soup kitchen) from social justice, which seeks to reform systems that affect the life and dignity of persons and communities (for example, advocating for unemployment and medical insurance for those who lose their jobs).[2] Sometimes, these levels of action—micro and macro—can even be pitted against one another. But this ignores the fact that charity and justice need each other: many charity organizations, like Catholic Charities, depend on government grants while the distribution of government benefits often depends on these local charity organizations that are in better contact with those in need.

Loaves and Fishes in a Complicated World

Why does the world have to be so complicated? When I think about the personal and social changes needed to care for the earth, I, like many others, can feel overwhelmed. At moments like that, I always think of the biblical story where Jesus miraculously feeds thousands of people. But before he does, someone steps forward and volunteers their five loaves and two fishes. I always wonder, "What is he thinking? He knows that isn't enough to feed everyone!" But it is from that meagre beginning that Jesus is able to do his work. The world is complicated, but the biblical message challenges people to bring their loaves and fishes.

On the issue of the environment, the pope is clear in his encyclical: people need both, and neither is sufficient on its own. He says, "Enforceable international agreements are urgently needed" (*LS* 173), and laments "weak international political responses" (*LS* 54). Concurrently, however, the pope notes the importance of little things like "avoiding the use of plastic and paper" or "using public transport and carpooling" (*LS* 211). He says, "We must not think that these efforts are not going to change the world. They

2. For pastoral resources on the relationship between and necessity of both charity and justice, see U.S. Conference of Catholic Bishops, "Two Feet of Love in Action," 2017, *http://www.usccb.org/beliefs-and-teachings/what-we-believe/catholic -social-teaching/two-feet-of-love-in-action.cfm*.

benefit society, often unbeknown to us, for they call forth a goodness which, albeit unseen, inevitably tends to spread"—possibly to
other levels of society (*LS* 212). Individuals must make different
choices about things that affect all of creation, and structures must
be put in place so people can change course together. You can't have
one without the other.

Waste and Technocracy[3]

Two key areas of the environmental crisis illustrate why each
approach needs the other: waste and technocracy. The pope has powerful things to say about both. First, most environmental issues are
about waste. The pope has constantly criticized the "throwaway culture," the "culture of waste," in which people have "not developed the
capacity to absorb and reuse waste and by-products" through a "circular model of production" that would capture waste and reuse it (*LS*
22). Instead, the current economy assumes people can extract unlimited resources from nature, and then throw them "away" when they
are "finished." Instead of a circular model, in which waste is mini-
mized, this model maximizes "through-put"—the more material we
mine, manufacture, and throw away, the bigger the economy grows.

Systems encourage waste, and so do individual choices. In my
recent move, I discovered that, like most Americans, I have way too
much stuff. What should I do with it all? I tried to "get rid of it," but
what exactly does that mean? Almost none of us have to deal directly
with all the waste we produce. I tried to follow the "reduce, reuse,
recycle" mantra. I especially tried to give away as much as I could,
but that was a job in itself. It was very tempting to put it all in the
trash, which means someone else takes it away and . . . well, who
knows? Maybe it gets exported to a landfill site abroad or travels as
far as the Great Pacific Garbage Patch—the patch of garbage that is
floating in the Pacific Ocean, currently estimated to be hundreds of
thousands of square miles in size.

---

3. For details on specific environmental issues mentioned in these sections, see
David Cloutier, *Walking God's Earth* (Collegeville, MN: Liturgical Press, 2014), and
Steven Bouma-Prediger, *For the Beauty of the Earth* (Grand Rapids, MI: Baker Aca-
demic, 2010).

When dealing with waste at both the macro and micro levels, it is important to consider that a large amount of damage caused by waste is generated "away" from the activities that produce it. Two major environmental crises of the past half-century were the death of forests in the eastern United States due to acid rain and the hole in the ozone layer that grew over the Antarctic. In each case, the culprit was waste from a substantial distance away. The acid rain was mostly caused by sulfur emitted by coal-burning power plants in the Midwest, whose emissions were carried into the atmosphere and combined with rain clouds. The ozone hole was caused by a class of aerosols and refrigerants that were being used by individuals and industries nowhere near the Antarctic.

In addition to highlighting how the effects of waste often occur far away from waste production, these stories also illustrate how micro and macro actions must combine to solve problems. Acid rain and the ozone hole are diminishing rapidly, due in large part to government regulation. Most likely the problem could not have been tackled successfully simply by encouraging people to switch out individual aerosol cans or air conditioners for new, "greener" models. Regulations were also needed to force power plants and manufacturers to develop other ways of delivering their products. Importantly, all competing businesses had to make the same investments. When the problem concerns the common good, laws must level the playing field, or else each company will resist being the first to pay the price to make the change.

For the most prominent problems mentioned in *Laudato si'*, the pope states clearly that both/and, macro/micro arrangements are necessary. Global warming is not a localized problem; in fact, the people affected most are likely to be populations that contributed little to the increase in greenhouse gases. It resembles the aforementioned problems in another way, too: no one is actually paying for their use of the atmosphere as a place to dump wastes. The chief problem today with the burning of carbon is that the waste products (carbon dioxide and methane) are being "dumped" into the atmosphere for free, without any economic disincentive. Hence the importance, for most economists, of a carbon tax—which really should be called a "waste tax," since it is merely a matter of making people take responsibility for the waste they produce. Not only would such a policy put a price on carbon, but it could provide revenue that could reduce other tax burdens that fall especially hard on the poor.

So why have international policy responses to ecological harm been so weak, filled with what the pope derides as "superficial rhetoric" and "perfunctory expressions of concern" (*LS* 54)? Part of the problem, Pope Francis says, is that "there are too many special interests, and economic interests" that "end up trumping the common good and manipulating information so that their own plans will not be affected" (*LS* 54). But these "special interests," such as energy companies, also serve peoples' individual wasteful choices. Thus there is no feasible way to address the problems of the "throwaway culture," and especially of using the atmosphere as an unlimited dumping space, without changing people's lifestyles. As the pope writes, "People may well have a growing ecological sensitivity, but it has not succeeded in changing their harmful habits of consumption which, rather than decreasing, appear to be growing all the more" (*LS* 55). The general consensus of the world scientific community is that the world must achieve an 80 percent reduction in carbon emissions within a couple of decades in order to avoid runaway, irreversible climate change. Certainly some of this reduction can be had by switching to renewable energy. But one cannot get around the fact that individuals will have to drastically cut their energy consumption, aided by smart sociopolitical changes.

In order to help people make difficult changes to their individual lifestyles, the pope develops a spirituality centered on the virtues—that is, good habits—of sobriety and humility. Sobriety, for him, is not about alcohol; rather, it is "a capacity to be happy with little," "a way of living life to the full" (*LS* 222–23). In contrast to those who live "dipping here and there, always on the lookout for what they do not have," this virtue enables us "to appreciate each person and each thing, learning familiarity with the simplest things and how to enjoy them" (*LS* 223). He sums this up in a pithy phrase that might be a personal motto: "Even living on little, they can live a lot" (*LS* 223). The habit of living a life characterized by *sobrietas* can be aided by legislation that encourages or prohibits certain actions, but ultimately it has to come from a conversion of heart and mind. So too with humility. In cultivating humility, the pope asks people to let go of "the possibility of limitless mastery over everything . . . when we exclude God from our lives or replace him with our own ego" (*LS* 223). Laws can help this, too, but they certainly cannot force it to happen.

As mentioned earlier, a second problem that requires attention to both individual and structural questions has to do with what the pope calls the "technocratic paradigm," naming it "the human origins of the ecological crisis" (*LS* 101). This might sound like a blanket criticism of technology, but the pope's argument is subtler than that. Technology is not bad; in fact, it is very good. He acknowledges the many ways it has benefitted humanity and, at one point, he quips, "Nobody is suggesting a return to the Stone Age" (*LS* 102, 114). That is why the pope is very careful to name the problem "the technocratic paradigm," which is a particular way of using technology in relation to natural resources.

Francis describes it as a new attitude toward nature itself, according to which we seek "to extract everything possible from [creation] while frequently ignoring or forgetting the reality in front of us" (*LS* 106).

Technological power becomes an end in itself, and people are guided not by genuine human ends or their creaturely limits but by an unadulterated desire to dominate creation. Just like Adam and Eve, whose disobedience of God was driven by the lustful desire to "be like God" (Gen. 3:5, NRSV), people want to be like God and exercise absolute control over creation. The pope points out that this is a distortion of the biblical mandate for humans to exercise "dominion" on behalf of the loving Creator (Gen. 1:26–28). In response, Francis writes that "we are not God" and must recognize that "each creature has its own purpose" and we must "discover in each thing a teaching which God wishes to hand on to us" (*LS* 67, 84–85).

Consider the example of a cow. What is a cow's nature, as created by God? Imagine the contented cow, domesticated yet respected as a creature with intrinsic goodness. My college town had as its slogan, "Cows, Colleges, and Contentment." But did the milk, cheese, or beef you most recently enjoyed come from a contented cow? Unless you paid a premium, it probably did not. Instead, it likely came from a poor creature in an all-controlling, profit-maximizing CAFO (Concentrated Animal Feed Operation) where cows are packed together in mud (and poop), filled with antibiotics to stop the inevitable sickness of the conditions, and force-fed an unnatural diet of corn. That is not even to mention the horror of most modern slaughterhouses. This cannot be what it means to allow a cow to praise God by existing as a cow.

The point here is not that people must all necessarily become vegans. Indeed, that claim would completely miss the point and fall into the false choice of either "using" nature destructively or "leaving it alone." Instead, the pope—faithful to the biblical call that humans should "cultivate and care for" creation (cf. Gen. 2:15)—is pointing to two different ways of using nature: one respects nature's integrity, especially as a true gift from God; the other views it instrumentally, as raw material to be controlled without limit. These two different ways of relating to non-human creation match perfectly with two importantly different ways of relating to other people: people can be treated with respect, or as material resources to be used up and discarded. Both are "using," in the sense that good human relationships involve mutual benefit. But, hopefully, the difference between a romantic partner who gains benefits from a relationship and a partner who is "using" someone for his or her own benefit is evident.

Unsurprisingly, the technocratic paradigm involves both structures and individual choices. This is true in the sense that technological systems of domination both enable and are enabled by individuals' choices. But there is also a subtler issue. The pope speaks about the "rapidification" of the society as a big problem, which "contrasts with the naturally slow pace of biological evolution" (*LS* 18). Change is a part of life, the pope acknowledges, but the pace of change is the question. Everything in life seems to move along faster and faster. Ironically, there are more time-saving conveniences than ever, and yet people work more hours and feel more time-stressed. Why is that?

Slowing down might seem to be the answer, but it is much easier to say that than to do. I tried for a time in the early 2000s (prior to smartphones) to avoid having Internet at home, so that email would only intrude at certain times. But I gave it up as more and more tasks in life came to depend on an Internet connection and quicker responses to emails became expected. This example shows that technological adoption is not just a matter of individual choice but of social structure.

The pope makes a further point about social structures: the technocratic paradigm is pushed along by the interests of those who seek to profit from it. As he says, "We have to accept that technological products are not neutral, for they create a framework which ends up conditioning lifestyles and shaping social possibilities *along the lines dictated by the interests of certain powerful groups*" (*LS* 107; italics added). No American writer has articulated this problem more clearly than Kentucky farmer Wendell Berry, who for decades has pointed out that the industrialization of agriculture and the ruination of rural places is directed by an economic system that favors big, technologically intensive agricultural methods over smaller, simpler techniques. As he writes in one essay, land is often "used solely according to the standards dictated by the financial system and not at all according to the standards dictated by the nature of the place."[4]

Ultimately, one cannot simply blame some evil companies. As Berry writes, "The root of the problem is always to be found in private life," for "there are not enough rich and powerful people to consume the whole world; for that, the rich and powerful need the help of countless ordinary people."[5] Hence, while Berry criticizes the activity of profit-driven corporations, he recognizes that those corporations are ultimately serving public demand—our demand. This is also exactly what Pope Francis says. Although he recognizes the need for renewable energy policies (*LS* 26), he is clear about the lifestyle changes needed: those in wealthy countries must "significantly limit their consumption of non-renewable energy" and break the habits of ecologically harmful consumerism (*LS* 52, 209). Here it is important to emphasize that Francis is reiterating traditional Catholic teaching. As the *Catechism of the Catholic Church* explains, "'Structures of sin' are the expression and effect of personal sins" (1869).[6]

---

4. Wendell Berry, "Conservation Is Good Work," in *Sex, Economy, Freedom and Community: Eight Essays* (New York: Pantheon, 1993), 27–43, at 28.

5. Ibid., 32.

6. *Catechism of the Catholic Church*, 2003, Libreria Editrice Vaticana, *http://www .vatican.va/archive/ccc_css/archive/catechism/p3s1c1a8.htm*. See also *Compendium of the Social Doctrine of the Church*, 2004, Libreria Editrice Vaticana, *http://www.vatican .va/roman_curia/pontifical_councils/justpeace/documents/rc_pc_justpeace_doc_20060526 _compendio-dott-soc_en.html*, 117–119.

Possible Responses

What are people called to do in the face of waste and technocracy? The response, of course, must be both structural and personal. It must combine elements of what Pope Francis calls "civic and political love" (*LS* 228) with the need for personal "ecological conversion" (*LS* 216). People's hearts must change, but so must their structures. At the structural level, people need to advocate for smart policies that make it, as Catholic thinker Peter Maurin put it, "easier to be good."

As mentioned, for example, one could advocate for a national carbon tax that would make carbon-intensive products and practices more expensive while directing the revenue to many pressing social needs, particularly assisting the poor. Additionally, one could urge lawmakers to shift subsidies from fossil fuels to renewable energy technologies so consumers are forced to pay the full economic price of climate-changing fuels and give a cost break on fuels that do not change the climate. Like most technologies, advanced renewable energy initially costs more, but in the long run, becomes cheaper and pays for itself. A subsidy makes it easier to bear the higher initial cost, especially for the poor. Either or both of these policy changes would make it easier for consumers and companies to select ecologically sustainable energy technologies. These examples illustrate that good laws can help form good habits.[7]

At the personal level, simple awareness should be the first step. The pope talks eloquently about the need for education in "ecological citizenship" (*LS* 211), which includes "a critique of the myths of a modernity grounded in a utilitarian mindset (individualism, unlimited progress, competition, consumerism, the unregulated market)" and "seeks . . . to restore the various levels of ecological equilibrium" (*LS* 210). Studies consistently reveal that some kind of environmental literacy, that is, the ability to recognize and understand how ecological systems work and are shaped, is one of the best predictors of environmental action.

---

7. That is, virtues. Cf. St. Thomas Aquinas, *Summa theologiae*, I–II, q.92, a.1. For an extended treatment of this topic, see Cathleen Kaveny, *Law's Virtues: Fostering Autonomy and Solidarity in American Society* (Washington, DC: Georgetown University Press, 2012), 28–33.

Awareness of waste and of technocratic domination, even far away from immediate daily life, can lead people to look at the key patterns of their lives very differently. But it is not enough to *feel* something when hearing about endangered species or destroyed oceans; one must *do* something. The pope insists such education cannot be "limited to providing information," but must go on "to instill good habits" so that people are "personally transformed to respond" (*LS* 211). In particular, there are four key lifestyle patterns to consider: how one gets energy (food and fuel), where one lives, how one works, and finally how one thinks about one's investments.[8] Paying attention to the planetary consequences of these daily patterns personally and in communities can lead to big changes.

Conclusion

The challenge of caring for our common home through personal conversion and civic love can seem overwhelming. But the good news is that there are many places to start, many connections to make (or re-make). Start walking or biking or carpooling. Find a local farmers' market or food cooperative. Learn to delight deeply in time at a local park, enjoying the gifts of creation. Buy one less thing every day—find the opportunity to say, "No." These small steps start to change the tenor of society, and people come to find others who are also trying to live differently and with whom they can engage in collective grassroots organizing and political advocacy. As they do, the energy builds for larger agreements around the world. Francis insists that people must have hope. At one point, he refers to Noah, and explains that the story means that "all it takes is one good person to restore hope!" (*LS* 71). With God's help, the promise of a creation that is a universal communion can be restored. But humanity must take the initiative, both individually and together.

---

8. David Cloutier, *Walking God's Earth* (Collegeville, MN: Liturgical Press, 2014).

Review Questions

1. According to the author, what is the relationship between personal choices and social structures?

2. Pope Francis explains two environmental problems that require both individual and structural change. What are they, and why are they so problematic in today's world?

3. What does Pope Francis mean by the "throwaway culture" and the "culture of waste"?

4. What are the virtues of sobriety and humility, and how does Pope Francis think they can help individuals better care for creation?

5. What are some of the most important personal responses suggested in this chapter? What are the key changes in larger social structures?

In-Depth Questions

1. In describing the way people deal with waste and technology, the pope is looking at daily life. Do you see these problems appearing in your own life? If so, what steps could you take individually and with others in your community to make a difference—even a small difference—regarding waste and technology?

2. Catholic social teaching insists on a "preferential option for the poor," and Pope Francis shows this in action. Yet, in U.S. society, the poor are often stuck in unsustainable patterns of action and structure and, worse, they cannot afford the sometimes-expensive solutions to ecological problems sold to the rich. What specific things might be done in the United States to help the poor fully participate in a more sustainable society?

3. Pope Francis emphasizes the importance of public policies in response to ecological challenges. He also laments that in politics, "there are too many special interests, and economic interests easily end up trumping the common good and manipulating information so that their own plans will not be affected" (*LS* 54). How might you—individually and with

others—advocate for better environmental policies and challenge the political influence of special interests?

4. What might things look like in your life and in society if technology was used as Pope Francis would like it to be used? What would need to change in order to realize this vision of technology?

5. The chapter identifies "four key lifestyle patterns to consider: how one gets energy (food and fuel), where one lives, how one works, and finally how one thinks about one's investments." What is one action you could take today in each area that would better care for creation?

Suggestions for Further Study

Ahern, Kevin. *Structures of Grace: Catholic Organizations Serving the Global Common Good.* Maryknoll, NY: Orbis, 2015.

Cloutier, David. *The Vice of Luxury: Economic Excess in a Consumer Age.* Washington, DC: Georgetown University Press, 2015.

———. *Walking God's Earth: The Environment and Catholic Faith.* Collegeville, MN: Liturgical Press, 2014.

DiLeo, Daniel R. "Consumption and Lifestyle Choices." In *The Theological and Ecological Vision of Laudato Si': Everything Is Connected,* edited by Vincent J. Miller, 217–234. London: T&T Clark/Bloomsbury, 2017.

PART 5

Catholic
Social Ethics

CHAPTER 11

Laudato si' and the Development of Catholic Social Teaching

DANIEL P. SCHEID

Laudato si': On Care for Our Common Home[1] builds on and extends the social teaching of the Catholic Church on ecology in significant and vital ways. In the introduction, Pope Francis definitively joins the encyclical to the Church's social teaching (*LS* 15) and demonstrates how the moral vision of *Laudato si'* continues in the tradition of his predecessors, including Pope Paul VI, Pope John Paul II, and Pope Benedict XVI (*LS* 3–7). While in continuity with the Church's tradition, *Laudato si'* also offers a fresh interpretation of a Catholic

Catholic Social Teaching

Catholic social teaching represents the Church's wisdom about how to build a just society amid the challenges of modern life. It addresses a broad array of issues, such as war, racism, poverty, and immigration. While the principles of Catholic social teaching are rooted in the Gospel and in a Christian moral vision, they are also grounded in reason and so can be useful in a pluralistic society for dialoguing across religious and cultural divides. They can help all who share in the goal of making our world more just, peaceful, and sustainable.

---

1. Pope Francis, *Laudato si': On Care for Our Common Home*, July 18, 2015, *http://w2.vatican.va/content/francesco/en/encyclicals/documents/papa-francesco_20150524_enciclica-laudato-si.html*.

theology of creation ("The Gospel of Creation") and draws on and reshapes ethical principles in order to address the contemporary ecological crisis.

This chapter will review certain principles of Catholic social teaching that Pope Francis employs in *Laudato si'*: the common good, solidarity, and the preferential option for the poor. Additionally, and in the context of the cosmological vision of *Laudato si'* and its framework of integral ecology, the chapter will examine how Pope Francis employs the interpretive power of these principles in a way that develops and deepens their scope.

The Common Good

The principle of the common good is "inseparable" from Pope Francis's understanding of integral ecology, because the common good is "a central and unifying principle of social ethics" (*LS* 156). The classic definition of the common good in Catholic social teaching comes from the Vatican II document *Gaudium et spes*, which describes it as "the sum of those conditions of social life which allow social groups and their individual members relatively thorough and ready access to their own fulfillment."[2]

Cultivation of the Common Good in *Laudato si'*

According to Pope Francis's ecological vision in *Laudato si'*, the ecological common good has three different dimensions. First, it represents the sum of concrete biological goods that humans and other creatures need to survive, such as clean air, water, and food, or adequate habitat space and appropriate shelter. Second, the common good is much more than the aggregate of these individual goods. For example, Francis says, "The climate is a common good, belonging to all and meant for all" (*LS* 23). The earth only has one climate, though it may affect different geographical areas in profoundly different ways. So when the earth's climate and its healthy functioning

---

2. Second Vatican Council, *Gaudium et spes*, December 7, 1965, 26, *http://www .vatican.va/archive/hist_councils/ii_vatican_council/documents/vat-ii_cons_19651207 _gaudium-et-spes_en.html*. Pope Francis cites this passage in *LS* 156.

are damaged, for example through excessive methane and carbon dioxide emitted by human activities, it has repercussions for everyone, no matter who generated the pollution. Since "everything is interconnected" in creation (*LS* 138), common goods are, by definition, held in common by all humanity. Thus climate policies—and this would also apply to other planetary goods like freshwater, oceans, and forests—must prioritize the one human family above other special financial and national interests (*LS* 54). Catholic social teaching has long stressed the "universal destination of goods," or the principle that "the goods of creation are destined for the whole human race."[3] The ecological common good thus emphasizes that the goods of creation are interrelated, such that they must be protected by all and for all.

Third, the theme of interconnectedness stretches the ecological common good to new dimensions. The human common good, for example, includes the personal dimensions of relationship, affection, and even love that binds societies together. Since humans are social in nature, the "sum total of social conditions" indicates that social bonds are inextricable from human flourishing. The conditions that make personal happiness possible do not simply exist in society, but they come through society and are made possible by society. The good of human persons includes their relationships; the good "exists 'between' persons in the relations that make them who they are."[4] An individual's health and wellbeing—bodily, emotionally, financially, socially—depends on the community in which the person lives.

In a similar way, various Catholic theologians have proposed broader visions of the common good, such as the planetary or cosmic common good.[5] Pope Francis points out that humans "are part of nature, included in it and thus in constant interaction with it" (*LS*

---

3. *Catechism of the Catholic Church*, 1993, Libreria Editrice Vaticana, 2402, *http://www.vatican.va/archive/ccc_css/archive/catechism/p3s2c2a7.htm.*

4. David Hollenbach, "The Common Good Revisited," *Theological Studies* 50 (March 1989): 86.

5. See for example Daniel P. Scheid, *The Cosmic Common Good: Religious Grounds for Ecological Ethics* (New York: Oxford University Press, 2016); Jame Schaefer, "Solidarity, Subsidiarity, and Preference for the Poor: Extending Catholic Social Teaching in Response to the Climate Crisis," in *Confronting the Climate Crisis: Catholic Theological Perspectives*, ed. Jame Schaefer (Milwaukee: Marquette University Press, 2012), 389–425; John Hart, *Sacramental Commons: Christian Ecological Ethics* (Lanham, MD: Rowman & Littlefield, 2006).

139). As such, the flourishing and well-being of living creatures, species, ecosystems, and air, water, and the earth itself are integral parts of human flourishing. Nonhuman creatures are important instrumentally, for human use and well-being, but also intrinsically—for themselves—because they belong to the goodness of creation (see Genesis 1).

Human dignity, then, is part of a larger category of creaturely dignity. This does not deny the uniqueness of humans, or that human dignity may represent an elevated form of creaturely dignity (*LS* 119). But creaturely dignity does assert that the relationships humans have to non-humans should include some form of affection or love. The ecological and planetary common good are essential for human flourishing, and likewise, human beings ought to commit themselves to cultivating the good of the planetary community to which they belong. In short, the cosmic common good aims for the integrity, sustainability, and well-being of the entirety of the planet. Only this vision of the common good adequately corresponds to an integral ecology and to an understanding of creation as "the order of love" (*LS* 77). Francis offers a real development of Catholic social teaching here, emphasizing the common good and human dignity in a broader framework of the "universal communion" of creation that "unites us in fond affection with brother sun, sister moon . . . and mother earth" (*LS* 92).

The common good includes other dimensions often overlooked in questions of ecological ethics. Pope Francis insists that the common good includes future generations. When we consider future generations, we see the earth differently: not as a possession to exploit, but as a gift that we are called to share with others. Hence, "intergenerational solidarity is not optional, but rather a basic question of justice, since the world we have received also belongs to those who will follow us" (*LS* 159). We could argue, again in light of Francis's cosmological vision and the theme of interconnectedness, that we owe future generations not just a viable earth, but a real community of creation in which all persons are accompanied on their life's journey by sisters and brothers of other species.

Intriguingly, when discussing justice for future generations, Francis raises the importance of ultimate questions about the meaning of social and economic goals. "What is the purpose of our life in this world? Why are we here? What is the goal of our work and all our efforts? What need does the earth have of us? It is no longer enough, then, simply to state that we should be concerned for future generations. We need to see that what is at stake is our own dignity" (*LS* 160). Francis seems to suggest that our global political and economic systems have lost sight of what is of utmost significance and meaning for the human person, and indeed that this shortsightedness has contributed to the ecological crisis. Francis insists on reintroducing the deeper questions of the human heart as part of the Church's role in fostering the common good: reminding the world of the ultimate priority of the common good, of the good of all members of God's creation, and that in pursuing this common good, we are fulfilling our own dignity.

Solidarity

The principle of the common good leads directly to the virtue of "solidarity and a preferential option for the poorest of our brothers and sisters" (*LS* 158). In Catholic teaching, solidarity signifies the expression of love and care for others, grounded in the reality of the one human family, and in the growing awareness of our increasing global interdependence. Pope John Paul II famously describes solidarity when he insists that it is "not a feeling of vague compassion or shallow distress at the misfortunes of so many people, both near and far. On the contrary, it is a firm and persevering determination to commit oneself to the common good; that is to say to the good of all and of each individual, because we are all really responsible for all."[6]

Cultivation of Solidarity in *Laudato si'*

Francis observes that the world continues to become more interdependent and injects an ecological dimension into this insight. He calls for a "new and universal solidarity," urging humans to use their talents to get involved in building a sustainable world and "redress the damage caused by human abuse of God's creation'" (*LS*

---

6. Pope John Paul II, *Sollicitudo rei socialis*, December 30, 1987, 38, *http:// w2.vatican.va/content/john-paul-ii/en/encyclicals/documents/hf_jp-ii_enc_30121987 _sollicitudo-rei-socialis.html.*

14). Rather than an ethical dictate or a divine command, solidarity, as Francis describes it, is the natural human response to witnessing suffering: "Solidarity and care cannot but well up within us, since we were made for love" (*LS* 58). If "creation is of the order of love" (*LS* 77), as an integral ecology suggests, then when humans become attuned to that reality the virtue of solidarity might arise and grow naturally, since that is what we were made for.

Yet solidarity is more than feelings of sadness or feelings of care; as a virtue—that is, a good habit—solidarity disposes people to act for the common good of all members of the community to which one belongs. For example, after concluding his overview of various aspects of earth's ecological crisis, or of "what is happening to our common home," Francis reminds us that the point of all this data is not "to satisfy curiosity, but rather to become painfully aware, to dare to turn what is happening to the world into our own personal suffering and thus to discover what each of us can do about it" (*LS* 19). The virtue of solidarity orients each person toward acting in the world, both in private daily acts and through broader social movements that advance the common good, which in this case is the good of the entire planet.

Fittingly, Pope Francis encourages solidarity between developed and developing nations, and he cites as an example the need for poor countries "to eliminate extreme poverty and to promote the social development of their people." Given the risks of climate change, poorer nations can and should work to develop their economies, but must do so using less energy-intensive methods. Solidarity thus calls richer nations to assist developing nations—not only for their own benefit and that of our marginalized brothers and sisters, but also for the planetary common good of all creation. Indeed, solidarity is crucial in light of the inequities inherent in the climate crisis, which has been caused by the energy-intensive development of wealthy nations and which will impact developing nations the most. Concretely, Francis calls for "the establishment of mechanisms and subsidies which allow developing countries access to technology transfer, technical assistance and financial resources" (*LS* 172).

The virtue of solidarity is typically understood as oriented to the common good of the one human family, and so promotes the participation of all human beings in the process of protecting and promoting the global common good.[7] Yet again, however, Pope Francis helps us understand that interdependence extends far beyond the human community; the "all" for which we are responsible is planetary. And so our feelings of distress as we understand the scope of the climate crisis should not awaken "vague compassion," but true, firm, and persevering determination to commit ourselves to the ecological common good of the entire earth.

Though Pope Francis does not use this term, his depiction of solidarity suggests another development of Catholic social teaching and could well be described as a virtue of "earth solidarity."[8] As Jame Schaefer explains, the virtue of earth solidarity "includes other species, abiota,[9] ecological systems, and the biosphere." Humans must learn to value non-human creatures intrinsically and see them all as fellow "contributors to and benefactors of a life-sustaining climate."[10] The earth, our "common home," is a home to more than just human beings. The ecological crisis has made us aware of our radical interdependence with all creation, and of the human responsibility to care for the common good of all creatures. The virtue of earth solidarity channels concern for the earth into concrete moral action for the good of the poor, for the good of nonhuman nature, and for the planetary and cosmic common good.

Preferential Option for the Poor and Vulnerable

The Catholic tradition calls all people to exercise particular concern for the poor and marginalized since they are most vulnerable to injustices that undermine their human life and dignity. Although this commitment to the poor and marginalized has been a pillar of Catholic social teaching since the Church's first great social encyclical (*Rerum novarum*, 1891),[11] it reaches back through Jesus (e.g.,

---

7. Meghan Clark, *The Vision of Catholic Social Thought: The Virtue of Solidarity and the Praxis of Human Rights* (Minneapolis: Fortress, 2014).

8. For a description of earth solidarity, see Scheid, *The Cosmic Common Good*, 82–100.

9. Non-living entities.

10. Schaefer, "Solidarity, Subsidiarity, and Preference for the Poor," 411.

11. Pope Leo XIII, *Rerum novarum*, May 15, 1891, *http://w2.vatican.va/content /leo-xiii/en/encyclicals/documents/hf_l-xiii_enc_15051891_rerum-novarum.html*.

Matt. 25:34–40; Luke 4:16–21) all the way to the Old Testament (e.g., Exod. 22:20–26; Prov. 31:8–9).

Cultivation of the Preferential Option for the Poor and Vulnerable in *Laudato si'*

Along with the virtue of solidarity, Francis insists on the centrality of the poor. In *Laudato si'*, Francis introduces a new category of the poor and vulnerable: the earth itself. "This is why the earth herself, burdened and laid waste, is among the most abandoned and mal-treated of our poor" (*LS* 2).

In particular, though, Francis focuses on the human poor, and indeed our difficulty or even inability to consider that justice for future generations is rooted in the same inability to adequately ensure justice for the poor. That is why Pope Francis urges us to think not only of future generations but of "today's poor, whose life on this earth is brief and who cannot keep on waiting" (*LS* 162). Integral ecology means that we have to begin seeing environmental and social problems together, not as isolated phenomena. The earth laid waste and the abandoned poor are victims of the same global processes. These are not, Pope Francis says, "two separate crises, one environmental and the other social, but rather one complex crisis which is both social and environmental" (*LS* 139). We need to pursue strategies that simultaneously combat poverty and protect nature. As Francis says, "A true ecological approach always becomes a social approach; it must integrate questions of justice in debates on the environment, so as to hear *both the cry of the earth and the cry of the poor*" (*LS* 49).

One way of understanding the link between solidarity and the preferential option for the poor is through Francis's discussion of "ecological debt," reflections that enrich traditional conceptualizations of these Catholic social teaching principles. There is, he says, a debt owed by developed nations toward developing nations, or the global North to the global South (*LS* 51–52), and the concept of "ecological debt" captures many distinct but interrelated claims.

First, the poor and those in developing nations are more vulnerable to the harmful effects of climate change and environmental degradation than the rich who have sufficient resources to enable them to adapt, though climate change ultimately imperils all nations to some degree. Justice calls the rich to help the poor respond to and cope with a changing earth.

Second, northern developed nations achieved their economic prosperity in part through excessive acquisition of southern mineral and energy sources; the resources in the global South made possible the development of technologies and wealth that the developed nations enjoy. More pointedly, the technologies that developing nations need from developed nations were made possible by the resources from developing nations. Hence, Francis appeals—based on the universal destination of goods—for the transfer of technologies to countries that need them, and whose resources enable the development of these technologies.

Third, developed countries gained their wealth as a direct result of burning fossil fuels, which, though unknown at the time, in turn brought about the climate conditions that now disproportionately imperil poorer nations. If we imagine that each nation is justly allotted a certain amount of fossil fuel energy to use and greenhouse gases to emit, then developed nations are indeed indebted to developing nations. The North has taken more than its share of environmental climatic space, and so owes the South some compensation for the unjust harm that its people now experience.

Fourth, the planetary common good requires preserving critical habitats and biodiverse hotspots for future generations. Indeed, there is a positive correlation between those places on earth where biodiversity most thrives, and the people in developing nations (often indigenous peoples) who have resisted industrialization and deforestation. The South should be compensated for not destroying, as the North has done, ecosystems that the earth now desperately needs to preserve.

Finally, the term "ecological debt" highlights the ethical absurdity of focusing on the "financial debt" of developing nations, which has imposed a major political and economic burden for decades.[12] Southern financial debt servicing—which often ties financial aid to the acceptance of economic policies that benefit the global

---

12. For extended treatment of this topic, see: John Sniegocki, *Catholic Social Teaching and Economic Globalization: The Quest for Alternatives* (Milwaukee: Marquette University Press, 2009).

North—has hindered economic growth in many Southern countries. Indeed, in some cases indebted nations have paid their initial loan off many times over but remain in debt due to astronomical interest rates.[13] At the same time, developed nations enjoy economic prosperity by borrowing the biocapacity of developing nations. Yet our global economic system predominately focuses on the financial debt that burdens southern countries and ignores the ecological debt incurred by the North. Thus, Pope Francis says, "The foreign debt of poor countries has become a way of controlling them, yet this is not the case where ecological debt is concerned. In different ways, developing countries, where the most important reserves of the biosphere are found, continue to fuel the development of richer countries at the cost of their own present and future" (*LS* 52). Pope Francis, like his predecessor Pope Benedict XVI, calls for "differentiated responsibilities" regarding financial and ecological debt whereby developed rich countries must offer assistance to developing countries and limit their own consumption of non-renewable energy (*LS* 52).[14]

Within his concern for the poor it is important to note that Pope Francis manifests a remarkable solicitude for indigenous peoples who embody in a particular way the intersection of the cry of the earth and the cry of the poor. Many indigenous peoples themselves have used the concept of "ecological debt" to "present their climate vulnerability as a continuation of a long history of colonial devastation."[15] Francis highlights their essential contribution to a sustainable earth. They are not, he says, "merely one minority among others, but should be the principal dialogue partners" from whom industrialized populations should learn (*LS* 146). For example, Francis observes that while the Scriptures outline a threefold relationship for human beings with God, with neighbor, and with the earth (*LS* 66), modernity has by and large omitted concern for the earth. On the other hand, indigenous peoples have long fought to preserve a sense

13. I thank an anonymous reviewer for this insight.

14. See Pope Benedict XVI, *If You Want to Cultivate Peace, Protect Creation, World Day of Peace Message*, January 1, 2010, 9, *https://w2.vatican.va/content/benedict-xvi/en/messages/peace/documents/hf_ben-xvi_mes_20091208_xliii-world-day-peace.html*; Pope Benedict XVI, *Caritas in veritate*, 2009, 49, *http://w2.vatican.va/content/benedict-xvi/en/encyclicals/documents/hf_ben-xvi_enc_20090629_caritas-in-veritate.html.*

15. Willis Jenkins, *The Future of Ethics: Sustainability, Social Justice, and Religious Creativity* (Washington, DC: Georgetown University Press, 2013), 45.

of commitment to their lands because they have a sacred dimension and are integral to identity. Where indigenous peoples enjoy sovereignty over their land, they care for it the best (*LS* 146). Francis notes the pressure placed on indigenous peoples to abandon their lands in the name of purported progress, and so emphasizes that solidarity demands a commitment to both the economic well-being and cultural heritage of indigenous peoples.

Conclusion

Throughout *Laudato si'*, Pope Francis issues an inspiring, hope-filled, and comprehensive moral vision that affirms and develops core principles of Catholic social teaching: the common good, solidarity, and the preferential option for the poor. Specifically, he advances an inclusive global and ecological common good, encourages the virtue of solidarity that pursues justice for all members of the "splendid universal communion" of creation (*LS* 222), and supports a preferential option for all those endangered by environmental degradation, to whom wealthy nations owe an ecological debt. Pope Francis thus issues a prophetic call that is rooted in the rich tradition of Catholic social teaching and so demonstrates how the Church in the face of modern ecological challenges is, like God in the words of Saint Augustine, "so ancient and so new."[16]

Review Questions

1. How does *Gaudium et spes* define the common good, and what is meant by the "cosmic common good"?

2. How does Pope John Paul II define solidarity, and how does Pope Francis describe his vision of a "new and universal solidarity" in *Laudato si'* (*LS* 14)?

3. Why does the Catholic tradition call all people to exercise a particular concern for the poor and marginalized? What category does Pope Francis add to this concern in *Laudato si'*?

---

16. Saint Augustine, *Confessions*, trans. F. J. Sheed (Indianapolis: Hackett, 2006), 10.27.38.

4. What are some aspects of the "ecological debt" owed to developing nations?

In-Depth Questions

1. Do you agree with Pope Francis that "the climate is a common good, belonging to all and meant for all" (*LS* 23)? Why or why not? How might this claim shift the ways that countries approach climate change?
2. Do you agree with Pope John Paul II that "we are all really responsible for all" (*SRS* 38)? If so, how do we balance caring for people close by with those who are far away (spatially and temporally)? If not, what are some of the obstacles to the forms of global solidarity that Pope Francis espouses?
3. Do you agree with the tradition of Catholic social teaching that we have a responsibility to exercise particular concern for the poor and marginalized? Why or why not?
4. What do you think of Pope Francis's vision of the "universal communion" of creation? Can you imagine feeling affection for the sun, the moon, or a river, or calling them "brother" or "sister"? Why or why not?

Suggestions for Further Study

Curran, Charles E. *Catholic Social Teaching, 1891–Present: A Historical, Theological, and Ethical Analysis*. Washington, DC: Georgetown University Press, 2002.

Deane-Drummond, Celia. "Technology, Ecology, and the Divine: A Critical Look at New Technologies through a Theology of Gratuitousness." In *Just Sustainability: Ecology, Technology, and Resource Extraction*, edited by Christiana Z. Peppard and Andrea Vicini, SJ, 145–56. Maryknoll, NY: Orbis, 2015.

Deberri, Edward P., James E. Hug, Peter J. Henriot, and Michael J. Schultheis. *Catholic Social Teaching: Our Best Kept Secret*. Maryknoll, NY: Orbis, 2004.

Door, Donald. *Option for the Poor: A Hundred Years of Catholic Social Teaching*. Maryknoll, NY: Orbis, 1992.

Himes, Kenneth R. *101 Questions and Answers on Catholic Social Teaching.* 2nd ed. Mahwah, NJ: Paulist Press, 2013.

Himes, Kenneth R., Lisa Sowle Cahill, Charles E. Curran, David Hollenbach, and Thomas Shannon, eds. *Modern Catholic Social Teaching: Commentaries and Interpretations.* Washington, DC: Georgetown University Press, 2004.

Hollenbach, David. *The Common Good and Christian Ethics.* New York: Cambridge University Press, 2002.

Massaro, Thomas. *Living Justice: Catholic Social Teaching in Action.* 3rd ed. Lanham, MD: Rowman & Littlefield, 2016.

O'Brien, David J., and Thomas A. Shannon. *Catholic Social Thought: The Documentary Heritage.* Maryknoll, NY: Orbis, 2010.

Peppard, Christiana Z. "Commodifying Creation?: Pope Benedict XVI's Vision of the Goods of Creation Intended for All." In *Environmental Justice and Climate Change: Assessing Pope Benedict XVI's Ecological Vision for the Catholic Church in the United States,* edited by Jame Schaefer and Tobias Winright, 83–102. New York: Lexington, 2013.

Pontifical Council for Justice and Peace. *Compendium of the Social Doctrine of the Church.* Vatican: Libreria Editrice Vaticana, 2004. Available online at *http://www.vatican.va/roman_curia/pontifical _councils/justpeace/documents/rc_pc_justpeace_doc_20060526 _compendio-dott-soc_en.html.*

Schaefer, Jame. *Theological Foundations for Environmental Ethics: Reconstructing Patristic and Medieval Concepts.* Washington, DC: Georgetown University Press, 2009.

Scheid, Daniel P. *The Cosmic Common Good: Religious Grounds for Religious Ethics.* New York: Oxford University Press, 2016.

CHAPTER 12

Peace on Earth, Peace with Earth: *Laudato si'* and Integral Peacebuilding

TOBIAS WINRIGHT

> *"It's not that global warming is* like *a world war. It* is *a world war. . . . The question is, will we fight back?"* —Bill McKibben[1]

Shortly after the resignation of Pope Benedict XVI in 2013, the international Catholic periodical *The Tablet* asked theologians what qualities they hoped his successor would have. I replied with this:

> The next pope should remind Catholics that we are, first and foremost, followers of a Lord who said, "Blessed are the peacemakers, for they will be called children of God" (Matt. 5:9). He should enable Catholics to participate intelligently in the Mass and to connect what we experience and do there with everyday life, thereby informing and forming us to "love and serve the Lord" by defending human life consistently against all threats, including unjust war, toxic wastes, abortion, euthanasia, climate change, the international and domestic proliferation of weapons and firearms, lack of access to affordable health care, and more.[2]

---

1. Bill McKibben, "A World at War," *New Republic*, August 15, 2016, *https://newrepublic.com/article/135684/declare-war-climate-change-mobilize-wwii.*

2. Tobias Winright, "A Humble Heart and a Thick Skin," *The Tablet* 267, no. 8989 (March 16, 2013): 11.

Put differently, I had in mind a pope who would bring together, or integrate, spirituality, discipleship, and a range of life-and-death moral issues at this crucial time in the twenty-first century. Shortly thereafter, Jorge Mario Bergoglio was elected the 266th pope and became the first to take the name Francis.

Initially, some people wondered whether he had taken the name in honor of Saint Francis Xavier, a fellow Jesuit. In response to this uncertainty, the new pope clarified that he took the name Francis to celebrate Saint Francis of Assisi. As Pope Francis put it, "For me, he is the man of poverty, the man of peace, the man who loves and protects creation; these days we do not have a very good relationship with creation, do we? He is the man who gives us this spirit of peace."[3] That is to say, Saint Francis of Assisi recognized the interrelatedness of creation in the way that I had hoped Pope Benedict's successor would.

In his *Canticle of the Creatures*, Saint Francis celebrates God's gift of creation with relationship language and refers to "Brother Sun," "Sister Moon," "Brother Wind," "Sister Water," "Brother Fire," and "Sister Mother Earth" as relatives, kin to each other and to humankind, before announcing, "Blessed are those who endure in peace." Accordingly, G. K. Chesterton writes that Saint Francis's legacy is partly the insight that humans "could be reconciled not only to God but to nature and, most difficult of all, to themselves."[4] In other words, Saint Francis shows us that reconciliation between humans and God coincides with reconciliation between humans and one another, and between humans and non-human nature.

As Pope Francis observed above, "We do not have a very good relationship with creation, do we?" Humans and the rest of nature are alienated from each other, even to the point of being adversaries. Indeed, as environmental activist Bill McKibben puts it, global warming can be conceived of as a "world war" underway between people and planet. In this context, reconciliation means transforming alienation into what Pope Francis alludes to as relationships between

---

3. Pope Francis, "Audience to Representatives of the Communications Media," March 16, 2013, *http://www.vatican.va/holy_father/francesco/speeches/2013/march /documents/papa-francesco_20130316_rappresentanti-media_en.html*.

4. G. K. Chesterton, *St. Francis of Assisi* (Garden City, NY: Doubleday, 1924; Image, 1957), 152.

persons, God, and creation, and which are defined by flourishing and goodness—not merely the absence of estrangement or adversarial conflict. In other words, reconciliation entails building authentic, lasting peace.

Given the need for contemporary reconciliation understood as peace, Pope Francis promotes peace both *on* earth (that is, between peoples) and *with* earth (that is, between people and planet). In his homily on the feast of Saint Francis on October 4, 2013, Pope Francis asked the saint to make us "instruments of peace," adding that God created our world "to be a place where harmony and peace can flourish. . . . Let us respect creation, let us not be instruments of destruction! Let us respect each human being. May there be an end to armed conflicts which cover the earth with blood."[5] Likewise, in his first apostolic exhortation, *Evangelii gaudium*, Pope Francis expressed concern for vulnerable people whose lives are at risk, and also observed that there are "other weak and defenceless beings"— indeed, "creation as a whole"—threatened at this time by human activity (*EG* 215).[6]

As peacemakers, Christians should not contribute to the destruction of others, whether people or planet, but should be protective keepers of our kin—both human and non-human. Pope Francis opens *Laudato si'* with reference to Pope John XXIII's 1963 encyclical *Pacem in terris*, which he says "not only rejected war but offered a proposal for peace" in the face of "nuclear crisis" (*LS* 3).[7] "Now, faced as we are with global environmental deterioration" (*LS* 3), the pope calls Christians—indeed, all people—to "watch over and protect the fragile world in which we live, and all its peoples"(*EG* 216) in order to build peace between and among all human and non-human parts of creation.

Against this background, the present chapter suggests that *Laudato si'* sets the stage for extending *pacem in terris* to include *pacem*

5. Pope Francis, "Homily of the Holy Father Francis: Pastoral Visit to Assisi," October 4, 2013, *http://www.vatican.va/holy_father/francesco/homilies/2013/documents /papa-francesco_20131004_omelia-visita-assisi_en.html.*

6. Pope Francis, *Evangelii gaudium*, November 24, 2013, *http://w2.vatican.va /content/francesco/en/apost_exhortations/documents/papa-francesco_esortazione -ap_20131124_evangelii-gaudium.html.*

7. Pope John XXIII, *Pacem in terris*, April 11, 1963, *http://w2.vatican.va/content /john-xxiii/en/encyclicals/documents/hf_j-xxiii_enc_11041963_pacem.html.*

cum terra.[8] Or, to paraphrase the *Gloria* of the angels proclaimed at Jesus's birth and repeated in the Catholic Mass, "Glory to God in the highest, and peace to God's people *and* earth" (cf. Luke 2:14). In particular, the chapter argues that—especially given his concept "integral ecology"—the connection Pope Francis makes in *Laudato si'* between peacebuilding and ecology calls for a new ethical paradigm termed "integral peacebuilding," which encompasses traditional Catholic perspectives on war and peace.

First, though, the supposed "war" between people and planet described by Bill McKibben needs further consideration.

War Metaphor: What Is It Good For?

As noted above, popular author and environmental activist Bill McKibben writes that global warming "*is* a world war."[9] As a theologian who writes about war and peace, I must admit that I initially took McKibben's words as a surprising metaphor. The metaphor of war is often used to galvanize efforts to address problems in society: there has been a war on poverty, a war on drugs, a war on crime, and a war on cancer. Although this war language can be compelling in these instances, it can also be problematic. For example, the "war on crime" idiom can unfortunately cause police to see themselves as a military-like force combating an enemy, rather than as serving and protecting their community in which even criminals are fellow citizens.

"But this is no metaphor," says McKibben with regard to the use of war language in reference to climate change. As he puts it,

> By most of the ways we measure wars, climate change is the real deal: Carbon and methane are seizing physical territory, sowing havoc and panic, racking up casualties, and even destabilizing governments. . . . Its first victims, ironically, are those who have done the least to cause the crisis. But it's a world war aimed at us all. And if we lose, we will be as decimated and helpless as the losers in every conflict—except

---

8. "Peace on earth" and "peace with the earth," respectively.

9. McKibben, "A World at War," italics in original. Subsequent references to McKibben will come from this article.

that this time, there will be no winners, and no end to the planetwide occupation that follows. . . . The question is not, are we in a world war? The question is, will we fight back? And if we do, can we actually defeat an enemy as powerful and inexorable as the laws of physics?

McKibben goes on to describe "the battlefield," "this siege," "the onslaught," and "overwhelming attacks" by "our foes." One example is ocean warming: "In the Pacific this spring, the enemy staged a daring breakout across thousands of miles of ocean, waging a full-scale assault on the region's coral reefs." In response, McKibben says that humanity's "only hope is to mobilize like we did in WWII," when the American government, citizens, and businesses transformed the U.S. economy from consumer- to military-based manufacturing virtually overnight via public policies, a sense of civic duty, and a shared commitment to sacrifice for the common good. Today, of course, the shift is not martial but sociopolitical and ecological: the U.S. must move away from fossil fuels, undue corporate influence, and consumerism toward clean energy, democracy, and material moderation. But for McKibben, the urgency and scale of the collective action needed to avoid climate change tipping points and runaway global warming warrants the analogy to World War II mobilization.

While I agree with McKibben's prognosis (the language of which has been echoed in popular headlines like "Religious Scholars Recommend Ways to *Combat* Climate Change"),[10] I would add that the natural world is not the "enemy"; rather, the "foe" is global warming. Nor, as McKibben admits, is this adversary sentient or evil. Instead, this threat, in connection with the laws of physics, is simply a physical consequence of human activity (technically referred to as *anthropogenic effects*), especially the use of fossil fuels such as coal and oil ever since the Industrial Revolution. Thus we might say, as the mid-twentieth century comic strip character Pogo once said, "We have met the enemy and he is us."[11]

---

10. Menan Khater, "Religious Scholars Recommend Ways to Combat Climate Change," *Daily News Egypt*, June 28, 2016, italics added, *http://www.dailynewsegypt .com/2016/06/28/religious-scholars-recommend-ways-combat-climate-change/*.

11. Walt Kelly, *Pogo: We Have Met the Enemy and He is Us*, 2nd ed. (New York: Simon and Schuster, 1987).

Laudato si' and the War Metaphor

Although Pope Francis does not go so far as to describe climate change and ecological degradation in military terms, he does refer to violence, war, and the environment in *Laudato si'*. At the very beginning of the encyclical, he writes, "The violence present in our hearts, wounded by sin, is also reflected in the symptoms of sickness evident in the soil, in the water, in the air and in all forms of life" (*LS* 2). At the outset, the pope confesses that all of the harms happening in nature are, at root, the result of human attitudes and activities that he names sinful "violence." The unjust aggressor threatening nature is, in Francis's view, humankind rather than some law of physics. And since humans are part of nature (*LS* 139), the violence that we do to nature is also an attack on ourselves—especially the poor and marginalized who are most vulnerable to the effects of environmental degradation (*LS* 48).

The violence done to humans via ecological harm can take many forms. For example, just as there are refugees of war, innocent people displaced by conflict who seek refuge elsewhere, Pope Francis recognizes that there now are many environmental refugees, innocent people who have done little to cause ecological harm but are forced to move because of ecological degradation. He writes,

> There has been a tragic rise in the number of migrants seeking to flee from the growing poverty caused by environmental degradation. They are not recognized by international conventions as refugees; they bear the loss of the lives they have left behind, without enjoying any legal protection whatsoever (*LS* 25).

One such example is the case of the Carteret Islanders, who are being forced by the rising South Pacific to relocate from their native home despite contributing practically nothing to the climate change that is melting global ice sheets.[12]

---

12. Bishop Bernard Unabali, "Keynote Address at the Catholic Consultation on Environmental Justice and Climate Change," in *Environmental Justice and Climate Change: Assessing Pope Benedict XVI's Ecological Vision for the Catholic Church in the United States*, ed. Jame Schaefer and Tobias Winright (Lanham, MD: Lexington, 2013), 257–62. The Carteret Islanders' story is also the subject of the documentary film *Sun Come Up*, directed by Jennifer Redfearn (Blooming Grove, NY: New Day Films, 2011).

In addition to population displacement via flooding or, for that matter, desertification, climate change and environmental degradation further injure humans by spoiling the resources on which people—especially the poor—directly depend. For example, potable water and fertile soil are often polluted or depleted by industries that relocate factories to developing nations where government environmental regulations are few or unenforced. These actions, Pope Francis observes, in turn cause "the premature death of many of the poor [and] conflicts sparked by the shortage of resources" (*LS* 48).

Amid resource shortages wrought and exacerbated by ecological degradation, "it is foreseeable," Francis warns, "that, once certain resources have been depleted, the scene will be set for new wars" (*LS* 57). Here it is worth pointing out that the U.S. military and its advisors have repeatedly recognized climate change as a national security threat.[13] As with most wars, such conflicts only worsen the condition of poor and vulnerable people. Thus Pope Francis employs the language of war and laments that the poor and "excluded" are "treated merely as *collateral damage*" to ecological harm (*LS* 49, italics added).

Although the pope highlights that war harms people, especially the poor, he concurrently emphasizes that war—especially modern war with its indiscriminate weapons of mass destruction—harms the environment. He observes, "War always does grave harm to the environment and to the cultural riches of peoples, risks which are magnified when nuclear power and biological weapons are born in mind" (*LS* 57). For these reasons, he calls on political leaders to "pay greater attention to foreseeing new conflicts and addressing the causes which can lead to them" (*LS* 57).

Ultimately, though, the incipient causes of war and environmental degradation are moral and spiritual. And so the solution is

---

13. Military Advisory Board, *National Security and the Threat of Climate Change* (Alexandria, VA: The CNA Corporation, 2007), 1; available at *https://www.cna.org /cna_files/pdf/national%20security%20and%20the%20threat%20of%20climate%20 change.pdf*; Daniel Moran, ed., *Climate Change and National Security: A Country-Level Analysis* (Washington, DC: Georgetown University Press, 2011); Suzanne Goldberg, "US Military Warned to Prepare for Consequences of Climate Change," *The Guardian*, November 9, 2012, *http://www.theguardian.com/world/2012/nov/09/us-military -warned-climate-change*; and National Intelligence Council, *Global Water Security: Intelligence Community Assessment* (Washington, DC: National Intelligence Council, February 2, 2012), 1, available at *http://www.fas.org/irp/nic/water.pdf*.

likewise moral and spiritual, not just political. Pope Francis writes that proposed solutions to ecological challenges "will be powerless to solve the serious problems of our world if humanity loses its compass, if we lose sight of the great motivations which make it possible for us to live in harmony, to make sacrifices and to treat others well" (*LS* 200). Here "harmony" is the moral and spiritual goal or end that humans are supposed to seek and build. Such harmony is not only meant for human society, but also for the rest of creation. An "ecological education," writes Pope Francis, should "seek also to restore the various levels of ecological equilibrium, establishing harmony within ourselves, with others, with nature and other living creatures, and with God" (*LS* 210, 213–14).

This discussion of harmony brings us back to what Pope Francis said earlier about how the sin in human hearts gives rise to alienation between humans and God, humans and each other, and humans and the rest of creation. The pope thus invites people to undergo a "profound interior conversion" or "ecological conversion" (*LS* 217) that enables reconciliation with God, one another, and "reconciliation with creation" (*LS* 218). Of course, by referring to "creation," the pope has in mind planet Earth. Recent Catholic eco-theology, however, engages current scientific understanding of the universe and is more cosmic in scope, for example, calling for "cosmological conversion," even as it addresses global concerns such as climate change.[14] Nevertheless, as Donna Schaper asserts, "Many think that ecology is all about nature when it is rather about peace."[15] Similarly, Pope Francis echoes and extends the peace prayer of Saint Francis—"Make me an instrument of your peace . . ."—to include nature. He writes, "Yet we are called to be instruments of God, our Father, so that our planet might be what he desired when he created it and correspond with his plan for peace, beauty and fullness" (*LS* 53).

The peace for which Pope Francis calls "is much more than the absence of war" (*LS* 225) and includes positive things like the

14. See, for example, Julia Brumbaugh and Natalia Imperatori-Lee, eds., *Turning to the Heavens and the Earth: Theological Reflections on a Cosmological Conversion; Essays in Honor of Elizabeth A. Johnson* (Collegeville, MN: Liturgical Press, 2016).

15. Donna Schaper, "Biblical Animal Prophecy Reveals Ecology Is All about Peace," *National Catholic Reporter*, July 11, 2016, https://www.ncronline.org/blogs/eco-catholic/biblical-animal-prophecy-reveals-ecology-all-about-peace.

aforementioned beauty and fullness. Again, a word that encompasses "peace, beauty and fullness" is *harmony*, and the Hebrew word for peace that connotes such harmony is *shalom*. Shalom existed in the world before humans sinned, and it is what God wills to be ultimately restored in creation.[16] As eco-theologian Norman Wirzba writes, shalom is "a deep and all-embracing reality," which is not "simply the absence of violence," but a more positive and reconciling vision.[17] Put differently, shalom upholds and promotes the integrity of all creation.

In order to bring about shalom amid contemporary ecological degradation, Pope Francis calls for "integral ecology," which builds on and brings together earlier references by Popes John Paul II and Benedict XVI to "human ecology"—which refers to a right ordering of persons—and "natural ecology" or "environmental ecology"—which refers to the right ordering of nonhuman creation.[18] Although integral ecology is a rich concept with many possible dimensions, there are two that seem especially important to the present discussion. First, integral ecology emphasizes humans' "serene harmony with creation" (*LS* 225). Next, integral ecology is based on a "fraternal love [that] can only be gratuitous; it can never be a means of repaying others for what they have done or will do for us. That is why it is possible to love our enemies" (*LS* 228).

---

16. For helpful accounts of biblical teaching on shalom, see Steven Bouma-Prediger, *For the Beauty of the Earth: A Christian Vision for Creation Care*, 2nd ed. (Grand Rapids: Baker Academic, 2010), 110, 116–17, 119, 144–45, 149, 180, 183; Dianne Bergant, "The Bible's Wisdom Tradition and Creation Theology," in *God, Creation, and Climate Change: A Catholic Response to the Environmental Crisis*, ed. Richard W. Miller (Maryknoll, NY: Orbis, 2010), 47. In her review of Willis Jenkins, *Ecologies of Grace: Environmental Ethics and Christian Theology* (New York: Oxford University Press, 2008), Christine E. Gudorf raises some interesting questions by noting that "there seems to be no consensus among Christian ethicists at large whether nature needs redemption, or if it does, what that redemption would entail. Would redemption mean the end of predation in nature, and the coming of the lion and the lamb laying down together in peace?" *Journal of the American Academy of Religion* 80, no. 1 (March 2012): 249.

17. Norman Wirzba, "Reconciliation through Christ," in, *Making Peace with the Land: God's Call to Reconcile with Creation*, ed. Fred Bahnson and Norman Wirzba (Downers Grove, IL: InterVarsity, 2012), 66.

18. For a reference to "human ecology" by John Paul II, see *Centesimus annus*, May 1, 1999, 39, *http://w2.vatican.va/content/john-paul-ii/en/encyclicals/documents/hf_jp-ii_enc_01051991_centesimus-annus.html*. I am grateful to Dan DiLeo for explicating these terms in this way via personal correspondence.

This reference to fraternal love alludes to Jesus's teaching about how Christians should love their enemies rather than apply the *lex talionis* ("law of retaliation") of an "eye for an eye and a tooth for a tooth" (Matt. 5:38–44). This passage appears in the Sermon on the Mount with another that brings this discussion of peace and ecology full circle: "Blessed are the peacemakers, for they will be called children of God" (Matt. 5:9). At the same time, however, these references to peace raise important questions: Does the Christian emphasis on love and peacemaking entail *pacifism*? If so, how are Christians and others expected to, as McKibben emphasized, *fight* climate change and environmental degradation?

In the Catholic tradition, peacemaking does not mean passivity; rather, it requires action. That is why Pope Francis proactively calls for all people to dynamically care for creation, and underscores that the activity for which he advocates "is essential to a life of virtue; it is not an optional or a secondary aspect of our Christian experience" (*LS* 217). Thus, just as we are each called to actively serve as "keeper" of our human sisters and brothers, so too are we called to actively care for creation and its members, which Saint Francis and Pope Francis recognize as our sisters and brothers.[19]

Given Pope Francis's call for people to care for creation, it is worth pointing out that his call references Genesis 2:15, in which humans are given the responsibility to "'till and keep' the garden of the world" (*LS* 67). As a former law enforcement officer, I appreciate how theologian Steven Bouma-Prediger, translates "till and keep" as a phrase that "is painted on the door of every Chicago police car," namely, "to serve and protect."[20] Pope Francis similarly writes, "'Tilling' refers to cultivating, ploughing or working, while 'keeping' means caring, protecting, overseeing and preserving" (*LS* 67). On this basis, he emphasizes "a relationship of mutual responsibility between human beings and nature," in which humans have "the duty to protect the earth and to ensure its fruitfulness for coming generations" (*LS* 67).

Before continuing, it should be noted that the connections between peace and ecology that Pope Francis lifts up in *Laudato si'* significantly develop and expand upon the connections made by his papal

---

19. Saint Francis of Assisi, "Canticle of the Creatures," in *Francis of Assisi: Early Documents*, ed. Regis J. Armstrong (New York: New City, 1999), 1:113–14; *LS* 1.

20. Bouma-Prediger, *For the Beauty of the Earth*, 64.

predecessors and fellow bishops. In his *1990 World Day of Peace Message*, John Paul II observed, "In our day, there is a growing awareness that world peace is threatened . . . by a lack of *due respect for nature*, by the plundering of natural resources."[21] Additionally, Pope Benedict XVI observed in his encyclical *Caritas in veritate* that "protecting the natural environment in order to build a world of peace is thus a duty incumbent upon each and all" (*CV* 14). Moreover, Benedict emphasized in his *2010 World Day of Peace Message, If You Want to Cultivate Peace, Protect Creation* (the title itself says a lot!), "The protection of creation and peacemaking are profoundly linked" (14).[22]

Here in the United States, the U.S. Catholic bishops have similarly connected peace and ecology. Soon after the First Gulf War, the bishops wrote in their 1991 statement *Renewing the Earth*,

> Clearly, war represents a serious threat to the environment, as the darkened skies and oil soaked beaches of Kuwait clearly remind us. The pursuit of peace—lasting peace based on justice—ought to be an environmental priority because the earth itself bears the wounds and scars of war. . . . These are not distinct and separate issues but complementary challenges. We need to help build bridges among the peace, justice, and environmental agendas and constituencies.[23]

21. Pope John Paul II, *Peace with God the Creator, Peace with All of Creation: Message of His Holiness Pope John Paul II for the Celebration of the World Day of Peace*, January 1, 1990, 1, italics in original, *http://www.vatican.va/holy_father/john_paul_ii/messages/peace/documents/hf_jp-ii_mes_19891208_xxiii-world-day-for-peace_en.html*. For a brief account of how John Paul II "expanded the tradition" of Catholic social thought on ecology, including in connection with the "role of war in causing environmental devastation" in this *World Day of Peace Message*, see John Hart, *What Are They Saying about Environmental Theology?* (New York: Paulist Press, 2004), 11–18. Hart also highlights John Paul II's call in *Ex corde ecclesiae* for Catholic institutions of higher education to study "serious contemporary problems" including "the promotion of justice for all . . . [and] the protection of nature" (14; *ECE* 32).

22. Pope Benedict XVI, *If You Want to Cultivate Peace, Protect Creation: Message of His Holiness Pope Benedict XVI for the Celebration of the World Day of Peace*, January, 2010, *http://www.vatican.va/holy_father/benedict_xvi/messages/peace/documents/hf_ben-xvi_mes_20091208_xliii-world-day-peace_en.html*.

23. United States Catholic Conference, *Renewing the Earth: An Invitation to Reflection and Action on Environment in Light of Catholic Social Teaching*, in *"And God Saw That It Was Good": Catholic Theology and the Environment*, ed. Drew Christiansen and Walter Grazer (Washington, DC: United States Catholic Conference, 1996), 337. Available online at *http://www.usccb.org/issues-and-action/human-life-and-dignity/environment/renewing-the-earth.cfm*.

Eight years prior, the bishops declared, "Peacemaking is not an optional commitment. It is a requirement of our faith" and its "unity and harmony extend to all of creation; true peace implied a restoration of the right order not just among peoples, but within all of creation" (*The Challenge of Peace* 333, 32).[24] Thus Pope Francis's integral ecology builds on the foundation and scaffolding of his predecessors, who also provided some nascent building blocks for what I call "integral peacebuilding."

Integral Peacebuilding: Pacifism, Just War, and Just Peacemaking

Peacemaking and protecting are certainly forceful imperatives in *Laudato si'* and Catholic theology more generally. But what do these terms actually entail? The U.S. Catholic bishops observe that whereas all Catholics are called and obligated to work for peace, it is "the *how* of defending peace which offers moral options."[25]

Traditionally, Catholics have had two paths for defending peace and protecting people: pacifism and just war. As noted, pacifism is not passivity; rather, it is nonviolence that recognizes that "all believers must defend the cause of justice, must protect human rights, must resist evil."[26] Just war is not "anything goes," killing as many enemies as possible; rather, it calls for armed enemy engagement according to moral criteria intended to govern when to embark on war (*jus ad bellum*), how to conduct war (*jus in bello*),

24. National Conference of Catholic Bishops, *The Challenge of Peace: God's Promise and Our Response*, May 3, 1983, http://www.usccb.org/upload/challenge-peace-gods-promise-our-response-1983.pdf. Three years later, the United Methodist Council of Bishops published their own pastoral letter: *In Defense of Creation: The Nuclear Crisis and a Just Peace* (Nashville: Graded Press, 1986). There the Council made a similar point to the Catholic bishops' when they said, "We write in defense of creation. We do so because the creation itself is under attack. Air and water, trees and fruits and flowers, birds and fish and cattle, all children and youth, women and men live under the darkening shadows of a threatening nuclear winter . . . , a crisis that threatens to assault not only the whole human family but planet earth itself" (11).

25. National Conference of Catholic Bishops, *The Challenge of Peace*, 73, italics in original.

26. Kenneth R. Himes, "Pacifism," in *The New Dictionary of Catholic Social Thought*, ed. Judith A. Dwyer (Collegeville, MN: Liturgical Press, 1994), 707.

and the ways by which to secure a just, lasting peace in the wake of war (*jus post bellum*).[27]

In recent years, pacifism and just war have moved closer together and produced in theological ethics a third option for peacebuilding: just peacemaking. The contributors to this option are mostly proponents of just war, but also include some pacifists.[28] Together, advocates for just peacemaking have identified ten practices—rather than principles or criteria—that are ethically normative, empirically observable, and demonstrably effective for preventing war:[29]

1. Support nonviolent direct action.
2. Take independent initiatives to reduce threat.
3. Use cooperative conflict resolution.
4. Acknowledge responsibility for conflict and injustice and seek repentance and forgiveness.
5. Advance democracy, human rights, and interdependence.
6. Foster just and sustainable economic development.
7. Work with emerging cooperative forces in the international system.
8. Strengthen the United Nations and international efforts for cooperation and human rights.
9. Reduce offensive weapons and weapons trade.

---

27. According to the *Catechism of the Catholic Church*, the traditional moral criteria of the just war doctrine are as follows:

> The damage inflicted by the aggressor on the nation or community of nations must be lasting, grave, and certain; all other means of putting an end to it must have been shown to be impractical or ineffective; there must be serious prospects of success; the use of arms must not produce evils and disorders graver than the evil to be eliminated. The power of modern means of destruction weighs very heavily in evaluating this condition. (2309)

The category of *jus post bellum* is relatively new in Catholic theological ethics. For more on this concept, see Mark J. Allman and Tobias L. Winright, *After the Smoke Clears: The Just War Tradition and Post War Justice* (Maryknoll, NY: Orbis, 2010).

28. Glen Stassen, ed., *Just Peacemaking: The New Paradigm for the Ethics of Peace and War*, rev. ed. (Cleveland: Pilgrim Press, 2008), 9.

29. Ibid., 35.

10. Encourage grassroots peacemaking groups and voluntary associations.[30]

Just peacemaking, therefore, serves as a corrective to both just war and pacifism—without doing away with either—by actively addressing the root causes of armed conflict, so as to avoid war altogether or, if that is not possible, make war truly a last resort.

In addition to the concept of just peacemaking, an interdisciplinary group of Catholic theologians, ethicists, political scientists, historians, sociologists, and active practitioners have advocated for just peacebuilding.[31] This group, which includes both pacifists and just war proponents, believes that "peacebuilding precedes and follows upon peacemaking" in several important ways.[32] Whereas peacemaking entails the important work of discrete conflict neutralization, peacebuilding enables the integral cultivation and preservation of lasting peace via initiatives that address "all phases of . . . protracted conflicts, in which pre-violence, violence, and post-violence periods are difficult to differentiate."[33] Thus Pope Francis's call for peace that protects both people and planet implicitly appeals to an already-existent and still-developing tradition of Catholic moral thought that seeks to build integral peace through attention to everything that would upset it.

Notably, the language of "just peace" has recently gained traction in the Catholic hierarchy. In April 2016, Pax Christi International and the Pontifical Council for Justice and Peace hosted a "nonviolence and just peace" conference at the Vatican that called for an end to the Catholic teaching and use of just war theory, as well as a papal encyclical "on nonviolence and Just Peace."[34] Pope Francis's *2017 World Day of Peace Message, Nonviolence: A Style of Politics for Peace*, similarly emphasizes active nonviolence as the "cure for our broken world,"

30. Ibid.

31. Robert J. Schreiter, R. Scott Appleby, and Gerard F. Powers, eds., *Peacebuilding: Catholic Theology, Ethics, and Praxis* (Maryknoll, NY: Orbis, 2010).

32. R. Scott Appleby, "Catholic Peacebuilding," *America*, September 8, 2003, http://americamagazine.org/issue/449/article/catholic-peacebuilding.

33. R. Scott Appleby, "Peacebuilding and Catholicism: Affinities, Convergences, Possibilities," in *Peacebuilding*, ed. Schreiter et al., 3.

34. For more, see *An Appeal to the Catholic Church to Re-Commit to the Centrality of Gospel Nonviolence*, available at http://www.paxchristi.net/news/appeal-catholic-church-recommit-centrality-gospel-nonviolence/5855#sthash.coYvEyKG.dpbs.

which includes not only wars, terrorism, and criminal activity, but also environmental devastation.[35] While this call is laudable, I think that, sadly, armed force in defense of innocent people—and to defend, for instance, elephants from poachers seeking their ivory and pushing them to extinction—will continue to be necessary at times. Whether it is called "just war," "just policing," "just defense," or what the United Nations now calls humanitarian intervention, the "responsibility to protect" (also abbreviated as "R2P"), I agree with Kenneth Himes that there is a "need to develop a general theory of armed intervention."[36]

Here, in light of Pope Francis's integral ecology, it seems that the development of an "integral peacebuilding" could be a move in the right direction. Such a framework could profitably combine elements of nonviolence, just war, just peacemaking, and just peacebuilding, to actively build lasting peace, care for our common home, and allow for prudential intervention when violence compromises peace on earth. In this vein, a number of theologians and ethicists have been imaginatively exploring these possibilities in recent years.[37] Especially

---

35. Pope Francis, *Nonviolence: A Style of Politics for Peace: Message of His Holiness Pope Francis for the Celebration of the World Day of Peace*, January 1, 2017, 2, *http://w2.vatican.va/content/francesco/en/messages/peace/documents/papa-francesco_20161208_messaggio-l-giornata-mondiale-pace-2017.html*.

36. Kenneth R. Himes, "Intervention, Just War, and U.S. National Security," *Theological Studies* 65 (2004): 149. See also, Tobias Winright and Mark Allman, "Protect Thy Neighbor: Why the Just-War Tradition Is Still Indispensable," *Commonweal* 143, no. 11 (June 17, 2016): 7–9.

37. Some examples include Daniel Cosacchi, "Earthly Destruction: War, the Environment, and Catholic Social Teaching" (PhD diss., Loyola University, Chicago, 2016); Laurie Johnston, "Just War Theory and Environmental Destruction," in *Can War Be Just in the 21st Century? Ethicists Engage the Tradition*, ed. Tobias Winright and Laurie Johnston (Maryknoll, NY: Orbis, 2015), 96–111; Matthew A. Shadle, "No Peace on Earth: War and the Environment," in *Green Discipleship: Catholic Theological Ethics and the Environment*, ed. Tobias Winright (Winona, MN: Anselm Academic, 2011), 407–25; and J. Milburn Thompson, "Treating Nature Nonviolently: Developing Catholic Social Teaching on the Environment through Nonviolence," in *Violence, Transformation, and the Sacred: "They Shall Be Called Children of God,"* ed. Margaret R. Pfeil and Tobias L. Winright (Maryknoll, NY: Orbis, 2012), 225–38. Erin Lothes Biviano also offers a creative use of just war theory and just peacemaking for evaluating fossil fuel use in an essay co-written with Christiana Z. Peppard, Julia Watts Belser, and James B. Martin-Schramm, "What Powers Us? A Comparative Religious Ethics of Energy Sources, Power, and Privilege," *Journal of the Society of Christian Ethics* 36, no. 1 (Spring/Summer 2016): 3–25, at 15–19. Also, Walter E. Grazer, in connection with a Religion and Environmental Ethics Project at the Berkley Center for Religion and International Affairs at Georgetown University, is working on using just war theory to develop principles for addressing climate change.

as Catholic conversations about just peace continue in the wake of *Laudato si'* and the Nonviolence and Just Peace Vatican conference, I urge people of faith and goodwill to consider "integral peacebuilding" as a way to frame peace discourse in the twenty-first century.

Conclusion

In keeping with the writings of Popes John Paul II and Benedict XVI, Pope Francis in *Laudato si'* emphasizes that peace and care for our common home—like everything in creation—are "absolutely interconnected" (*LS* 92).[38] Although Catholic theologians and ethicists often focus on either peace or ecology, the time has come for the work done in each field to more deeply inform that of the other and, in turn, their shared project of building *peace with* [and between] *all of creation*, both human and non-human (*1990 WDP*). To this end, interdisciplinary efforts to develop the category of "integral peacebuilding" are, in my view, urgent and welcome.

Review Questions

1. Why does Bill McKibben think that climate change is a world war? For what response does he call?
2. According to Pope Francis, how does ecological degradation do violence to human and non-human creation?
3. If peace is "much more than the absence of war" (*LS* 225), as Pope Francis says, what does peace entail?
4. Explain the difference between peacemaking and peacebuilding.
5. What does the author mean by "integral peacebuilding"?

In-Depth Questions

1. War is a powerful reality in our world. Given its connotations, do you think describing climate change as a "world war" is an effective rhetorical move? Why or why not?

---

38. Here Pope Francis quotes the Conference of Dominican Bishops, Pastoral Letter *Sobre la relación del hombre con la naturaleza*, January 21, 1987.

2. McKibben says that adequate attention to climate change will require a transformation of U.S. society on the order of that which helped the Allies win World War II. Do you agree? If not, why? If so, what do you think are the three most important structural changes necessary?

3. As noted, Pope Francis's insight that ecological degradation can lead to war is echoed by the U.S. military's recognition that climate change is a national security threat. Do you think more widespread knowledge of the U.S. Armed Forces' position on climate change could alter climate change discourse in the United States? If so, how? If not, why?

4. The author describes the differences between pacifism, just war, just peacemaking, and just peacebuilding. To which do you find yourself most drawn? Why?

5. Do you agree with the author that "integral peacebuilding" could provide an important framework by which to build integral peace that protects both persons and planet? Why or why not?

Suggestions for Further Study

Biviano, Erin Lothes, et al. "What Powers Us? A Comparative Religious Ethics of Energy Sources, Power, and Privilege." *Journal of the Society of Christian Ethics* 36, no. 1 (Spring/Summer 2016): 3–25.

Cosacchi, Daniel. "Earthly Destruction: War, the Environment, and Catholic Social Teaching." PhD diss., Loyola University, Chicago, 2016.

Johnston, Laurie. "Just War Theory and Environmental Destruction." In *Can War Be Just in the 21st Century? Ethicists Engage the Tradition*, edited by Tobias Winright and Laurie Johnston, 96–111. Maryknoll, NY: Orbis, 2015.

Shadle, Matthew A. "No Peace on Earth: War and the Environment." In *Green Discipleship: Catholic Theological Ethics and the Environment*, edited by Tobias Winright, 407–25. Winona, MN: Anselm Academic, 2011.

Thompson, J. Milburn. "Treating Nature Nonviolently: Developing Catholic Social Teaching on the Environment through Nonviolence." In *Violence, Transformation, and the Sacred: "They Shall Be Called Children of God,"* edited by Margaret R. Pfeil and Tobias L. Winright, 225–38. Maryknoll, NY: Orbis, 2012.

Contributors

Michael Agliardo, SJ (PhD, University of California, San Diego; STL, Weston Jesuit School of Theology), is Executive Director of the U.S. Catholic China Bureau. His doctoral research focused on religion and public life, especially religion and environmental issues. That research also examined religious pluralism, both how particular religious traditions grapple with religious diversity and the way pluralism affects society as a whole. He continues to explore religion, environmental issues, and public life, and how these intersect. He also has an area focus on China.

Drew Christiansen, SJ (PhD, Yale University), is Distinguished Professor of Ethics and Global Human Development at Georgetown University and a Senior Research Fellow at the Berkley Center for Religion, Ethics, and World Affairs. He is a former director of the United States Conference of Catholic Bishops (USCCB) Office of International Justice and Peace and president and editor in chief of the Jesuit weekly *America*. He was the lead consultant on the US bishops' environmental 1993 pastoral "Renewing the Earth" and architect of the bishops' environmental justice program. He is coeditor with Walter Grazer of *And God Saw That It Was Good: Catholic Theology and the Environment* (Washington, DC: United States Catholic Conference, 1996).

David Cloutier (PhD, Duke University) is Associate Professor of Moral Theology and Ethics at The Catholic University of America. Among his publications are the award-winning *Walking God's Earth: The Environment and Catholic Faith* (Collegeville, MN: Liturgical Press, 2014); *Reading, Praying, Living Pope Francis's Laudato Si': A Faith Formation Guide* (Collegeville, MN: Liturgical Press, 2015); and *The Vice of Luxury: Economic Excess in a Consumer Age* (Washington, DC: Georgetown University Press, 2015). He has authored dozens of professional and popular articles, coedits the professional blog *catholicmoraltheology.com*, and served for eight years as the Board President of the Common Market, the consumer food cooperative of Frederick, Maryland.

Daniel R. DiLeo (PhD, Boston College) is Assistant Professor and Director of the Justice and Peace Studies Program at Creighton University. His research focuses on Catholic theological ethics, with particular emphasis on public theology and Catholic social thought. He is especially interested in climate change, and works to bring Catholic theological ethics into the public square to shape civic discourse, policy, and action on this issue. He has published in the *Journal of Catholic Social Thought* and *Horizons*, and contributed chapters to edited volumes on ecology and theology. Since 2009 he has been Project Manager at Catholic Climate Covenant.

Walter Grazer teaches in the Catholic Studies Program at Georgetown University, focusing on ecology and Catholic social thought. He also has a consultancy in the area of religion and the environment. Formerly he served in several positions with the United States Conference of Catholic Bishops, including Manager of the Environmental Justice Program; Senior Policy Advisor for Religious Liberty, Human Rights, and European Affairs; and Deputy Director for Migration and Refugee Services. He is coeditor with Reverend Drew Christiansen, SJ, of *And God Saw That It Was Good: Catholic Theology and the Environment* (Washington, DC: United States Catholic Conference, 1996). Mr. Grazer holds a MA in International Relations, a MSW in Social Work and a BA in Philosophy.

Msgr. Kevin W. Irwin (STD, Ateneo San Anselmo, Rome) is Dean Emeritus and Research Professor at the School of Theology and Religious Studies at The Catholic University of America. He is the author of eighteen books, two of which received awards from The Catholic Press Association: *Sacraments: Historical and Liturgical Theology* (First Prize, 2016) and *What We Have Done, What We Have Failed to Do: Assessing the Liturgical Reforms of Vatican II* (Second Prize, 2014). He is the author of *A Commentary on Laudato Si': Examining the Background, Contributions, Implementation and Future of St. Francis's Encyclical* (Mahwah, NJ: Paulist Press, 2016) and is presently revising his signature work *Context and Text: Method in Liturgical Theology* (Collegeville, MN: Liturgical Press, 1994).

Richard W. Miller (PhD, Boston College) is Associate Professor of Systematic Theology and Associate Professor of Sustainability Studies at Creighton University. His research interests include the mystery of God, divine providence and human suffering, and the ecological crisis. He has published in the *Heythrop Journal*, *Theological Studies*, *New Blackfriars*, *The Journal of Religion and Society*, and the *Journal for Peace & Justice Studies*. He is a contributor to and editor of seven books including *God, Creation, and Climate Change: A Catholic Response to the Environmental Crisis* (Maryknoll, NY: Orbis, 2010), which won a 2011 Catholic Press Association of the United States and Canada book award in the faith and science category.

Dawn M. Nothwehr, OSF (PhD, Marquette University), holds the Erica and Harry John Family Endowed Chair in Catholic Theological Ethics at Catholic Theological Union in Chicago. Her research engages environmental ethics through the lens of Franciscan theology, particularly the effects of global climate change on people bearing the burdens of poverty. Equal interests are the religion-science dialogue, and the ethics of power and racial justice. She teaches environmental ethics, racial justice, and fundamental moral theology, and serves on the Encyclical Working Group for the Archdiocese of Chicago, charged with the implementation of *Laudato si'*. She is the author of *Ecological Footprints: An Essential Franciscan Guide for Faith and Sustainable Living* (Collegeville, MN: Liturgical Press, 2012). Nothwehr is the presenter of the popular lecture series "God's Creation: A Course on Theology and the Environment" (Now You Know Media, 2016).

Nancy M. Rourke (PhD, Maynooth College in Ireland) is Associate Professor of Religious Studies and Theology and Director of the Catholic Studies Program at Canisius College. She teaches in the areas of world religions and Catholic ethics, and her research is in the areas of Catholic ecological ethics and bioethics. She is coeditor of *Theological Literacy in the Twenty-First Century* (Grand Rapids: Eerdman's, 2002), has contributed chapters to several edited volumes on ecology and theology, and has been published in *Irish Theological Quarterly*, *Environmental Ethics*, and *National Catholic Bioethics Quarterly*. She has also served as a peer reviewer for the College Theology Society annual book award.

Jame Schaefer (PhD, Marquette University) is Associate Professor of Systematic Theology and Ethics at Marquette University where she focuses on relating theology, the natural sciences, and technology. Her publications include *Theological Foundations for Environmental Ethics: Reconstructing Patristic and Medieval Concepts* (Washington, DC: Georgetown University Press, 2009), *Confronting the Climate Crisis: Catholic Theological Perspectives* (Milwaukee: Marquette University Press, 2011), and the inaugural "Animals" entry in *New Catholic Encyclopedia* (2013). She worked with an international team commissioned by the Higher Education Secretariat of the Society of Jesus to create *Healing Earth* (*http://healingearth.ijep.net/*) and is currently leading a three-year project for the Religion and Conservation Biology Working Group of the Society for Conservation Biology aimed at facilitating the collaboration of religious communities and conservation researchers and practitioners. Prior to academia, she served in environmental and energy policy positions by appointment of local, state, national, and bi-national governments.

Daniel P. Scheid (PhD, Boston College) is Associate Professor of Theology at Duquesne University, where he teaches in the areas of theological ethics, religion and ecology, and Christian social ethics. His research explores interreligious ecological ethics, and he has published essays in the *Journal of Inter-Religious Studies* and the *Journal of Religion & Society*, as well as several edited volumes. In his book *The Cosmic Common Good: Religious Grounds for Ecological Ethics* (Oxford: Oxford University Press, 2016), he draws on Catholic social thought to construct what he calls the "cosmic common good," a new norm for interreligious ecological ethics that can also be found in Hindu, Buddhist, and American Indian religious traditions. Dr. Scheid and his wife live in Pittsburgh with their three children.

Mary Evelyn Tucker (PhD, Columbia University) and **John Grim** (PhD, Fordham University) have appointments in the Yale School of Forestry and Environmental Studies as well as the Divinity School and the Department of Religious Studies. They direct the Forum on Religion and Ecology at Yale, and teach in the joint MA program in religion and ecology. Together they have organized ten conferences at Harvard University on religion and ecology and edited a groundbreaking series on religions and ecology. Along with Brian Thomas Swimme, Mary Evelyn and John created a multi-media project called *Journey of the Universe* (*http://journeyoftheuniverse.com*), which includes an Emmy award winning film, a book, and a DVD series titled *Journey Conversations* that includes twenty interviews with leading scientists, educators, and environmentalists. They published *Ecology and Religion* with Island Press in 2014. They are editors of the Ecology and Justice series with Orbis Books that currently has nineteen books. They are currently President and Vice-President of the American Teilhard Association.

Tobias Winright (PhD, University of Notre Dame) is the Mäder Endowed Associate Professor of Health Care Ethics and an Associate Professor of Theological Ethics at Saint Louis University. His research focuses on bioethics, war and peace ethics, ecological ethics, and criminal justice ethics. Among his publications, he edited *Green Discipleship: Catholic Theological Ethics and the Environment* (Winona, MN: Anselm Academic, 2011); coedited *Environmental Justice and Climate Change: Assessing Pope Benedict XVI's Ecological Vision for the Catholic Church in the United States* (Lanham, MD: Lexington, 2013); and coauthored *After the Smoke Clears: The Just War Tradition and Post War Justice* (Maryknoll, NY: Orbis, 2010). From 2012 to 2017 he was coeditor of the *Journal of the Society of Christian Ethics.*

Index

Note: The abbreviations *n* and *s* that follow page numbers indicate footnotes and sidebars, respectively.

217

159s, 174, 183, 186–88. *See also*
climate change; extinctions;
global warming; pollution
as moral issue, 29
ecological debt, 37, 189–93
ecological degradation, 9, 17, 28,
37, 52, 64–65, 74, 103, 105, 114,
116n6, 133, 138n6, 144n26, 148,
189, 192, 200–204, 210–11
ecological diversity. *See* diversity
ecological economics, 72
ecological education, 38, 43, 160n6,
162–63, 202
ecological equilibrium, 177, 202
ecological ethics, 185
ecological exploitation. *See*
exploitation
ecological integrity, 66, 76
ecological justice, 65–66, 73–77
ecological literacy, 71, 158n4
ecological problems, four major,
140n16
ecological-societal concerns, 151
ecological theology, 35, 42, 95–112.
See also liberation ecological
theology
ecological virtues, 110, 154, 158–59,
161, 163–64
*Ecologies of Grace: Environmental
Ethics and Christian Theology*
(Jenkins), 203n11
ecology, 10n3, 16n5, 36, 37. *See also*
"deep ecology"; *Earth Charter;*
environmental ecology; human
ecology; integral ecology;
liberation ecological theology;
mental ecology; social ecology
cosmology and, 64–79
environment and, 16n5, 31–43
equity and, 74

four ecologies, 106–7
new paradigm of, 110
peace and, 12, 205
Ecology and Justice Series on
Integral Ecology (Orbis Books),
74–75
Ecology and Liberation (Boff), 102–3
"Ecology and Poverty: Cry of the
Earth, Cry of the Poor" (Boff
and Elizondo), 101–2, 106n47
economic development, 34, 207
economic justice, 28, 76
Economic Justice for All (National
Conference of Catholic
Bishops), 46n4
Economics of Climate Change, The
(Stern), 126n38, 131n67
economy/economics, 12, 16, 27,
40, 45–51, 54–55, 60, 88–89,
104, 114n2, 126n38, 131n67,
171, 199. *See also* capitalism;
ecological economics; globalization; *specific topics*, e.g., ecological
debt; inequality
world, 19
ecosystems, 21, 68, 71, 74, 83,
109, 120–21, 124–25, 130–31,
145–46, 156
Ecuador, 44
ecumenism, 21, 31–32, 39–41, 53.
See also dialogue; interfaith
collaboration; unity
education, 26, 47, 57–58, 73, 76–77,
102, 151–52, 158, 159s, 177–78,
205n21. *See also* ecological
education
environmental, broadening goals
of, 148
egoism, 88
Elizondo, Virgilio, 101–2

emissions, 119, 126, 146n31,
172–73
employment, 170. *See also* labor;
workers, concern for
encyclicals, 10n3, 52. *See also specific
titles of encyclicals*
endangered species, 106, 147, 178
enemy/enemies
love for, 204
"We have met the enemy and he
is us," 199
energy, 180. *See also* fossil fuels;
renewable energy
consumption, 24, 173, 176, 191
energy companies, 173
environment, 16n5, 46. *See also*
habitat
Christian beliefs regarding,
16n5
Christian theology of, 83
ecology and, 16n5, 31–43
recent teaching on, 16–27, 66–71
environmental ecology, 33, 102–3,
106, 203
environmental education, 148
environmental impact assessments,
146n31
environmentalism, 47–51, 54, 61,
103
environmental issues, 10, 33, 38, 45,
49, 51–52, 55, 57, 61, 77, 116n6,
171
Environmental Justice Program
(EJP), 33, 54, 76, 195
environmental literacy, 177
Environmental Protection Agency
(EPA), 56
episcopal conferences, 25, 32, 34,
37, 42, 66, 152. *See also specific
conferences*, e.g., CELAM;

United States Conference of
Catholic Bishops
environment, recent teaching on,
25–27
equity, 27, 74, 76
erotic enchantment, 110
eschatology, 86, 90, 145n27
eternal law of God, 46
ethics, 19n16, 158n4, 183. *See also*
Catholic social ethics; ecological
ethics; theological ethics; virtue
ethics
Evangelical Environmental
Network, 32, 49–52
Evangelii gaudium (Francis), 25, 35,
81, 197
Evangelium vitae (John Paul II), 22
evangelization, 25–26, 81–82
Eve (biblical character), 174
evil, 58, 85, 145, 157, 176, 199,
206–7
evolution, 19n19, 65s, 68, 75, 78,
101–4, 107, 143–44, 175
and creation, 71–73
creative, 84–86
Ex corde ecclesiae (John Paul II),
205n21
exploitation, 17, 19n6, 67–68, 71,
75, 95s, 139, 160
extinctions, 35, 72, 115, 118, 121,
125, 129–31, 209

F

faith, 25, 164. *See also* Christianity
family, 25, 54, 87, 151–53
God's, 98
human, 31, 34, 184, 186–87,
206n24
universal, 72, 138n7, 139

typhoons, 44
"tyrannic anthropocentrism," 28

U

UNESCO, 146*n*30
United Nations, 17, 21, 39, 142,
   143*n*21. *See also* Intergov-
   ernmental Panel on Climate
   Change (IPCC); Sustainable
   Development, Conference of the
   UN on
United States
   climate change/sea level rise and,
      127–28
   Constitution of, 46
   military, 201, 211
   reception of *Laudato si'* in, 44–62
United States Conference of
   Catholic Bishops (USCCB),
   27, 32–34, 41, 47*n*7, 55–57, 59,
   146*n*29, 170*n*2, 205*n*23, 206*n*24.
   See also *Global Climate Change:
   A Plea for Dialogue, Prudence and
   the Common Good; Renewing the
   Earth*
unity, 11, 42, 80, 82–83, 206. *See also*
   ecumenism
universal communion, 23, 28, 68, 72,
   103–6, 139, 143*n*21, 147, 150,
   178, 185, 192–93
universal destination of goods, 184,
   190
universe, 69, 100, 144. *See also*
   cosmology; creation; universal
   communion
Universe Story, The (Swimme and
   Berry), 69*s*, 75
University of Georgia, 152
utilitarianism, 38, 95*s*, 177

V

values, 161–62
Vatican, 39. *See also* Francis *and
   other individual popes;* Vatican II
   conservative officials in, 71
   Pontifical Academy of Sciences,
      113*n*1
Vatican II, 15–16, 33, 66, 86, 99,
   183. See also *Gaudium et spes*
vice/vices, 154–56, 161–64
Vietnam, 127
violence, 38, 68, 105, 160, 200, 203,
   208–10. *See also* war
virtue/virtues, 38, 161–66, 204. *See
   also* cardinal virtues; ecological
   virtues; theological virtues;
   specific virtues, e.g., awareness
virtue ethics, 154–67
virtue theories, 154, 156, 161, 164–65
"virtuous cooperator" model, 144*n*26
vocation, 164–65
volunteers/voluntary associations,
   208
vulnerable people. *See* marginaliza-
   tion; poor and vulnerable people;
   preferential option for the poor
   and vulnerable

W

war, 21. *See also* civil war; nuclear
   weapons; *specific wars*
   just, 206–10
   metaphor, 198–206
   world war, global warming as,
      195–96, 198–99, 210
waste, 28, 114, 137*n*5, 140–43,
   155–61, 195. *See also* littering;
   recycling
   and technocracy, 171–79